An

ANCIENT
BLUEPRINT
FOR THE SUPERNATURAL

DESTINY IMAGE BOOKS BY
DENNIS AND JENNIFER CLARK

Flowing in the River of God's Will

A Practical Guide to Self-Deliverance

Releasing the Divine Healer Within

The Supernatural Power of Peace

Deep Relief Now: Free, Healed, and Whole

Live Free

Breaking Soul Ties

Visit Drs. Dennis and Jennifer Clark online at
www.forgive123.com.

Visit the online school directed by Jason Clark at
http://training.teamembassy.com.

Jason's full testimony is available as *Grace Transforms* in CD and
DVD format at
www.forgive123.com.

ENDORSEMENTS

This book was hidden by God but discovered to help usher in the greatest revival in history—the global glory!

SID ROTH
Host, *It's Supernatural!*

It seems we are facing right now a time in history when Holy Spirit is bringing the old wells of wisdom to the surface again. While many might think, "Well that's in the past," I urge you to take a good look at the wells that are brought forth through this book, *An Ancient Blueprint for The Supernatural.* What's wonderful is that the very teachings of the first disciples of Jesus, and their way of life, still challenge our current mindset and society today. Their research changed the lives of Drs. Dennis and Jen Clark and their church. I'm sure it will transform yours as well.

ANA WERNER

I found *Ancient Blueprint for the Supernatural* fascinating with regard to the cultural context of first century Jewish followers of Jesus. It was inspiring to learn about how well-educated and familiar with the scriptures they were, and how dedicated they were to teaching the Gentiles about spiritual living. I feel like I could meditate on the *Didache* and it would be like meditating on the beatitudes, or the Proverbs. The book is also filled with many practical bits of information that serve as a guide in how to practice being in the Spirit more actively. A very enriching and practical read.

JASON HASSING
Messianic Jewish believer in Jesus

An

ANCIENT BLUEPRINT

FOR THE SUPERNATURAL

*The Lost Teaching of the Apostles,
Hidden for Such a Time as This*

Drs. Dennis & Jennifer Clark

CONTENTS

PREFACE

AS its full title states, *The Lord's Teaching to the Twelve Apostles for the Gentiles* [Nations], the *Didache* was framed by Jewish apostles as a training program for the apprenticeship of Gentiles in the Way of Life prior to joining the Messianic community. The roots of the *Didache* go deep into Jewish tradition and belief, which is not surprising because Christianity has Jewish roots. Jesus was a Jewish rabbi and His disciples were Jewish disciples. Gentiles were grafted into the holy root of Israel. Jesus is the promised Messiah for both Jew and Gentile.

> *If the first portion of the dough is holy, the batch is also holy. And if the root is holy, so are the branches. But if some of the branches were broken off, and you, being a wild olive shoot, were grafted in among them and became a partaker with them of the root and richness of the olive tree, do not boast against the branches. If you boast, remember you do not sustain the root, but the root sustains you* (Romans 11:16-18).

In deference to the Jewish roots of our faith, we have used the text of the Modern English Version (MEV) for most Scripture verses, changing the anglicized Greek word *Christ* to the anglicized Hebrew word *Messiah*.

May the Lord of Legions be pleased to bless us through the holy vine of His servant David that He made known to us through His servant Yeshua as we study the wellspring of the *Didache*. To Him be glory forever.

—TOBY JANICKI

SPECIAL INTRODUCTION FROM THE PUBLISHER

"GOD, why aren't we currently seeing the level of miracles, signs, and wonders that *they* saw in the New Testament and in the early Church?"

I try to be as honest as possible in my conversations with the Lord, since He already knows what I'm thinking, and, according to Scripture, knows what I'm going to ask Him before I utter a single word (see Matt. 6:8).

Biblically speaking, we have access to the *same* Holy Spirit who was poured out on the Day of Pentecost. There is no sound biblical evidence of the Spirit being released from heaven then withdrawn completely (cessation theory) or withdrawn to be released at certain, strategic times and seasons. As Dr. Michael L. Brown claims, "I am Charismatic *because* I am sola-Scriptura." In other words, "I believe in the present-day power and demonstration of the Holy Spirit because I hold strictly to what Scripture teaches. And that power is available now because that Person (Holy Spirit) has been poured out!"

God answered my question. When I asked about *not* seeing the measure of supernatural activity that we read about in the Book of Acts and in early church history (first 300-500 years of the Church, post-Pentecost), the Holy Spirit gently reminded me that those who have operated in the greatest manifestation of miracles in their day, built their discipleship and doctrine on biblical foundations that came from *another day.* Their lives were established on ancient standards and they preached eternal truth. Every generation that has exchanged the ancient and timeless truths of the *"apostles' teaching"* for something relevant and crowd pleasing has lived beneath the supernatural standard that is clearly attainable through the Holy Spirit.

In contemporary society, we think that in order to be "relevant" to culture, we need to water down the message. A.W. Tozer in the compilation book, *Voice of a Prophet*, notes that "one of the gods of the modern church" is a misguided passion to be relevant. The greatest, most relevant people will be those who carry a message from another age—heaven—that, when proclaimed, applied and demonstrated, will release the power and reign of heaven *here* on Earth.

God wants to release an unprecedented measure of His supernatural power *through* His people. What is the key? We need to both proclaim and live by a message that heaven considers worthy of confirming with *"accompanying signs"* (Mark 16:20 NKJV).

I remember studying *The Didache* while completing my Master of Divinity work at Regent University. I'm amazed at how, in society's unrelenting rat race to become relevant, some of the most powerful words to live by are always those that are timeless and ancient. Such is the case with the *Didache* and this amazing accompanying book that Drs. Dennis and Jen Clark have put together.

Covering everything from moral character to the end times, from Holy Communion to baptism, from ministry protocol to the practices of Christian living, *The Didache* is a simple compilation of Bible-based standards that are meant to serve as foundational, yet practical guidelines for living the Christian life. *The Didache* is not Scripture, but it's absolutely Scripture based and Bible saturated. It's a discipleship guide that shows contemporary believers how to walk the ancient paths. And it's these paths that heaven desires to confirm with the signs and wonders we have all been longing to see demonstrated!

Heaven is not holding the Holy Spirit hostage. When we believe that God is waiting for some strategic, "one day, someday" time to re-release the Holy Spirit into the planet, it's easy to bypass our sacred responsibility as believers to live biblically and walk in faith *today*. The only One *yet to come* is Messiah Jesus, who at His second coming will split a real, literal sky and return to a real, literal Mount of Olives. In the meantime, we have been given a gift that is beyond comprehension—the gift of God Himself in the Person of the Holy Spirit.

What is the life that is attractive to the fire and power of the Spirit? It's the "Romans 12:1" life that is wholly yielded and surrendered to God as a *living sacrifice*. I believe *The Didache* practically shows us what this looks like and, through the empowerment of the Spirit, how to do it.

LARRY SPARKS
Publisher, Destiny Image
MDiv, Regent University

THE LOST
TEACHING

CHAPTER 1

THE LOST TEACHING
OF THE APOSTLES

IT was like the plot of a mystery novel or gripping thriller. An ancient first-century manuscript, lost in the distant past, is stumbled upon by a young Greek Orthodox cleric who was browsing in a dimly lit library, tucked away in a far corner of the Middle East. The year was 1873. The cleric's name was Philotheos Bryennios. The place was Istanbul, Turkey.[1]

> The Jerusalem Monastery possesses, like most convents, a library.
> It is preserved in a small stone chamber, erected for that purpose.
> ...It receives scanty light through two strongly barred windows. Its
> entrance is adorned with holy pictures. It contains about a thousand
> bound volumes. ...Among the books of this library [was discovered]
> one of the rarest treasures of ancient Christian literature.[2]

Sandwiched between the pages of an unnoticed primitive book, or codex,[3] containing a total of seven manuscripts was a single, complete, bound copy of a long-lost text entitled *The Teaching (Didache) of the Lord through the Twelve Apostles to the Gentiles*. The word *didache* (pronounced "did-ah-KAY") means "teaching" or "training." The medieval scribe who created the copy signed it "Leon, scribe and sinner, 11 June 1056."

The ancient manuscript contained a long-lost text.

Scholars and historians were at first enthralled. Then skeptical. Theories and speculations abounded. Who wrote it? When was it written? Was it based on other documents or did it stand alone? How could it have been overlooked? Was it a fake or could it be authentic? How could it have been lost so long? Was it one document or was it pieced together from several sources? Scholars studied it intensively and theories abounded. It was the subject of heated debate for many years. Finally, the dust began to settle and its true worth revealed.

What an astonishing discovery! Who would have ever thought such a significant first-century document, that had disappeared for almost two thousand years, would resurface centuries later? It is as though a great prize hidden by the hand of God for a generation yet to come. As the Lord announced to Daniel concerning his prophecies, it was concealed for our day: The *"words...closed up and sealed until the time of the end"* (Dan. 12:9).

The *Didache* was hidden for a generation yet to come.

Few ancient documents can survive the ravages of time. Most early writings were inscribed on papyrus, a form of paper much like our paper today, which is fragile and easily destroyed by mold and water damage. Parchment, on the other hand, is much more durable and can survive intact for centuries.[4] This particular text of the *Didache* was written on parchment and bound together with several other documents in book form. It is the only intact copy of the *Didache* in existence.

Until Bryennios made his discovery, small fragments had been found in various locations such as Egypt and Syria, but this is the only complete version of the entire manuscript ever found. Both the short title, *Didache*, and expanded title, *Teaching (Didache) of the Lord through the Twelve Apostles for the Nations*, is referred to by name in texts written by early church fathers such as Origen, Athanasius, Clement of Rome, and others who held the *Didache* in high esteem. This important document is now preserved in the library of the Orthodox Patriarch of Jerusalem, where it is catalogued as *Codex Hierosolymitanus 54*.[5]

The early church fathers highly esteemed the *Didache*.

Almost overnight, everyone in Europe, England, and America was astonished that such an ancient and important work had gotten lost, but after nearly fifteen hundred [years] a single copy had surfaced. When the first English translation was released...on 20 March 1884 in the New York bookstores, five thousand copies were sold on the first day. (Sabatier:5) Nonetheless, during the first years after its publication, some scholars dismissed Bryennios's find on the grounds that it was "a modern forgery." It was almost as though a document (a) lost for nearly fifteen hundred years and (b) overlooked repeatedly by scholars cataloguing the library was not allowed to show up so unexpectedly. After a few years, however, the judgment of authenticity prevailed.[6]

> Everyone was astonished that such an important work had been lost.

WHO AUTHORED THE *DIDACHE*?[7]

The *Didache* itself identifies the authors of the training as the apostles: *The Teaching of the Lord through the Twelve Apostles for the Nations* [Gentiles]. Although authorship is still a topic of scholarly debate, it is widely believed that the framers were indeed the twelve Jewish apostles. Moreover, it is clearly a Jewish document. "When one compares the teaching of the *Didache* to the New Testament, it seems certain that the essential thrust of the book follows the same path as the teachings of the apostles and breathes the spirit of our Master Yeshua."[8]

WHAT IS THE PURPOSE OF THE *DIDACHE*?

What if the first-century apostles appeared to us today with their own discipleship manual? In a sense, that is exactly what has happened.

> The entire system of the *Didache* displays little taste for negotiating, defining, and defending the exalted titles and functions of Jesus. Rather, the *Didache* is taken up with the business of passing on the Way of Life revealed to its authors by the Father through His servant Jesus.[9]

What did this training program generate in the first centuries? The *Didache* produced believers who were full of purity, passion, and power the likes of which the world had never seen. They turned the world upside down!

Gospel of the kingdom. The most common way the gospel is presented today is that our sins are forgiven. It is indeed wonderful news that allows us to be reconciled with God. However, we are told in Romans 3:23 that Jesus has solved another great problem we face due to the fall in the Garden. *"For all have sinned and fall short of the glory of God"* (NKJV). Adam and Eve sinned and were separated from God. They were also separated from the glory they once knew in the Garden.

Forgiveness of sins through the blood takes care of our sin dilemma: *"All have sinned."* However, Jesus preached that we are not only rescued *from* something but also brought *unto* something. Our redemption includes restoration to a heavenly realm that is available to all who seek it. Because of Messiah, our heavenly Father has *"delivered us from the power of darkness and conveyed us into the kingdom of the Son of His love"* (Col. 1:13 NKJV).

Jesus is a King with a kingdom. A "kingdom" is the territory ruled by a king. He has authority over the people, laws, and enterprises of the kingdom he rules. When we speak of the Lordship of Jesus, we are actually speaking of His authority over His kingdom. Under His Lordship, we are ruled by Him. Unlike modern kingdoms in the earth today, in which individuals become subjects of a monarch because of physical birth, we must first be born again and then allow Jesus to reign over us as our Lord and Master. Although we once lost the glory, through the way opened by Jesus we can experience the glory again. Jesus came as our pioneer, or captain, leading us back into the presence and glory of God. Jesus is now *"bringing many sons"* and daughters *"to glory"* (see Heb. 2:10).

In the book of Matthew alone, Jesus speaks of the *gospel of the kingdom* of heaven fifty-one times. In the Book of John, Jesus tells us that we can still be present on earth yet know God in a heavenly realm. *"At that day you will know that I am in My Father, and you in Me, and I in you"* (John 14:20 NKJV). And: *"If anyone loves Me, he will keep My word; and My Father will love him, and We will come to him and make Our home with him"* (John 14:23 NKJV).

> The kingdom of God is the very centerpiece of Jesus' teachings. Matthew speaks instead of the "kingdom of heaven." However, a number of passages in Matthew are virtually identical to those in Mark and Luke, except for the substitution of "kingdom of heaven"

for "kingdom of God." Thus, the same reality is intended. The Gospel of John mentions the kingdom only twice but refers many times to the closely related concept of eternal life...

However, the kingdom initiated by Jesus is not the earthly kingdom that was widely inferred from the Old Testament prophesies. It is a spiritual kingdom that is now growing in the hearts of men and women, and it will find its fulfillment in the eventual sovereign rule of God and defeat of all evil. Those people who choose to belong to God's kingdom and serve Him, are those who are destined to inherit eternal life in God's presence.[10]

Because of Jesus, we can connect with the heavenly realm so we can live in a heavenly way on earth—not just forgiven sinners but sons and daughters of a heavenly King who is accessible. *"But he who is joined to the Lord is one spirit with Him"* (1 Cor. 6:17). *"Even when we were dead in trespasses,* [our heavenly Father] *made us alive together with Messiah...and raised us up together, and made us sit together in the heavenly places in Messiah"* (Eph. 2:5-6 NKJV).

Revelation 2:7 tells us that Jesus has opened the glory-filled atmosphere once found in the Garden of Eden to the children of God: *"To him who overcomes I will give permission to eat of the tree of life, which is in the midst of the Paradise of God."* We can receive and appropriate the same promises and inheritance as the early church. *"The promise is to you and to your children, and to all who are afar off, as many as the Lord our God will call"* (Acts 2:39 NKJV).

A glorious Church. Members of the early church lived on earth but were truly citizens of heaven and representatives of God in heaven. They were children of another world. Acts 4:33: *"And with great power the apostles gave witness to the resurrection of the Lord Jesus. And great grace was upon them all"* (NKJV). The term "great grace" could be translated as mega-grace. Grace is not just unmerited favor, although that is included. Grace is also the personal presence of Jesus empowering us to live as sons and daughters of God.

Believers during the early centuries tapped into power that seems missing in our churches today. No wonder the early church is the gold standard to which we must look. We can rediscover the Way walked by the first believers in the Messiah—if we are willing to pay the price.

On the Day of Pentecost, the glory of God was poured out. God's glory might be defined as the holy radiance of the presence of God, or "the burning splendor of the presence of the Lord."[11] God's glory cannot be separated from His holiness. "The radiant presence of glory of the holy God expressed the innermost nature of deity."[12] Numerous passages in Scripture link God's holiness and glory (see Exod. 3:5; 15:11; 29:43; 40:43; Isa. 6:1-6).

Following the incident in Acts 5:1-10 when Ananias and Sapphira lied to the Holy Spirit and were struck dead, we are told that *"great fear came on the entire church and on all those who heard these things"* (Acts 5:11). Holiness is required to come into the presence of God and His glory. The High Priest under the old covenant prepared his heart before he dared enter the Holy of Holies on the Day of Atonement. Although the practice of tying a rope to the ankle of the High Priest before he entered the Most Holy Place in case his heart preparation was inadequate and he was struck dead in the presence of God is not found in Scripture, it has its origins in Jewish literature.

> The Talmud...[tells] us that there was a very real sense of fear on the part of the other worshippers who were waiting to see if the High Priest would emerge from the Sanctuary alive. The Talmud says: "He (the High Priest) would pray a short prayer (as he exits) the outer chamber. He would not extend his prayer so as not to alarm the (people of) Israel." This does seem to imply that there were times when the High Priest did not emerge from the Holy of Holies. Furthermore, the Mishna says: After the Yom Kippur Service; "They would give him (the High Priest) back his (ordinary) clothes to wear, and accompany him back to his house, where he would make a festive meal for his beloved (family and friends) to celebrate his emergence from the Holy sanctuary in peace." Again, this clearly shows the fear that must have existed for the possibility that the High Priest may not survive the day.[13]

The early church revealed what the New Testament calls a *glorious church.* As believers, we are cautioned to prepare ourselves while on earth. Jesus *"loved the church and gave Himself for it, that He might sanctify and cleanse it with the washing of water by the word, and that He might present to Himself a glorious church, not having spot, or wrinkle, or any such thing, but that it should be holy and without blemish"* (Eph. 5:25-28). "Spots" refer to internal *moral blemishes* and "wrinkles" are *disobedient actions*.

Jesus Himself tells us to watch and be ready in the parable of the wise and foolish virgins (see Matt. 25:1-13). In Hebrews 12:14, we are exhorted to prepare diligently: *"Pursue...holiness without which no one will see the Lord."* In the Book of Revelation, the Bride must get ready: *"Let us be glad and rejoice and give Him glory, for the marriage of the Lamb has come, and His wife has made herself ready"* (Rev. 19:7).

In addition, the final chapter of the *Didache* urges believers to be diligent. The Messianic community is told that their key concern should be holiness of life. They are cautioned to be watchful, faithful, and in fellowship with one another. *Didache* 16:1-2 says, "Be watchful over your life—do not let your lamps be snuffed out, and do not let your loins be ungirded—but be ready, for you do not know the hour in which our Lord is coming. Gather together frequently, seeking those things appropriate for your soul, because a lifetime of faithfulness will not benefit you if you have not been perfected by the end."

What if the twelve apostles appeared to us with their own discipleship manual?

The *Didache* contains a transformative step-by-step training program for Gentile novices to prepare them for active participation in Messianic communities. It "encapsulated the...practice by which non-Jews were initiated into the altered habits of perceiving, judging, and acting" within the Jesus movement during the first centuries after the birth of the church.[14]

> This *Didache* reveals more about how [Messianic believers] saw themselves and how they lived their everyday lives than any book in the...Scriptures. It is not a gospel and, accordingly, it does not attempt to offer guidance by narrating the life of Jesus. In fact, it is older than the canonical gospels and was written in the generation following the death of Jesus. Nor is the *Didache* a letter like the writings of Paul. In fact, the *Didache* was created at the time of Paul's mission to the Gentiles, but it shows not the slightest awareness of that mission or of the theology that undergirded it.[15]

When carefully examined, the *Didache* demonstrates an extraordinary unity in the progression of topics by which mentors trained novices in a carefully designed and well-ordered way. The new Gentile believers were guided by spiritual mothers and fathers through a long apprenticeship that led to the formation of true disciples who were transformed in beliefs, mindset, and behavior. It lays out a clear program for training novices to be full, active members in a community of fellow believers.

> No document...is as descriptive, as organized, and as comprehensive as the *Didache* when it comes to offering evidence about the community that lies behind the text. ...By following the training of candidates through their prebaptismal training all the way to their final admonitions regarding the last days, one stands to gain a comprehensive overview of the Way of Life lived within...mid-first-century [believing] communities.[16]

The *Didache* is an extension of the Great Commission!

THE JEWISHNESS OF THE EARLY CHURCH

The Jews rightly saw themselves as a truly unique people both by birth and belief, adherents of an historical religion instituted by God Himself. These early Messianic believers were simply Jews to whom a new way of living the covenant had been revealed.

They were still within the Jewish fold, having a rich history as God's chosen people. The first-century church met as Messianic Jews in homes, synagogues, and at the Temple in Jerusalem. They numbered themselves among the Jews God had delivered from slavery in Egypt, worshipers of the God of Abraham, Isaac, and Jacob, and lovers of the Holy Scriptures. Later, believers in the Messiah and Jews underwent a real separation, but not until after many years had passed.

Messianic believers were Jews with a new way of living the covenant.

TOTAL COMMITMENT

What did it mean to become a believer in the Jewish Messiah? Even early on, believing in Jesus stirred up persecution—at first subtle, then blatant, and finally ferocious. Total commitment was required to enable believers to endure rejection, pain, suffering, and, sometimes, death. After all, the Messiah Himself had told them: *"Blessed are you when men revile you, and persecute you, and say all kinds of evil against you falsely for My sake. Rejoice and be very glad, because great is your reward in heaven, for in this manner they persecuted the prophets who were before you"* (Matt. 5:11-12). And: *"They will hand you over to be persecuted and will kill you. And you will be hated by all nations for My name's sake"* (Matt. 24:9).

> ## Total commitment was required.

At the time of His ascension, Jesus gave His disciples final instructions. He told them to train up other disciples. He didn't say to lead people in a prayer of conversion and give them a booklet and a Bible. Rabbi Jesus told them to make true disciples by teaching others just as Jesus had taught them. Jesus had already demonstrated to them that a lengthy apprenticeship was required to transform novices into true disciples by the time and effort He had poured into them.

> *Yeshua came and talked with them. He said, "All authority in heaven and on earth has been given to me. Therefore, go and make people from all nations into talmidim [disciples], immersing them into the reality of the Father, the Son and the Ruach HaKodesh [Holy Spirit], and teaching them to obey everything that I have commanded you. And remember! I will be with you always, yes, even until the end of the age"* (Matthew 28:18-20 CJB).

In fact, the *Didache* is an extension of the Great Commission itself: *"Go... and make disciples"* (Matt. 28:19).

> ## "Go make disciples."

The Gentile Problem

For years following the day of Pentecost, the apostles taught fellow Jews exclusively. In Acts chapter nine, the first serious persecution took place under Saul and, almost overnight, believers fled the city, many going south to Judea and others dispersing as far north as Antioch, a Gentile city. Paul was converted on the road to Damascus and disappeared from the scene for many years. When the persecution ended, many believers who had fled the city returned to Jerusalem while others remained in Judea to evangelize and plant churches.

Then, much to the astonishment of everyone, the Lord sent Peter forth on a new mission in answer to the prayers of a Roman centurion, a Gentile God-fearer, who was living in the Mediterranean seaport town of Caesarea Maritima. Peter arrived at Cornelius' house and began preaching. Much to everyone's amazement:

> *The Holy Spirit fell on all those who heard the word. All the believers of the circumcision who had come with Peter were astonished, because the gift of the Holy Spirit had been poured out even on the Gentiles.... Then Peter continued, "Can anyone forbid water for baptizing these, who have received the Holy Spirit as we have?" So he commanded them to be baptized in the name of the Lord* (Acts 10:44-48).

Gentiles can be followers of the Jewish Messiah!

At first, the early church baptized new believers at the time of conversion, but this practice of instant baptism changed at some point during the course of the first decade. (This is the scriptural reasoning behind our practice of baptizing immediately after conversion.) However, by the time Gentiles began becoming followers of the Jewish Messiah and being welcomed into local assemblies, believers were required to demonstrate transformed lives prior to baptism.

Later, by the end of the third century, the points of *Didache* were taught for a few weeks during the season of Lent, followed by an elaborate ceremony during which new believers were baptized and welcomed into the church. Without the requirement of holiness of life, churches became filled with mostly nominal believers, much like today. Instead of requiring holiness, the church leaders encouraged the practice of "letting the tares grow with the wheat" (see Matt. 13:26-30). This practice has led to the low-level faith we see so often today.

Although scholars disagree about the actual dates, a logical timeline based on the events recorded in the Scriptures and the fact that a need for the discipleship of Gentiles had arisen might look something like this:

AD 30	Day of Pentecost
AD 38	Saul persecutes the church
AD 38	Believers flee from Jerusalem; some go south to Judah, some as far north as Antioch, some return to Jerusalem
AD 38	Paul is converted
AD 38	Peter goes to Cornelius' house and Gentiles become followers of the Jewish Messiah
AD 41	Barnabas is sent to Antioch because a new church community has formed
AD 42	Barnabas brings Paul to Antioch
AD 43	Paul and Barnabas leave for the first missionary journey
AD 48	Council of Jerusalem
AD 49	Paul writes Galatians
AD 50-70	Gospel of Mark
AD 50-70	Gospel of Matthew
AD 60	Gospel of Luke
AD 61	Book of Acts
AD 85	Gospel of John

When Gentiles began to come into the fold, the apostles needed a new discipleship strategy. That Paul needed such a plan in the church at Corinth is abundantly clear!

Do you not know that the unrighteous will not inherit the kingdom of God? Do not be deceived. Neither the sexually immoral, nor idolaters, nor adulterers, nor male prostitutes, nor homosexuals, nor thieves, nor covetous, nor drunkards, nor revilers, nor extortioners will inherit the kingdom of God. **Such were some of you** (1 Corinthians 6:9-11).

The apostles needed a discipleship strategy for Gentiles.

Not only would the Jews have needed a discipleship strategy for Gentile believers following the conversion of Cornelius, but this same teaching would be a useful tool for Barnabas in Gentile Antioch in AD 43 and, soon afterward, for the first missionary journeys taken by Paul and Barnabas and later missionary journeys. It is believed that the apostle Paul was familiar with the *Didache* and referred to it in the following verses:

*But thanks be to God, for you were slaves of sin, but you have obeyed from the heart **that form of teaching** to which you were entrusted* (Romans 6:17).

*Holding firmly **the trustworthy word that is in accordance with the teaching**, that he may be able both to exhort with sound doctrine and to convince those who oppose it* (Titus 1:9).

A PAGAN CULTURE

The first converts to the new Jesus movement were Jewish, believed in one God, had been carefully trained from childhood about morality, and knew the Torah. Gentiles, however, came from a thoroughly pagan culture, worshiped many gods, and were ignorant of all that was written in the Scriptures. They needed a complete shift of worldview, a basic understanding of right and wrong, and a transformed Way of Life.

In the Gentile world of the first few centuries, sexual immorality, including pedophilia, was widely accepted, human life was expendable, the killing of infants by exposure was common, a multitude of gods were worshiped, and involvement with witchcraft and other forms of the occult was prevalent. Is our modern culture so very different from that of the early centuries as far as pagan influence in beliefs and lifestyle? Our culture today is surely just as corrupt as the pagan Greco-Roman culture of the ancient world.

ONE NEW MAN

Today, it's sad to say that the reverential culture of ancient Israel as a nation no longer exists as it once did. Large numbers of Jews have adopted a secular lifestyle and don't have a grip on the morality of the Torah as they did during Bible times. Now many Jewish believers need the *Didache* as much as Gentiles. During the transition from the early centuries to the modern world, so much has been lost that there is very little difference between the spiritual needs of either Jew or Gentile. Considering Paul's revelation of one new man, we believe that now is the time to form the *full* body of Messiah—one body in the Spirit made up of Jew and Gentile—a brand-new species of being. One new creation. One new man.

> For He Himself is our peace, who has made both one, and has broken down the middle wall of separation, having abolished in His flesh the enmity, that is, the law of commandments contained in ordinances, so as to create in Himself **one new man** from the two, thus making peace, and that He might reconcile them both to God in one body through the cross, thereby putting to death the enmity (Ephesians 2:14-16 NKJV).

WHY DO WE NEED THE *DIDACHE* WHEN WE HAVE THE BIBLE?

How much difference is having the Bible making among believers these days? Are believers making a first-century impact on the world as we know it? Many don't seem to be reading it much, and those who do don't seem to know it very well, much less apply it effectively to their lives. It is quite common for believers to gravitate toward only those teachings that fit their chosen lifestyle while disregarding the verses they dislike. Based on our personal experience, it seems that many young believers who grew up in the church rarely read their Bible, don't know much beyond basic Bible stories (if that), and seldom incorporate biblical principles into their lives.

On the other hand, many believers have more faith in what they see on the news or read on social media than the Bible. Few seem to be changed enough by their faith to reflect Jesus more than the world. We must admit that most believers today bear little resemblance to Jesus as far as holiness, radical commitment, and selfless love. Question: Is the world turning to Jesus based on how believers live?

Perhaps we need something more.

Is the world turning to Jesus based on how we live?

Perhaps we should look back to the time when the fledgling church was pure, passionate, and powerful and learn the way of discipleship as taught by the apostles. Perhaps the *Didache* was hidden by God only to be released for an end-time generation: *"Who knows if you haven't come to the kingdom for such a time as this?"* (Esther 4:14 WEB).

Our own church has already been profoundly affected by studying and living in the Way of Life as taught by the *Didache*. Lives are being changed, consciences made more sensitive, and relationships are being healed.

WHAT DOES IT MEAN TO BE A BELIEVER?

If we are to properly understand the *Didache* and its purpose, we must reflect upon what it means to be a believer. When we look back to the early church, it is clear that being a believer in Jesus involved far more than knowing about Him, believing certain facts, agreeing to certain doctrinal points, or as behavior modification.

Jesus was an observant Jew, was a Jewish teacher and was called Rabbi by many, and had disciples who hung on His every word. The first-century church was a Jesus movement within the Jewish community. They were Jews who believed Jesus was the Jewish Messiah, the fulfillment of the promises of God to the Jewish people.

The disciples who became the twelve apostles lived as disciples in the fullest sense of the word. Moreover, they lived together in close relationship as did all the believers in the early church. "In a context like this 'being a believer' is more akin to seeking to join a community rather than simply giving assent to a set of teachings or expressing a personal preference."[17]

And continuing daily with one mind in the temple, and breaking bread from house to house, they ate their food with gladness and simplicity of heart (Acts 2:46).

The Hebrew word for "disciple" is *talmid* (plural *talmidim*), meaning those who leave all they have known in the past to learn and practice the ways of their teacher. They endeavor to not only learn what their teacher knows but to become the same kind of man he is. That is what was practiced by the early disciples and should be practiced now. Men and women who look and love like Jesus should be the goal of all who follow Him.

This practice of rabbis choosing *talmidim* was not a rare practice among the Jews. What *was* uncommon was for certain rabbis to seek out followers and tell them, "Follow me." *"You did not choose Me, but I chose you"* (John 15:16). It was not the ordinary way things were done but not unheard of.

No one can come to Me unless the Father who has sent Me draws him (John 6:44).

The first disciples left their homes and spent three years immersed in the life and teaching of their Rabbi. They walked with Him, dined with Him, laughed with Him, were rebuked by Him, and sat at His feet to learn from Him. It was like total immersion when learning a new language.

How did Jesus train His followers to be *talmidim*? They became His apprentices during His three years on earth. Their Rabbi taught them to rejoice with Him at a wedding and they witnessed a great miracle in which water became wine. He taught them to have compassion on the multitudes. After teaching parables, He called His disciples aside for in-depth instruction. Rabbi Jesus sent the disciples out to minister with no money, no food, and no place to stay (see Mark 6:7-9). Their Master showed how to answer antagonists and how to love the sick, poor, outcasts, and children. And Rabbi Jesus taught them how to die.

That's radical. Not only were Jesus' *first* disciples radical, centuries later He still had radical disciples trained by the apostles' teaching—the *Didache!*

The Challenge for Today

Based on our observations, few believers today seem to exhibit the passion, purity, and power of the early church.

- Pastors look the other way when unmarried believers live together.
- Killing babies through abortion is rampant.
- Killing the elderly through euthanasia is becoming commonplace.
- The worship of pagan gods through participating in new age and occult activity is glamorized and excused.
- The Bible is only selectively believed by churchgoers, especially those younger than forty.
- Far too many churches preach a watered-down gospel.
- As the late evangelist Steve Hill pointed out, we are being swamped with an avalanche of heretical teaching.[18]

> Few believers today demonstrate the passion, purity, and power of early church.

The truth is, for the most part our churches are being changed by culture rather than influencing the culture for good. Something is clearly wrong with whatever we are doing now. More than ever, we need to equip believers to be powerhouses and lights in this dark world. Perhaps this is why the *Didache* has been restored to us.

ENDNOTES

1. Istanbul, Turkey was formerly known as "Constantinople." After the collapse of the Ottoman Empire in 1923, the new Republic of Turkey officially changed the name of Constantinople to Istanbul.
2. Philip Schaff, *The Oldest Church Manual Called the Teaching of the Twelve Apostles* (Edinburgh, Scotland: T&T Clark, 1885), 2-4.
3. A codex is an ancient book made of stacked, handwritten pages stitched together along one side. At first used by early Christians primarily for the

Scriptures and other revered texts, eventually it replaced the earlier scrolls and wax tablets. It had a number of advantages in that it could be opened to any page in the text, text could be written on both sides, and it could contain long texts that could not be contained on a single scroll. In the early centuries, it was a frequent practice to bind the four Gospels and Book of Acts together, and complete Bibles were commonplace.

4. Parchment is an ancient writing material made from specially prepared animal skins.

5. Thomas O'Loughlin, *The Didache: A Window on the Earliest Christians* (Grand Rapids, MI: Baker Academic, 2010), 1-3.

6. Aaron Milavec, *The Didache: Faith, Hope, and Life of the Earliest Christian Communities,* 50-70 C.E. (Mahwah, NJ: The Newman Press, 2003), 5.

7. Jonathan A. Draper, "The Holy Vine of David Made Known to the Gentiles through God's Servant Jesus: 'Christian Judaism' in the Didache," in *Jewish Christianity Reconsidered: Rethinking Ancient Groups and Texts* (ed. Matt Jackson-McCabe; Minneapolis, MN: Fortress, 2007), 281; Clayton N. Jefford, "Authority and Perspective in the Didache" in *The Didache: A Missing Piece of the Puzzle in Early Jewish Christianity* (Atlanta, GA: SBL Press, 2015), 57.

8. Toby Janicki, *The Way of Life: The Rediscovered Teachings of the Twelve Jewish Apostles to the Gentiles* (Jerusalem, Israel, US Distribution: Marshfield, MO: Vine of David Publishing, 2017), 13.

9. Aaron Milavec, *The Didache: Text, Translation, Analysis, and Commentary* (Collegeville, MN: Order of Saint Benedict, 2003), 40.

10. "The Kingdom of God," *Christian Bible Reference Site*; retrieved April 27, 2020 from https://www.christianbiblereference.org/jkingdom.htm.

11. Donald D. Demaray, ed., *The Daily Wesley*, trans. Paul Gerhardt (Anderson, IN: Bristol House, 1994), 48.

12. George Allen Turner, *The Vision Which Transforms* (Kansas City, MO: Beacon Hill Press, 1964), 17.

13. Milavec, ix.

14. Ibid.

15. Rabbi Gavin Michal, "Did the High Priest have a Rope Tied around His Ankle?" *Kotz Blog*, March 4, 2018; retrieved April 27, 2020 from https://www.kotzkblog.com/2018/03/166-did-high-priest-have-rope-tied.html?m=0.

16. Milavec, *The Didache: Faith, Hope, and Life of the Earliest Christian Communities,* xxv.

17. Milavec, *The Didache: Text, Translation, Analysis, and Commentary*, 40.

18. Steve Hill, *Spiritual Avalanche: The Threat of False Teachings that Could Destroy Millions* (Lake Mary, FL: Charisma House, 2013).

CHAPTER 2

CLASH OF CULTURES

WE should never take for granted just how much Jesus shaped the world in which we live. Looking back over the centuries, it is striking to realize what an immense impact He has made. Jesus challenged the status quo and introduced an entirely new way of thinking. His influence is inescapable. Jesus wasn't a president, emperor, or military hero, yet His influence has profoundly affected almost every arena of life—religion, science, government, education, art, charity, morality, as well as the belief in human dignity itself.

Jesus was the Man who changed everything.

HOW JESUS CHANGED THE WORLD

Except for the Jews, the ancient world was steeped in pagan religion and practices, including infant sacrifice. Concepts of right and wrong that we take for granted were unheard of in Greco-Roman society. To pagans, babies were valuable only if they were mentally and physically sound...and the correct gender. It was accepted practice to place unwanted babies outside in fields or forests to die of starvation, from inclement weather, or be devoured by wild animals if they were deformed, handicapped, or for any other reason, including being born a female.

Before Jesus, women were first the property of their fathers and then of their husbands. They were seen as intellectually inferior to men and not even worth educating. Treated as second-class citizens since time immemorial—property of males, dominated, second-class citizens—women were elevated by Jesus to a status equal with men. Jesus was the great emancipator of women.

The early church followed the example of their Master.[1] A compelling case has been made that two-thirds of the church of the first two centuries was composed of women due to the favorable environment of believing communities.[2] Not only were they considered to be equal with men, worthy of respect, and allowed to minister and even have their own ministries, but, for the first time, the same standards of holiness and purity were applied to men and women alike.

Jesus was the Man who changed everything!

Often, to appease angry gods, first-born children were sacrificed for the hope of gaining a better life in some way (rain, prosperity, a good harvest, and so forth). The bronze statue of the god, Molech, contained a gaping pit filled with fire into which the "worshipers" dropped live infants.[3] *"You shall not give any of your children to offer them to Molech, and so profane the name of your God: I am the Lord"* (Lev. 18:21 ESV).

Even among the Jews who did consider human life to be precious, many still viewed the crippled, diseased, lame, or blind as inferior beings, unable to mirror the glory and holiness of God. The coming of Jesus shifted the world's assessment of human life because He taught that *every* person is made in the image of God. Whether a king or deformed beggar child, all are equal in the eyes of God.

During World War II, Dutch clockmaker Corrie ten Boom was sent to a concentration camp for hiding Jews in her home to save them from the Nazis. As Corrie explained to Lieutenant Rahms, her Nazi interrogator, "'God's viewpoint is sometimes different from ours—so different that we could not even guess at it unless He had given us a Book which tells us such things.' I knew it was madness to talk this way to a Nazi officer. But he said nothing so I plunged ahead. 'In the Bible I learn that God values us not for our strength or our brains but simply because He has made us. Who knows, in His eyes a half-wit may be worth more than a watchmaker. Or—a lieutenant.'"[4]

Jesus' beginnings were humble. He taught about compassion, love, human worth, dignity, and hope. He demonstrated righteousness, truth, and justice. He "told the truth in love" by comforting the suffering and chastising the religious and arrogant.

The coming of Jesus shifted the world's view of human life.

Jesus spoke of the necessity of being compassionate for the imprisoned, having mercy for sinners, being charitable toward the poor, and feeding the hungry. He said that when you helped the least of these it was the same as if you had ministered to Him! Believers throughout history have responded to the words of Jesus caring for the sick, feeding the hungry, building hospitals and orphanages, starting schools, forming prison ministries, and ministering in leper colonies. Why? Because their Master, Jesus, was merciful.

Because of Jesus, the notion of the strong winning and the weak losing in a dog-eat-dog world was turned upside down. Jesus came preaching, "Love your enemies" and that we should pray for those who do us wrong. Once only the strong and powerful were winners. Now the ones who loved the most were the winners.

The world would never have voted Jesus most likely to succeed.

His life and teaching simply drew people to follow Him. He made history by starting in a humble place, in a spirit of love and acceptance, and allowing each person space to respond. He deliberately placed Himself on a collision course with Rome, where He would have been crushed like a gnat. And He was crushed.

And yet...

Jesus' vision of life continues to haunt and challenge humanity. His influence has swept over history like the tail of a comet, bringing His inspiration to influence art, science, government, medicine, and education; He has taught humans about dignity, compassion, forgiveness, and hope. ...Jesus is history's most familiar figure. His impact on the world is immense and non-accidental.[5]

Jesus was on a direct collision course with Rome.

THE KING OF THE JEWS

Jesus was the long-promised Jewish Messiah, the so-called King of the Jews. Or so His followers believed.

Now Jesus stood before the governor [Pontius Pilate]. *And the governor asked Him, saying, "Are You the King of the Jews?" Jesus said to him, "It is as you say." ...When they had twisted a crown of thorns, they put it on His head, and a reed in His right hand. And they bowed the knee before Him and mocked Him, saying, "Hail, King of the Jews!"* (Matthew 27:11, 29 NKJV)

The day He was crucified it looked as if He was passing off the world stage only to fade away into history past. His disciples didn't know what to do. They had thrown in their lot with Him and He had been their "answer."

Now He was dead. Crucified. Their hopes were dashed. We can't even imagine the depths of their despair. They were choking with bewilderment and disappointment. It looked like their failed movement was at an end.

EARTHQUAKE

However, the Resurrection reawakened their dreams. Then, the Day of Pentecost came. The devil had made his biggest mistake ever. An earthquake shook the entire world! No wonder the veil in the Temple was torn apart from top to bottom. No wonder the dead were raised and walked the streets of Jerusalem. No wonder the system of time itself was changed to begin with "*anno Domini*," the year of our Lord.

An earthquake shook the entire world!

Prior to this event, God had always been restricted to a *place* on earth. The Garden. The Tabernacle. The Temple in Israel. Then, Jesus Himself. But now God indwelt the *followers* of Jesus! *"For we are the temple of the living God; even as God said, I will dwell in and with and among them and will walk in and with and among them, and I will be their God, and they shall be My people"* (2 Cor. 6:16 AMPC). God was no longer confined. He lived in mobile, walking temples who would spread His message and presence to the four corners of the earth.

> *How beautiful upon the mountains are the feet of him who brings good news, who proclaims peace, who brings good news of happiness, who proclaims salvation, who says to Zion, "Your God reigns!"* (Isaiah 52:7)

A Roman Problem

The Jesus movement was in its infancy. Believers faced the external opposition of persecution and, almost from the earliest days, the internal opposition of heresies. Could this new movement survive?

At first Messianic believers were seen as a Jewish problem and were viewed as just another Jewish sect. Roman officials tolerated them at first because, after all, the Jews kept to themselves for the most part and made little difference within the Roman Empire as a whole. These believers were an entirely new species in society. They were a new race with a new way of life that was not Jewish, Roman, or Greek. (The early Jesus movement was the fulfillment of the Jewish hope for their Messiah. A separation between Messianic believers and Jews occurred later).

When the Gentiles began following Jesus, things changed and both Jewish and Gentile believers began to be eyed with suspicion by the governing authorities. Believers refused to worship the Roman gods or the Roman emperor. By refusing to cooperate, and even worse, by adding formerly law-abiding Roman citizens to their ranks, they were disrupting the stability of the Roman Empire spiritually and economically.

> Believers were a new race with a new way of life.

To the Romans, their gods were useful to the government for establishing a unified citizenry and keeping order. Adding in the worship of Roman emperors, Greek gods, or any others was of no concern as long as Roman worship was included.

It was the exclusivity of the Jesus movement that caused problems because they would worship no other God. Judaism had been tolerated mostly because of their unique ethnic identity and Jews seemed to pose little threat to Rome, except when they revolted against harsh Roman rule. In such cases, however, it was not a religious but a governmental problem. Before long, though, believers in the Way became particular targets of Rome.

PERSECUTION

Full-blown persecution of Messianic believers by the Romans started small but exploded during the second century AD. Unlike the Jews, these troublesome believers were evangelistic and therefore posed a serious threat to Rome. They were winning over Roman citizens to this new Way of Life in an alarming way. It was seen as a major threat to the stability of the Roman Empire.

To discourage those who might elect to join their numbers, public executions became both a form of entertainment and warning. It reached the point that simply accusing someone you didn't like of being a believer practically guaranteed they would be taken into custody and executed. It took strong faith to endure the threat of death. It also took a unified community to fortify that faith.

> It took strong faith to endure the pressure under threat of death.

REACHING THE WORLD

For years after the ascension of Jesus, the church in Jerusalem went nowhere else. The Jesus movement remained right there in Jerusalem. It wasn't until Peter's revelation and visit to Cornelius around AD 40 that Jewish believers even dreamed that Gentiles could be believers and not until later were churches planted in other locations.

Once the Lord made it clear that Gentiles *could* be followers of Jesus, however, the apostles realized that specialized training would be required to transform pagan believers into worthy members of the new Jesus movement. The twelve did what any good church leaders would do. They prepared a training program called the *Didache*. Eventually this teaching would spread throughout the known world.

PAGAN VS. JUDEO-CHRISTIAN MORALITY

The expression "Judeo-Christian ethic" refers to morality based on the laws of God as taught in the Bible. As in ancient times up to the present day, it is a moral way of living that is timeless and exists outside of the ever-shifting winds of culture. Only Jews and believers in Jesus have lived according to the Scriptures. The very foundation of Western civilization was based upon the absolute and unchanging laws of God. The phrase "Judeo-Christian" first became commonplace in the 1940s, recognizing the value system and worldview common to Jews and believers.

> **Only Jews and believers in Jesus have lived according to the Scriptures.**

Jews were carefully taught the Scriptures from an early age and trained in morality of life. They saw the world in a different way from the rest of the world. It was not a matter of behavior but the measure of life itself. The early Messianic believers were Jews and lived as Jews. For the first believers, it was a change of belief more than a change of lifestyle.

As far as Gentile believers in Jesus, *everything* changed. A new lifestyle needed to be practiced and absorbed to prepare Gentiles for joining a community of believers. When the apostles introduced the *Didache*, its use resulted in transformed lives. The "clash" needed to be removed before unity could happen, but it required a change of worldview, a change in living, a change of spirituality, and a change of behavior. It required "walking out their faith" until it became internal reality.

> **The *Didache* was designed to produce a transformed life.**

MODERN-DAY PAGANISM

Thirty years ago, who would have ever dreamed that a scientist would actually recommend cannibalism, the eating of humans, as a serious practice to protect the environment. Yet a recent article in *The Washington Times* states just that.[6] It is clear also that occult practices are becoming increasingly popular. Moreover, the demand for traditional exorcism is rising dramatically.

> In partnership with Summit Ministries, Barna [Research] conducted a study among practicing Christians in America to gauge how much the tenets of other key worldviews—including new spirituality, secularism, postmodernism and Marxism—have influenced Christians' beliefs about the way the world is and how it ought to

be. Barna's new research found strong agreement with ideas unique to nonbiblical worldviews among practicing Christians.

Here are a few notable findings among practicing Christians:

- 61% agree with ideas rooted in New Spirituality.

- 54% resonate with postmodernist views.

- 36% accept ideas associated with Marxism.

- 29% believe ideas based on secularism.[7]

Witchcraft and other pagan religious practices increased in the U.S. over the past few decades, with millennials turning to astrology and tarot cards as they turn away from Christianity and other tradition-ally dominant Abrahamic religions. ...With 1.5 million potential practicing witches across the U.S., witchcraft has more followers than the 1.4 million mainline members of the Presbyterian church.[8]

Priests are fielding more requests than ever for help with demonic possession, and a centuries-old practice is finding new footing in the modern world. ...Father Vincent Lampert, the official exorcist for the Archdiocese of Indianapolis... [said] in early October that he'd received 1,700 phone or email requests for exorcisms in 2018, by far the most he's ever gotten in one year.[9]

Apparently, given the state of the church, our concern as pastors should not only be the discipleship of new believers, but perhaps the believers already sit-ting in our Sunday services need a refresher in what we should believe and how we should live as believers. Is it possible all of us need the *Didache* as an anti-dote for the paganism flooding our world today?

ENDNOTES

1. Rodney Stark, *The Rise of Christianity: How the Obscure, Marginal Jesus Movement Became the Dominant Religious Force in the Western World in a Few Centuries* (New York, NY: HarperOne, 1996), 101.

2. Although Paul has been accused of failing to abide by the teachings and actions of Jesus concerning women, in fact a close examination of the Scriptures with cultural issues and local problems taken into consideration proves otherwise.

In Galatians 3:28, Paul himself declares, "There is neither Jew nor Greek, slave nor free, male nor female, for you are all one in Christ Jesus." This cut to the quick of the provocative daily prayer of Jewish males at that time, "Blessed are you, O God, King of the Universe, Who has not made me..." and conclude, respectively, "a *goy* [Gentile]," "a slave," and "a woman." Paul, a Pharisee, knew exactly what he was saying and what he was coming against. The main reason for this morning prayer was that even though Gentiles, slaves, and women were considered human beings, they were not qualified to participate in certain privileges that were reserved for Jewish males. Although there are numerous other examples, one particularly noteworthy mention is made in Romans 16:7 of Junia (called in several translations by the nonextistent male name "Junias"). Paul refers to her as an apostle: *"Greet Andronicus and Junia, my kinsmen and fellow prisoners, who are noteworthy among the apostles, who also came to Messiah before me."*

Not only did Paul *not* discriminate against women in ministry, he openly praised them for their work in the ministry of the church. Paul speaks of twenty-nine individuals in Romans 16 and, of that number, he mentions ten females. He sanctions the work of eight of them concerning their work in the ministry. Phoebe, in particular, is praised for her work as a deaconess. Priscilla is cited for her being part of a husband-wife team, and Paul calls them "fellow workers."

Of several controversial verses mentioned in the New Testament in which Paul is accused of misogyny, one notable one is found in 1 Corinthians 11:34-35 and is regularly used today to disqualify women from ministry. However, when this passage is considered within its cultural context, we are dealing here with a specific problem caused by followers of the goddess Artemis who claimed that mankind was birthed from Artemis alone without male involvement and that women were superior to men. These female followers were disrupting the church with their teaching and practices. Therefore, Paul told the church to restrict their platform of influence and said they should remain silent. See Rev. Rick McKinniss' excellent bookwork, *Equally Yoked: What the Bible Really Teaches about God's Ideal for the Genders* (Maitland, FL: Xulon Press, 2009).

3. In our day, millions of infants are sacrificed every year on the altar of the mother's convenience. Recently, an actress lifted her Oscar statuette high and rejoiced that aborting her unborn baby had made it possible for her to win the trophyx.

4. Corrie ten Boom, *The Hiding Place* (Old Tappan, NJ: Chosen Books, 1984, originally published in 1971), 148.

5. John Ortberg, *Who Is This Man? The Unpredictable Impact of the Inescapable Jesus* (Grand Rapids, MI: Zondervan, 2012), 12. Pronouns referring to Jesus have been capitalized by the author.

6. Cheryl K. Chumley, "Cannibalism: Scientist Says Eating Humans Could Save Earth," *The Washington Times*, September 6, 2019; retrieved February 26, 2020 from https://www.washingtontimes.com/news/2019/sep/6/cannibalism-whacked-scientist-says-eating-humans-c.

7. "Competing Worldviews Influence Today's Christians," Barna Research, May 9, 2017; retrieved February 26, 2020 from https://www.barna.com/research/competing-worldviews-influence-todays-christians.

8. Benjamin Fearnow, "Number of Witches Rises Dramatically Across U.S. As Millennials Reject Christianity," *Newsweek*, November 18, 2018; retrieved February 26, 2020 from https://www.newsweek.com/witchcraft-wiccans-mysticism-astrology-witches-millennials-pagans-religion-1221019.

9. Mike Mariani, "American Exorcism," *The Atlantic*, December 2018; retrieved February 26, 2020 from https://www.theatlantic.com/magazine/archive/2018/12/catholic-exorcisms-on-the-rise/573943.

CHAPTER 3

LITERACY IN THE ANCIENT WORLD

SOME scholars and historians have proposed that the majority of people in the ancient world, including the Israelites, were illiterate, estimating that the average literacy rate in the ancient civilized world was only around 10 to 15 percent.[1] Many other scholars, researchers and archaeologists, however, believe that this percentage is far too low.[2] Theories of rampant illiteracy have now been called into question by new archeological discoveries showing that literacy was indeed commonplace in ancient Israel as well as the entire Greco-Roman world in general well before the first century.

Literacy was commonplace in ancient Israel.

Why is the matter of ancient literacy so important? What is at stake for our faith?

Believe it or not, there are more topics and arguments in biblical studies judged by an ancient literacy yardstick then meets the eye. Brian J. Wright, author of *Communal Reading in the Time of Jesus*, debunks much of the earlier scholarship on the subject of ancient literacy and explains a possible agenda behind claims of illiteracy in the early church.

> Let me [Brian J. Wright] give you just four specific examples within biblical scholarship to illustrate my point [that an effort is being made in academia to discredit Jesus and the apostles through faulty scholarship]:
>
> 1. If a fisherman like Peter wasn't wealthy, was from a rural area, and had no formal education, then he couldn't have composed

the letters ascribed to him, like 1 Peter. Therefore, it is said, 1 Peter is a forgery.

2. If writing materials were limited and costly [and they were neither],[3] few people were literate, and the way traditions were passed along were predominately by word of mouth, then in all likelihood it wasn't until much later that [believing] communities developed a strong textual tradition or agreed upon which books belonged [in the canon of Scripture]. Therefore, it is argued, the New Testament writings are historically unreliable, and we can't really know which texts should be considered Holy Scripture.

3. If mass illiteracy prevailed in the first century AD, and if Jesus's family was from a so-called remote area, then the James who wrote the Book of James is probably not the "brother" of Jesus as traditionally understood.

4. If literacy was relatively non-existent, then there are most likely concocted stories and details in the New Testament in order to make certain people, even Jesus, look more educated and literate than they really were (e.g., John 7:53–8:11).

Did you notice? Authorship, interpretation, authority, and the reliability of the Scriptures are no small matters to believers. If, however, the scholarly consensus is wrong about ancient literacy and the impact book culture had on early Christianity, then these types of arguments will need to be abandoned or amended.[4]

The importance of literacy for a nation or empire is difficult to overestimate. Illiteracy produces dependence and precludes the ability to deal effectively in the currency of ideas, engage in more than rudimentary business enterprises, or function as a nation of laws.

ARCHAEOLOGY AND ANCIENT LITERACY

It seems that more people could read and write in Israel than previously thought, reaching at least as far back as the first Temple period around 600

BC. "Even the lowest soldier in the [ancient] Judaic army was literate," states an analysis recently published in the *Proceedings of the National Academy of Sciences* in 2016.[5]

Researchers used a combination of archaeology, Jewish history, and computer processing to show that soldiers, as well as ordinary Israeli citizens, not only wrote but wrote skillfully. "There is something psychological beyond the statistics," Israel Finkelstein, professor of archaeology at Tel Aviv University, told *The New York Times*. There is an understanding of the power of literacy. And they wrote well, with hardly any mistakes."[6]

Why is this important? With widespread literacy, discipleship would not have relied upon oral tradition alone, but almost everyone could read the Scriptures and literature such as apologetics, books, letters, and the *Didache*. (Although few individuals possessed a personal copy of the Torah, they could read it in the local synagogue.)

The ancient Jews produced the loftiest literature the world has ever known—the Torah. As a result, Jewish society was a jewel in the midst of the debauchery and brutality of the Greco-Roman culture. Would it be thought likely that people who treasured Torah would neglect such skills as reading and writing? Isn't it more likely that they would deeply invest in teaching their children to become informed and educated about their most prized resource—the Torah?

LITERACY IN THE GRECO-ROMAN WORLD

The "widespread use of the written word among...communities has now been clearly demonstrated throughout the western part of the early Roman empire.[7] A recent study of ancient civilization in *Archaeology International* states: "The creation of [the Roman Empire can be] viewed as the triumph of superior Latin- and Greek-speaking communities over illiterate barbarians. ...The skills of reading and writing were benchmarks for the advance toward civilization. ... The Roman empire was bound together by writing."[8] Of course, it is assumed that, if one can write, one can read.

The literacy rate across the rest of the Greco-Roman world also appears to be much higher than previously believed. In findings in 2011 from the *Iklaina Archeological Project*, the discovery of a tablet believed to be 3,400 to 3,500 years old "throws back the advent of widespread literacy across this region of the eastern Mediterranean Basin."[9]

> *But continue in the things that you have learned and have been assured of, knowing those from whom you have learned them, and that since childhood you have known the Holy Scriptures, which are able to make you wise unto salvation through the faith that is in Messiah Jesus* (2 Timothy 3:14-15).

JEWISH DISCIPLESHIP

Without question, life-long devotion to [Torah study] has been the hallmark of the Jewish people. Of the five books of the Pentateuch, Deuteronomy in particular stresses the importance of studying and reviewing the commandments. In the passages that we recite as the first paragraph of the Shema, we are told to "recite [God's teachings] when at home and when away, when lying down and when rising up" (Deuteronomy 6:7).[10]

In ancient Israel, nothing was more important to study than the *Torah*. Beginning in the family, children were to be thoroughly educated in God's Word. Fathers were particularly charged with teaching the words of the *Torah*, and the home was the first "school" attended by children.

In ancient Israel, nothing was more important than learning *Torah*.

A formal educational system, however, was instituted only after the return of the captives from the Babylonian exile. "The effects of the exile upon the Hebrews were far-reaching. Babylon at that time was the most advanced centre of culture and learning in the world. There schools, libraries, and literature were already ancient. In contact with this environment the Hebrews came to understand the importance of the school and literature."[11]

In ancient Babylon, the Jewish people observed a highly effective and sophisticated system of education right before their eyes. The lessons they learned there were not forgotten.

Following the Babylonian captivity, when the Israelites returned to their own land, God used the priest Ezra (480–440 BC), a *scribe of the law of the God of heaven,* to make a covenant whereby the Jewish people consecrated themselves to obey *Torah* (Ezra 7:12). Ezra reasoned that all the evil that had befallen the Israelites throughout the centuries could have been averted if they had known and obeyed God's Law. The Jewish people must *know* God's law to obey it. Therefore, a new educational system needed to be established to supplement the education provided within the family circle. This marked the beginning of the school movement in Israel.

Ezra laid a foundation for the future of Judaism. From this time forward the *Torah*, the five books of Moses, became the constitution of the nation and secured the continuation of the biblical heritage of the Jewish people.

At this time, the Jewish people consecrated themselves anew to God and His Word. A new order of scribes arose who were dedicated to teaching, guarding, and preserving the Scriptures. Synagogues were instituted as centers for formal Jewish worship in local communities and to provide schools for education. The Jewish people also began to study the Scriptures intensely because they realized that failure to know God's law and teach it to their children was the reason for their captivity in the first place. It was to this renewed Israel that God sent His Son Jesus centuries later.

> **Synagogues were instituted to provide centers for worship and education.**

Later, in keeping with this emphasis on education, "Simeon ben-Shetach, a Pharisee scholar and brother of Queen Alexandra Salome who reigned from 78-69 BC, was the first of several to issue a decree that children should go to school." He made attendance at school compulsory in Jerusalem as early as 75 BC. "Simeon ordered that schools be established in the larger cities in which the young might receive instruction in the Holy Scriptures as well as in the traditional knowledge of the Law."[12] Subsequently, other decrees extended the requirement.

> **The primary object of Jewish education was to know God and His Word.**

Long before the birth of Jesus during the first century, education and attendance at school was a great priority for the Jewish people. School curriculum revolved around learning *Torah*, or Jewish written law. Studying *Torah* was considered an act of worship, even more so than praying. Jesus would have followed the typical educational plan as other boys his age.[13] "The only schools were those connected with the synagogues. A local *Torah* teacher called the *hazzan* was paid by the local community. The only school-book was the Hebrew scriptures. A synagogue presupposed a school, just as in our country a church presupposes a Sunday-school."[14]

School curriculum revolved around learning *Torah*.

With the exceptions of the Sabbath and feast days, school was held every day. "When the children came to school...they had already learned from their parents select Proverbs and verses from the Psalms, and had been taught the significance of the various religious ceremonies."[15]

Studies for boys started when they were around five or six years of age in the elementary school, *bet sefer*, or "house of the book." Between six and ten they were taught reading and writing, mostly from the Pentateuch as text, and a little arithmetic.[16] After age twelve or thirteen, the best students were able to continue their studies in secondary school, or *bet midrash*, "house of interpretation," where pupils learned the more complicated oral interpretation of the *Torah*. When they weren't in school, boys worked alongside their fathers to learn a trade.

> The method of learning in the Jewish elementary school was not unlike that of other [people in this part of the world]. Frequent repetition was required for the purpose of committing a text [to memory] and obtaining a distinct pronunciation. ...Writing was taught by following the copy on a wax tablet with a stylus, and when the pupil was more advanced, on papyrus or parchment with a pen.[17]

By adulthood, Jews knew most of the Scriptures by heart. If an individual recited a passage, the audience would know immediately whether or not it was accurate. Jesus, in keeping with His culture, would simply begin with, *"It is written..."* knowing His audience would recognize it.

By adulthood, Jews knew most of the Scriptures by heart.

When Jesus was speaking to crowds of ordinary people (as well as religious authorities) in the Gospels, He asked His hearers, *"Have you not read?"* seven times in the gospels. Jesus quoted the *Torah* saying, *"It is written,"* twenty-one times, indicating that reading and writing were not unusual accomplishments.

"Have you not read?"

In addition to regular services twice on the Sabbath, two services were scheduled during the week. Over the course of a year, the Pentateuch, the first five books of the Bible, was read aloud in its entirety. Portions of the Prophets and Writings were also read. The whole scroll was read in sequence beginning immediately after the seven-day autumn festival, Sukkot. *Simhat Torah*, "rejoicing with/of the *Torah*," is a Jewish holiday that celebrates the end of the annual cycle of *Torah* readings and the beginning of the new.

Although few girls went to school like boys (they were primarily taught by their mothers at home), it did not mean that girls were not educated in *Torah*. "There was no differentiating between boys and girls when it comes to knowing the Law—both [would] have known the main parts of the Mosaic Law."[18] All Jews attended services twice every Sabbath and twice during the week. At these times, everyone was instructed in the Scriptures by oral readings and teachings.

> Jesus was born, grew up, and spent His ministry among people who knew Scripture by memory, who debated its application with enthusiasm, and who loved God... (Deuteronomy 6:5). Understanding this helps us to understand the great faith and courage of His followers who left Galilee and went to the whole world to bring the good news. Their courage, their message, the methods they used, and their complete devotion to God and His Word were born in the religious communities in the Galilee.[19]

ENDNOTES

1. William V. Harris, *Ancient Literacy* (Cambridge, MA: Harvard University Press, 1991); Catherine Hezser, *Jewish Literacy in Roman Palestine* (Tubingen: Mohr Siebek, 2001).

2. Alan Millard, *Reading and Writing at the Time of Jesus* (New York, NY: New York University Press, 2000).

3. Papyrus, the paper of the ancient world, was widely available and not expensive." Stanley E. Porter and Andrew W. Pitts, "Paul and his Bible: His Education and Use of the Scriptures of Israel," *Journal of Greco-Roman Christianity and Judaism* 5 (2008), 9-41.

4. Brian J. Wright, "The Triumph of Christianity's Reading Practices: How Some Faulty Assumptions Swept Biblical Scholarship," Baptist 21, February 20, 2018; retrieved February 27, 2020 from https://baptist21.com/blog-posts/2018/triumph-christianitys-reading-practices-faulty-assumptions-swept-biblical-scholarship; Brian J. Wright, *Communal Reading in the Time of Jesus* (Minneapolis, MN: Fortress Press, 2017).

5. Jon Miltimore, "Study: Literacy in Ancient Israel Was 'Far More Widespread than Previously Known,'" *Intellectual Takeout*, April 15, 2016; retrieved November 10, 2019 from https://www.intellectualtakeout.org/blog/study-literacy-ancient-israel-was-far-more-widespread-previously-known; Matthieu Richelle, "Epistles: When did Literacy Emerge in Judah?" *Biblical Archaeology Review* 46.2 (2020).

6. Ibid.

7. John Wilkes, "The Pen Behind the Sword: Power, Literacy, and the Roman Army," *Archaeology International*, 2001, 5, pp. 32-35; retrieved January 2, 2020 from http://doi.org/10.5334/ai.0510.

8. Ibid.

9. Philippe Bohstrom, "Unknown Monumental Palace Rewrites Ancient Greek History," *Haaretz*, January 30, 2017; retrieved January 2, 2020 from https://www.haaretz.com/archaeology/MAGAZINE-unknown-palace-rewrites-ancient-greek-history-1.5492227.

10. Eliezer Diamond, adapted from *The Observant Life,* May 20, 2012, "A Brief History of Torah Study," *The Rabbinical Assembly*; retrieved February 19, 2020 from https://www.rabbinicalassembly.org/story/brief-history-torah-study.

11. Sonya Schoeman, "Early Hebrew Education and Its Significance for Present-Day Educational Theory and Practice," *HTS*, V. 53, Number 1&2 (1997), 412.

12. "Education in Ancient Israel," *American Bible Society*; retrieved February 19, 2020 from http://bibleresources.americanbible.org/resource/education -in-ancient-israel.

13. Wilhelm Bacher and Jacob Zallel Lauterbach, "Simeon ben-Shetach," *Jewish Encyclopedia* (The unedited full-text of the 1906 Jewish Encyclopedia); retrieved February 23, 2020 from http://www.jewishencyclopedia.com/ articles/13717-simeon-ben-shetah.

14. Jari Metsämuuronen, "How Jesus Learned the Scriptures: Modern Reflections of the Educational Practices at the Beginning of the Common Era," *Research Gate*, 2019, 10.13140/RG.2.2.18529.15203; retrieved January 8, 2019 from https://www.researchgate.net/publication/330497075_How_Jesus_Learned _the_Scriptures_Modern_Reflections_of_the_Educational_Practices_at_the _Beginning_of_the_Common_Era.

15. Selah Merrill, *Galilee in the Time of Christ* (London, UK: The Religious Tract Society, 1885, reprinted in Columbia, SC February 21, 2020), 88.

16. Frank Pierrepont Graves, *A History of Education before the Middle Ages* (Honolulu, HI, University Press of the Pacific, 2004, reprinted from the 1925 edition), 128.

17. Ibid., 129-131.

18. Jari Metsämuuronen, 7.

19. Ray Vander Laan, "Rabbi and Talmidim," That the World May Know; retrieved February 3, 2020 from https://thattheworldmaynow.com/ rabbi-and-talmidim.

CHAPTER 4

THE DISCIPLESHIP OF JESUS

IMAGINE trekking through the Galilean countryside with Jesus, following in His footsteps when climbing the Mount of the Beatitudes, sitting at His feet as He explained the parables, breaking bread with Him, marveling at His miracles, hearing Him spar with the scribes and Pharisees, and seeing Him weep with compassion for Lazarus. We can only imagine what it would have been like to know Jesus during His earth walk, but we can understand a great deal about Jesus' childhood and the culture of His day.

What was special about the region of Galilee and what would it have been like for a young boy to grow up there?

What would it have been like to walk in the footsteps of Jesus?

The ruins of the Temple in Jerusalem had been awe-inspiring, certainly, but my imagination failed me (Jennifer) somewhat in comparison to Galilee. As soon as we set foot in the region of Galilee, it was like a dream come to life as we gazed at the beauty of the land. The fields, valleys, and gentle mountains were a carpet of green, flowers bloomed everywhere, and, in the distance, misty blue and purple mountains circled the lake.

The Sea of Galilee (in truth not a saltwater sea but a large freshwater lake), also called the Lake of Gennesaret, was sparkling blue with small waves softly lapping upon the sands. Much to my delight, a charming boat, built to somewhat resemble those vessels that sailed it 2,000 years ago, glided slowly across the calm waters. It was easy to imagine Rabbi Jesus walking along the shore, talking with fishermen, climbing the hills with His disciples, and reading from the *Torah* in the synagogues.

THE REGION OF GALILEE

The land of Galilee is perhaps one of the most beautiful regions in Israel. At the time of Jesus, it was known for its prosperity, wealth, and low cost of living. A common saying of the time advised, "If anyone wishes to be rich, let him go north" to Galilee. Located in northernmost Israel, it is characterized by a lush landscape, gentle low hills, grassy valleys, fruit trees, small farming communities (or kibbutzim), historical sites, and picturesque villages. Divided into two parts, upper Galilee is known for its treacherous high peaks divided by narrow gorges and, to the south, lower Galilee, whose rolling hills surround the Sea of Galilee, forming a gentler terrain.

From the water's edge, we traveled up to higher ground and stepped upon the Mount of Beatitudes, also known as Mount Eremos in Greek, which is possibly the location where Jesus preached the Sermon on the Mount. The breathtaking vista overlooks the lake and, on the other side, the misty Golan Heights can be seen in the distance. The spacious slope leading down to the water could accommodate a large crowd, and experts say the acoustics are perfect so a speaker could easily be heard. Below us, we could observe the Sower's Cove, thought to be where Jesus taught the Parable of the Sower (see Mark 4:1-9) from a boat near shore.

A CARPENTER WHO BUILDS

Jewish families often lived in family housing complexes called *insulae* (singular *insula*) designed for a multi-generational extended family, constructed around an open courtyard. The insula is referenced in the New Testament as "household," meaning "an extended family living together." As sons married, they added to the insula. After asking a girl to marry him, the son would return to his village and build new rooms onto his father's home.

The Jewish family unit was called *bet av* meaning "the house of a father." When a man married and had children, he founded a family or "built a house." Townships and villages of Galilee provided a more rural setting than larger towns so more land was available for homesteads. The father generally taught his sons the family trade while the mother schooled the girls in household management.

> It was common to live with extended family members in an *insula*.

Although it has been commonly believed that Jesus was a carpenter who made wooden furniture, the gospels describe Joseph, the earthly father of Jesus, as a *tekton,* which means "a carpenter who builds," referring to a stonemason and general contractor. Noted Hebraic scholar James W. Fleming explains, "Jesus and Joseph would have formed and made nine out of ten [building] projects from stone either by chiseling or carving the stone or stacking building blocks."[1] Jesus would have known how to use wood; however, most of the time He would have shaped and laid stone. Because stone was so plentiful in Israel, it was the main building material of that day. Eldest sons were trained to take over the family business; therefore, Jesus would have been taught building skills and good business practices by Joseph. It is possible that Jesus, along with His brothers, worked alongside Joseph in constructing their own family home.

> Jesus was a *tekton*, or stonemason.

Although Jesus lived in the rural village of Nazareth, only a short distance away was the city of Sepphoris, called the "the crown jewel of Galilee." It was built by Herod Antipas, the son of Herod the Great, and was the capital of Herod's kingdom. Passing nearby was the Via Maris, the "Way of the Sea," the great international highway and trade route of the civilized world linking Israel, Egypt, Rome, and empires to the east. This put Galilee at the crossroads of the ancient world and later was key in the spread of the gospel to the world.

> Galilee was at the crossroads of the ancient world.

Jesus and his family "were engaged in a trade, had a home, and so far as we can tell should not be classified with landless peasants, or tenant farmers. ...His family was not merely pious, they were devout, and the evidence we have suggests that devout Jews especially insisted that their sons learn to read so they could take their turn reading *Torah* in the synagogue."[2]

Sepphoris, the capital of Galilee, was located a few miles away from Nazareth. It was a wealthy city built by King Herod to be the "crown jewel of the Galilee." From Nazareth, Jesus could have easily observed the splendor of Sepphoris with its secular culture, wealth, and power that so contrasted with the humble Nazareth. Sepphoris was a booming metropolis built on a hilltop. It could be seen for miles. ...It had all the trappings of a modern wealthy city of the Roman Empire. It boasted an elaborate water system with a cistern a thousand miles long. Rich villas with mosaic floors lined its modern streets. ...Jesus may have helped construct buildings in Sepphoris.[3]

The seaport city of Caesarea Maritima, seventy miles from Nazareth, was the location of the house of Cornelius where the Holy Spirit was first poured out upon the Gentiles. "Much of the city was built with imported marble, and the city had an elaborate sewer system that was cleansed by the sea."[4] Caesarea Maritima boasted one of the most amazing seaports in the ancient world. At the southern end of the harbor stood a great lighthouse whose fires burned day and night to guide ships carrying Roman soldiers, spices, olive oil, and grain along with the finest marble and granite to be used as building material by local stonemasons throughout Galilee.

> Because stone was plentiful in Israel, rocks and stones were the main building materials.

LIVING STONES

When Jesus taught the parable of the house built on a rock, He understood the importance of building on a proper foundation from His own experience. Jesus also called Himself the Cornerstone and said He is the Builder of His church, using living stones as the building material. Consider these verses of Scripture: *"Therefore everyone who hears these words of mine and puts them into practice is like a wise man who built his house on the rock"* (Matt. 7:24 NIV). Also: *"The stone which the builders rejected has become the chief cornerstone"* (Matt. 21:42). And finally: *"On this rock I will build My church"* (Matt. 16:18).

> *Coming to Him as to a living stone who is rejected by men, but chosen by God and precious, you also, as living stones, are being built up*

into a spiritual house as a holy priesthood to offer up spiritual sacrifices that are acceptable to God through Jesus [our Messiah] (1 Peter 2:4-5).

> You also, as living stones, are being
> built up into a spiritual house.

THE CHILDHOOD OF JESUS

Children were considered to be a sacred trust given by God and it would be hard to overstate the tender bond between parents and children. It is difficult to imagine a world more oriented to piety and more dedicated to raising up children *"in the discipline and instruction of the Lord"* (Eph. 6:4).

The childhood of Jesus has been the subject of much speculation and even some fanciful notions. In fact, it is doubtful that His childhood was different from that of other Galilean children. Jesus attended school, took part in the services at the local synagogue, and learned a trade from His father, Joseph. In other words, His was a typical Jewish upbringing.

> Children are a sacred trust given by God.

The early years of Jesus' life and His later ministry were spent among people who knew Scripture by memory, who studied and discussed it fervently, and whose highest goal was to love and please God (see Deut. 6:5). God insured that Jesus would have the upbringing necessary for the preaching of the gospel message of *malchut shemayim*, or "the kingdom of heaven." From this same region, His disciples would be prepared to join a new Messianic movement and eventually take the good news to the world.

> God chose Galilee for His Son.

"In the days of [Messiah], the pious Jew had no other knowledge, neither sought nor cared for any other [knowledge]...than that of the law of God. ...To the pious Jew, on the contrary, the knowledge of God was everything; and to prepare for or impart that knowledge was the sum total, the sole object of his education."[5] From infancy children were immersed in an atmosphere of reverence. They heard their father nightly say the Shame,[6] participated in Sabbath worship and prayers with their family, heard the chant of the Psalms in services, and saw their father touch his finger to the *mesusah* while saying a benediction each time he passed through the doorway to their home. Jewish children were not educated for the sake of learning like the Greeks, but solely to love and serve God by knowing His law.

From infancy children were immersed in an atmosphere of reverence.

"What we know of the Galileans would quite prepare us for expecting that the gospel should have received at least a ready hearing among many of them. ... Galilee was the great scene of our Lord's working and teaching, and the home of His first disciples and apostles."[7] Galileans were known as hot-blooded yet warm-hearted, impulsive and generous, hard-working and brave. Their theology differed from the Judeans in that they were less legalistic while at the same time exhibited "more earnest practical piety and strictness of life, and less adherence to those Pharisaical distinctions which so often made void the law."[8]

> The people of Galilee were the most religious Jews in the world in the time of Jesus. This is quite contrary to the common view that the Galileans were simple, uneducated peasants from an isolated area. This perspective is probably due to the comments made in the Bible, which appear to belittle people from this area. ...The Galilean people were actually more educated in the Bible and its application than most Jews [in general].
>
> More famous Jewish teachers come from Galilee than anywhere else in the world. They were known for their great reverence for Scripture and the passionate desire to be faithful to it. This translated into vibrant religious communities, devoted to strong families, their country, [and] whose synagogues echoed the debate and discussions about keeping the Torah.[9]

More famous Jewish teachers come from Galilee than anywhere else in the world.

Far from being backward and uneducated, Galileans displayed great reverence for God and pursued the study of Scripture intensely. Contrary to the negative views of some, "Galilee was a place where Jewish cultural life and a firm attachment to Judaism flourished well before the destruction of the Second Temple. Apart from Jerusalem, it even excelled the other parts of the land of Israel in these respects."[10]

> Jesus was born, grew up, and spent His ministry among people who knew Scripture by memory, who debated its application with enthusiasm, and who loved God... (Deuteronomy 6:5). Understanding this helps us to understand the great faith and courage of His followers who left Galilee and went to the whole world to bring the good news. Their courage, their message, the methods they used, and their complete devotion to God and His Word were born in the religious communities in the Galilee.[11]

Jews from Judea were prejudiced against the Galileans, primarily because of the local dialect they spoke. Due to this, Galileans unfairly suffered the scorn of their countrymen to the south. *"After a while those who stood by came to Peter and said, 'Surely you also are one of them, for your accent betrays you'"* (Matt. 26:73). Galileans, it seems, were also falsely perceived as "uneducated" according to elite standards of higher education: *"Now when they saw the boldness and unfettered eloquence of Peter and John and perceived that they were unlearned and untrained in the schools [common men with no educational advantages], they marveled; and they recognized that they had been with Jesus"* (Acts 4:13 AMPC).

The research of noted Israeli scholar and historian Gedalyah Alon (1901-1950)[12] and others, has largely refuted such negative perceptions of Galileans. Sadly, however, many scholars researching this subject have overlooked Alon's research as well as that of others who reached similar conclusions because they were written in Hebrew. In truth, many Galileans were numbered among the Pharisees and sages.[13]

Many Galileans were numbered among the Pharisees and sages.

The Jewish inhabitants who lived here were knowledgeable about the *Torah* and the various applications made by their tradition. They were determined to live God's word and to pass their faith and knowledge and lifestyle on to their children.[14] It was into this world that Jesus was born and raised as a child, eventually being respected as Rabbi by His followers. Jesus went to school and worshiped at the synagogue just like all the other boys in Galilee, including those who later became His disciples.

> Torah study was a remarkable feature in Jewish life at the time of the Second Temple and during the period following it. It was not restricted to the formal setting of schools and synagogue, not to sages only, but became an integral part of ordinary Jewish life. The Torah was studied at all possible times, even if only a little at a time. ...The sound of Torah learning issuing from houses at night was a common phenomenon. When people assembled for a joyous occasion such as a circumcision or a wedding, a group might withdraw to engage in study of the Law.[15]

Some extremely gifted students sought out a famous rabbi and left home to travel with him for a lengthy period of time after completing their formal education. A few rabbis of great authority, however, personally selected students and extended a personal invitation, saying, "Come, follow me."

> There is much more to a *talmid* than what we call student. ...*A talmid* wants to be like the teacher, that is to become what the teacher is. That meant that students were passionately devoted to their rabbi and noted everything he did or said. This meant the rabbi-*talmid* relationship was a very intense and personal system of education. As the rabbi lived and taught his understanding of the Scripture his students (*talmidim*) listened and watched and imitated so as to become like him.[16]

"Come, follow me."

AS ONE HAVING AUTHORITY

For a teacher to be called "rabbi" was a sign of formal recognition and respect of status and authority. It literally means "my master." Itinerant preaching was a common practice in ancient Israel. However, it did not mean that one called *rabbi* had attended a special institute of higher learning. These teachers were mostly ordinary workers such as farmers, vinedressers, or potters.

Many of them worked seasonally, traveling and teaching in the months when they were free. Rabbis interpreted the Torah, explained the teachings, and told parables. Some traveled from village to village, teaching in synagogues. Though they relied on the hospitality of others, rabbis were never paid. They often took disciples who would study under their direction for years, traveling with them wherever they went.[17]

> Rabbis interpreted the *Torah*, explained the teachings, and told parables.

For a teacher to be addressed as "rabbi" was a formal recognition of their authority based on their teaching. A disciple showed reverence for doing God's will by being obedient to his rabbi and, by being his servant, allowed himself to be corrected to be perfected in humility. When His disciples called Him "Rabbi," they recognized Jesus as one worthy of their respect. *"Then Jesus turned, and seeing them following, said to them, 'What do you seek?' They said to Him, 'Rabbi' (which is to say, when translated, Teacher)"* (John 1:38 NKJV).

Certain teachers of the law merely repeated interpretations they had learned from others. A few rabbis, however, had such great spiritual authority that they could teach new revelation, use parables to give new meaning to old truths, and reinterpret the Scriptures. Jesus was recognized as One with extraordinary authority: *"They went to Capernaum, and immediately on the Sabbath He entered the synagogue and taught. They were astonished at His teaching, for He taught them as one having authority, and not as the scribes"* (Mark 1:21-22).

When discussing parables, it is crucial to note that the parables of Yeshua in the Gospels have many similarities to parables in rabbinic literature. They have a common structure, similar motifs, themes, forms, and plots. They both instruct, often with the same theological message. Yeshua's teaching through parables was a blending of old and new... *"Therefore every scribe instructed concerning the kingdom of heaven is like a householder who brings out of his treasure things new and old"* (Matthew 13:52). ...The new is not a rejection of the old, but rather a breath of fresh life infused into an old message. Torah is not canceled, but reinterpreted.[18]

Jesus demonstrated how to live by His life; He also preached the gospel of the kingdom of the heavens, used parables as a major teaching device, and, finally, after the resurrection He appeared to two disciples traveling on the road to Emmaus and opened their understanding to Messiah in all the Scriptures: *"And beginning with Moses and all the Prophets, He explained to them the things concerning Himself in all the Scriptures"* (Luke 24:27).

The crowds who listened to Jesus would have recognized His rabbinic style of teaching. In Matthew 21, the crowds and even the small children were shouting praises after He preached and healed people who suffered physical afflictions.

The angry priests and scribes confronted Jesus indignantly because the children cried out, "Hosanna to the Son of David!" They said, "Don't You hear what these children are saying?" insisting that Jesus rebuke the children. Instead, Jesus rebuked the priests and scribes, saying, *"Have you never read, 'Out of the mouth of babes and nursing infants You have perfected praise'?"* It was a typical rabbinic technique to "hint at Scripture."

> *Then the blind and the lame came to Him in the temple, and He healed them. But when the chief priests and scribes saw the wonderful things that He did, and the children crying out in the temple and saying, "Hosanna to the Son of David!" they were indignant and said to Him, "Do You hear what these are saying?" And Jesus said to them, "Yes. Have you never read, 'Out of the mouth of babes and nursing infants You have perfected praise'?"* (Matthew 21:14-16 NKJV)

"Hosanna to the Son of David!"

Everyone knew the Scriptures so well that they would easily have been able to finish the verse in their own minds. Jesus was pointing to the rest of the verse which says, *"From the mouths of children and nursing babies you have ordained praise on account of your adversaries, so that you might put an end to the vindictive enemy"* (Ps. 8:2 NET).

The psalmist is saying that God's glory is so great that even children instinctively worship Him, to the shame of those that hate Him. In the same way, the children who acclaimed Jesus were responding to His ministry the way His interrogators should have, but refused to do.[19]

The next time you read the gospels, consult the references to the Old Testament when Jesus quotes scripture. You may be surprised to learn what He is actually saying!

WORLD CHANGERS

When He began His time of ministry, Rabbi Jesus invited twelve disciples, eleven of whom were Galilean by birth, to follow Him. They were His apprentices for approximately three years. During that time, they often failed to obey and failed to understand. *"Having eyes, do you not see? Having ears, do you not hear?"* (Mark 8:18). James and John earned the nickname "sons of thunder," and their mother asked if they could sit on the right and left hands of Jesus in the kingdom. Peter denied Jesus three times. And all of them ran away at the Cross.

When Jesus died on the Cross, they became broken men. Their knowledge of *Torah* wasn't enough. Their self-effort was in vain. Peter, the one who thought himself strong, denied Jesus three times. The disciples were ready to be empowered by the Holy Spirit. That was the whole point. No one can live up to God's requirements in the flesh. The discipleship by Jesus wasn't enough. The best man-made discipleship program isn't enough. Spiritual prowess must be included for disciples to stand.

> No one can live up to God's requirements in the flesh.

These very *talmidim* became the twelve apostles who instructed the first Jewish believers, wrote the *Didache*, discipled Gentile believers, and thereby *"turned the world upside down"* (Acts 17:6). The *Didache* was framed by the best—the Galileans who were discipled by Jesus Himself.

> They turned the world upside down.

ENDNOTES

1. James W. Fleming, *The Jewish Background of Jesus* (LaGrange, GA: Biblical Resources, 2004), 11.

2. Ben Witherington, "Reading and Writing in Herodian Israel," *Patheos: The Bible and Culture*, November 2, 2011; retrieved February 26, 2020 from https://www.patheos.com/blogs/bibleandculture/2011/11/02/reading-and-writing-in-herodian-israel-was-jesus-an-illiterate-peasant-part-one.

3. Ray Vander Laan, *Life and Ministry of the Messiah* (Grand Rapids, MI: Zondervan, 1990, 2009), 34.

4. Ibid., 198-199.

5. Alfred Edersheim, *Sketches of Jewish Social Life in the Days of Christ* (New York, NY: Originally published in 1876 by James Pott & Co. Publishing. This edition was independently published in 2016), 84.

6. The Shame is the most important prayer in Judaism and is recited often multiple times a day, reaffirming the Jewish people to Judaism. made up of three scriptural texts (Deut. 6:4–9, 11:13–21; Num. 15:37–41), which, together with appropriate prayers, is an integral part of the evening and morning services. The name comes from the initial word of the scriptural verse "Hear, O Israel: The Lord our God is one Lord" (Deut. 6:4), which conveys the idea "hear and obey."

7. Edersheim, *Sketches of Jewish Social Life,* 30.

8. Ibid., 84.

9. Ray Vander Laan, "Rabbi and Talmidim," That the World May Know; retrieved February 3, 2020 from https://www.thattheworldmayknow.com/rabbi-and-talmidim.

10. Schmuel Safrai, "The Jewish Cultural Nature of Galilee in the First Century," *Immanuel 24/25*, 187; retrieved January 14, 2019 from http://www.etrfi.info/immanuel/24/Immanuel_24_147.pdf.

11. Vander Laan, "Rabbi and Talmidim."

12. Alon Gedalyahu, *The History of the Jews in the Land of Israel during the Period of the Mishnah and the Talmud* (Ann Arbor, MI: Eisenbrauns Publishing, 1977), 318-323.

13. Safrai, "The Jewish Cultural Nature of Galilee in the First Century," 148.

14. Edersheim, *Sketches of Jewish Social Life,* 83-93.

15. Schmuel Safrai and Menahem Stern, eds., *The Jewish People in the First Century* (Amsterdam, NH: Brill Academic Publishing, 1976), 968.

16. Vander Laan, "Rabbi and Talmidim."

17. Ann Spangler and Lois Tverberg, *Sitting at the Feet of Rabbi Jesus* (Grand Rapids, MI: Zondervan, 2009, 2018), 31-32).

18. "Parables, Pt. 2," *Jewish Jewels*, August 1, 2016; retrieved April 17, 2020 from https://www.jewishjewels.org/news-letters/parables-pt-2.

19. Spangler and Tverberg, 41.

A GOD-ENCOUNTER

CHAPTER 5

THE BEGINNING

by Jason Clark

STUMBLING from the bedroom to the kitchen, my body shouted at me as I gasped for breath. Only a few feet and I was completely winded. It was classic all right. The flu. Wheezing, coughing, bone-aching, hacking up a storm, head pounding, and burning with fever. Every horror story I'd ever heard about the flu was happening to me. Almost the sickest I'd ever been in my life, I just about crawled back to the bedroom and only stayed upright by steadying myself on the walls. Too sick to eat, I made it back to bed and collapsed into the crumpled sheets. I've only had the flu a few times in my life, but this was one of the worst times.

"There's too much work that needs to get done and here I am stuck in bed!" would have been my usual way of thinking. Ordinarily, it made me angry to be sick. Frustrated at myself and irritated that God had let it happen. Before I stopped caring if I was sick, I had to humble myself before God, receive forgiveness for bad attitudes, saying in my heart, "Lord, I don't want this sickness to come between us. I want to feel Your presence even if I'm sick like this."

"GOD, I ONLY WANT YOU"

Then, I yielded to Jesus in me, down in my heart, to feel His peace. The only thing of any importance was staying in communion with God—that was my goal.

The miracle, however, was that I stopped caring about how horrible I felt. Not even able to eat, I decided just give it to the Lord as a fast and spend my time in prayer. After a few days, God's presence suddenly fell on me, surrounding and filling me so powerfully that my heart absolutely melted. He became all I wanted. Only He mattered. Nothing else had any meaning. It was so amazingly wonderful to be so wrapped in God's love that I really didn't care how ill I was. It didn't matter if I was healed or stayed sick. Nothing mattered but Him. Whatever happened, good or bad, was immaterial because He became everything to me.

Noting mattered but Him!

Who was I? The person thinking these strange thoughts couldn't be me? "I can't do anything else so I think I'll just stay here and enjoy being with God." As if I had a choice in the matter. Sick, well, live, die. It's all God and only God. My throat choked up and tears started to well up and flow out of my eyes. I wiped them away before they ran into my ears.

God loving me and me loving God in return had become my world. This wasn't me. Who was I? Jesus was in me living my life. I'd heard it preached and read about it in books but now it was so real. A replaced life. Galatians 2:20 was really happening to me. It was glorious! "Joy unspeakable and full of glory" despite being sick as a dog. *I have been crucified with Messiah; it is no longer I who live, but Messiah lives in me"* (Gal. 2:19-20 TLV).

Jesus was in me living my life.

His love was so unbelievably powerful. All I wanted to do was stay lost in His presence forever. Even though I didn't care at the time if I ever got well, it was obvious that this needed to be shared at church. But right now, only this time spent with the Lord had any meaning. As the days and nights merged into each other, God touched one thing after another in my heart. It wasn't just God's love for me, but love flowing out toward others. It was holiness and love blended together.

As soon as I felt better, I called my father to tell him what was going on with me. He's the senior pastor of my church and I'm the senior associate pastor. Dad, Jennifer, my father's wife, and I had been reading and sharing and praying for this experience, which we call the replaced life, for about a year. People have called it different things through the centuries but that's what we call it.

After driving over to Dad and Jen's house, I laid out all that had happened to me. Then I prayed for them. Nothing. Every day for about a week I went over to their house or called on the phone saying, "Did you get it?" Finally, when I said, "All things are possible if you believe," the Holy Spirit fell on Dad and he started laughing. Dad prayed impartation for Jen and the experience was hers. Sunday was coming up so you know what that means. Of course, I'd be speaking in light of my experience.

> All things are possible if you believe.

At church Sunday, we shared what had happened, had an altar call, and the majority of those present received the replaced life. Afterward, a leader from another ministry who had been present testified that this impartation of holiness was leading up to the next awakening. Strangers came looking for the rented room where we meet because they said they could feel holiness there.

> *It is his doing that you are united with the Messiah Yeshua. He has become wisdom for us from God, and righteousness and holiness and redemption as well!* (1 Corinthians 1:30 CJB)

At that time, we didn't have any idea that God was ordering our steps toward the discovery of the *Didache* for our own discipleship program. Soon, it would all make sense.

CHAPTER 6

MAKING TRUE DISCIPLES

by Jennifer

DURING the late fall of 2008, we moved the meeting location for our small core group of believers into a suite of rooms located in an office park. Dennis says he knew that we wouldn't gather a large crowd because the main room was small. As we began to set up for church services, the Lord said, "You are not a church. I want you to create an upper room to birth a church." And He gave us Ephesians 2:22: "Build a *'dwelling place of God in the Spirit'*" (NKJV). Understanding that we were to build people by making disciples, we then concentrated on unifying a family, preparing a bride, and equipping an army. God doesn't need large numbers, but He does require great commitment.

In our morning prayer time soon after we had relocated, I (Jennifer) suddenly saw myself lifted up above the earth, and as I looked down flashes like bolts of lightning began striking small groups of believers who were earnestly seeking God all over the earth, like small versions of Pentecost! As bursts of fire rained down, the entire earth began to glow with the glory of God. Golden light began to pulsate and gleam until it covered the whole world. *"But truly as I live, all the earth will be filled with the glory of the Lord"* (Num. 14:21).

This vision has never lost its power.

LIVING SACRIFICE

Beginning in the summer of 2016, as we entered into a time of intense prayer during which we laid our lives down before the Lord, we cried out for the Holy Spirit to live in us as fully as He did in Jesus during His earth walk.

When the Holy Spirit visited Rees Howells asking for a full surrender, He told Rees, "I am a Person. I am God, and I am come to ask you to give your body to Me that I may work through it. I need a body for My temple (1 Cor. 6:19), but it must belong to Me without reserve."[1] In other words, if the Holy Spirit was to be in complete control, then Rees must get out of His way. This is same the question He was asking us. Considering the dire conditions in the earth today, we said, "Yes," crying out like David facing Goliath, *"Is there not a cause?"* (1 Sam. 17:29 NKJV). How could we possibly say, "No!" to the One who gave everything for us?

If ever there was a time when God needed sold-out warriors, that time is now. For this purpose, we placed ourselves on the altar of God: *"I beseech you therefore, brethren, by the mercies of God, that you present your bodies a living sacrifice, holy, acceptable to God, which is your reasonable service"* (Rom. 12:1 NKJV). As Kathryn Kuhlman said, "The Heavenly Father does not ask for golden vessels. He does not ask for silver vessels. God asks for yielded vessels—those who will submit their will to the will of the Father."

God is preparing a bride for His Son, *"a glorious church, not having spot, or wrinkle, or any such thing, but that it should be holy and without blemish"* (Eph. 5:27). And: *"Let us be glad and rejoice and give Him glory, for the marriage of the Lamb has come, and His wife has made herself ready"* (Rev. 19:7).

During this time, the Holy Spirit began dealing with me about any hope, or dream, or aspiration that I was reluctant to relinquish. "What if I asked you to lay down everything you're doing now and completely hid you away in intercession?" It went on and on: "What if...what if...what if?" On each question He wrestled with me until my heart said, "If I have You, I have everything. You are the 'one thing' I seek."

> One thing I have asked from the Lord, that will I seek after—for me to dwell in the house of the Lord all the days of my life, to see the beauty of the Lord, and to inquire in His temple (Ps. 27:4).

SIGNPOSTS IN HISTORY

As we inquired of the Lord, He prompted us to look to the past for signposts in history. Who has gone before us and found what we're looking for? After the outpouring of holiness and love spearheaded by Jason, we immersed ourselves in the writings of John Wesley (1703–1791), the great cleric, theologian, and evangelist, because what he taught had made an almost unparalleled impact on the culture of England. He not only founded the Methodist movement there, he was a maker of disciples. Never content with church as usual, Wesley had a vision for a true faith like that of the early church.

Searching through historical documents, reading about the giants of the faith, and paying close attention to those who not only ushered in revival but changed the culture through the disciples they made, we continually asked, "What made the difference?" As we studied John Wesley, it was clear that he was satisfied with nothing less than primitive Christianity. Wesley was our "mentor" who led us to the discipleship program of the church in the first centuries and prompted us to study the *Didache*.

The early church immersed new believers in a form of training that enabled them to cross a bridge from their old culture into an entirely new way of life. In the more modern version of discipleship, we glimpse the other side of the bridge as penned by John Wesley.

> Here is the sum of the perfect law, the circumcision of the heart. Let the spirit return to God that gave it, with the whole train of its affections. Other sacrifices from us He would not: but the living sacrifice of the heart hath He chosen. Let it be continually offered up to God, through Christ, in flames of holy love.
>
> And let no creature be suffered to share with Him; for He is a jealous God. His throne will He not divide with another; He will reign without a rival. Be no design, no desire, admitted there, but what has Him for its ultimate object. This is the way wherein those children of God once walked, who being dead, still speak to us. "Desire not to live but to praise His name; let all your thoughts, words, and works tend to His glory." "Let your soul be filled with so entire a love to Him that you may love nothing but for His sake."[2]

The apprenticeship plan of the *Didache* was rigorous and designed to conform disciples to Jesus, prepare them for life in a community of believers, and equip them to be effective witnesses in a hostile environment. This training program communicated very clearly that discipleship is not for a few special Christians but for all Christians, not an option but an expectation, not an addition to conversion but an essential feature of conversion."[3] Moreover, they aptly used the metaphor of an athlete training for competition.

> Paul uses runners in the Greek games as examples of how we are to live as Christians. The first thing to notice is the utmost tension, energy, and strenuous effort pictured by athletes straining for the finish line in hope of the glory of winning. "This is the way to run," says Paul, "if we want to attain our potential."
>
> This requires steady, intense concentration or focus of the runners. They cannot afford to become distracted by things off to the side of their course. If they do, their effectiveness in running will surely diminish. Keeping focused requires control—not allowing distractions to interfere with the responsibility at hand. "Seek first the kingdom of God and His righteousness," says Jesus (Matthew 6:33). ...Paul then says the victorious runner sets Christians an example of rigid self-control: "Everyone who competes for the prize is temperate in *all* things." It is not only a matter of concentrating while he is racing, but in all areas of life because his whole life impacts on the race.[4]

CHURCH AS IT COULD BE

> The [discipleship plan of the *Didache*] enabled converts to become functional disciples and thus helped for a community of Christians whose example of faith and obedience provided a clear and winsome alternative. ...[The] movement excelled at setting and maintaining high standards of membership. Considering the cultural climate, nothing short of a rigorous training program would have sufficed. ...[Together this produced] one of the most effective training programs in the history of the church.[5]

In 2015, I (Jennifer) dreamed of an old church building in a downtown section of a city that had seen better days. Entering the front door, the dinginess and old, musty smell were oppressive. While others in the building were looking through wallpaper books and making plans to redecorate, I was transfixed by a picture of a brand-new church in vibrant emerald green, symbolic of resurrection life.

Resurrection life in the church is the supernatural life of Jesus formed in stones that are alive with His life—*living* stones. Not our flesh but the *life of Jesus* as a reality in transformed believers. Church as it *could* be. Church as it *should* be. Nothing less could satisfy!

It grieved me to think of merely covering over the moldy walls with paint and paper, making only surface repairs when it needed a complete overhaul. A remodel of something run-down wouldn't work—an extreme makeover from the foundation up was required.

John Wesley had this same vision.

> Wesley had a vision for the true faith.

WESLEY'S HOLY CLUB

In young adulthood, Wesley had banded together with a group of friends and formed a Holy Club to draw closer to God. Wesley pointed out that believers in England at that time were so nominal in their faith that he faced a pagan culture, almost as wicked as the Greco-Roman world during the time of the early church. During the eighteenth century, England was sunk in deep darkness. Newborns were left on the street to die and 97 percent of infants born to poor mothers living in workhouses died within a few short years.[6]

COLLAPSE OF MORALITY

Sir William Blackstone (1723–1780), the renowned British jurist whose *Commentaries on the Laws of England* became the best-known description of the doctrines of English law, visited the churches of all major clergymen in London and lamented that he "did not hear a single discourse which had more Christianity in it than the writings of Cicero."[7]

In most of the sermons he heard, Blackstone couldn't even tell whether the preacher was Hindu, Buddhist, or Christian by what was said! In 1738, Bishop Berkeley lamented that morality and Christianity had collapsed "to a degree never known in any Christian country."[8]

Can God change a depraved nation deeply submerged in what has been described as a moral and spiritual cesspool? This question may well be asked in our day concerning modern-day America. The answer has profound implications and places all of us in the center of the bull's-eye. Yes, He can and will, but all of us play a role in bringing about such transformation. How was England changed in one generation? By the discipleship of ordinary believers under the tutelage of one man who had a vision for church in the mold of the primitive church.

God can change an entire nation.

ACCOUNTABILITY GROUPS

At the very beginning of the movement, Wesley established accountability groups for believers to "watch over one another in love" as he and his friends had done for each other This practice became "the engine of holiness in early Methodism."[9] Although all believers were expected to attend class meetings, the more intimate band meetings were the "driving force behind Methodists' testimonies to growth in holiness."[10]

> The band meeting was *the place* where people who had experienced God's pardoning love and had entered in to a saving relationship with Jesus...gathered to pursue more. ...Wesley probably did not expect every member of a band meeting to have significant sins to confess every week. But he persistently encouraged, even implored, Methodists to gather together in band meetings because he wanted them to commit to a place where they could be fully known and be fully loved.[11]

> Band meetings were intended to be "little families of love," where people were able to sound [know the depths] of one another's lives to the bottom, to know each other deeply and completely in order to experience the depths of God's perfect love, and be made holy through dwelling in this love and bring all of their lives unto the light of God's grace.[12]

The Methodist movement was empowered by the experience of the replaced life as well as other encounters with God. The truth is, we can't live as a true believer in Jesus in our flesh. *"It is the Spirit who gives life. The flesh profits nothing"* (John 6:63). The replaced life is Jesus living His life through us. When we give up, Jesus takes over.

The next step we took was the establishment of Wesleyan-style small groups for discipleship.[13] Wesley said that these groups were the core and resulting fire of the Methodist movement. When the Methodist church was transplanted to America, Bible studies and prayer meetings replaced accountability groups and the dynamic impact of the band meetings was lost.

Watch over one another in love.

The early Methodists didn't pray for revival. They lived in revival and God was in their midst. *"Pursue peace with all men, and the holiness without which no one will see the Lord"* (Heb. 12:14). The fire and core of their movement came from the small accountability groups in which the hearts of believers were kept aflame with the love of God.

> One of the most important and lasting contributions that the Methodist movement made to the church is the rediscovery and systematic implementation of class meetings [small groups for accountability] as a means of grace for spiritual vitality. In many ways, what led to the success of John Wesley's evangelism ministry and the sustenance of the Methodist movement, in contrast to some of his colleagues, was the value he placed on shared communal life.[14]

CONVERTS VS. DISCIPLES

George Whitefield (1714–1770), a great evangelist during the First Great Awakening in America, commented on Wesley's discipleship, saying, "My Brother Wesley acted wisely, the souls that were awakened under his ministry he joined in class [small groups], and thus preserved the fruits of his labor. This I neglected, and my people are as a rope of sand."

> This was in keeping with the theological emphasis Wesley placed on sanctification—it would not be enough to "get people [born again]"

through field preaching or revival meetings, God desires that we orient our entire affections toward him. Wesley implemented several types of small groups such as classes, bands, select societies, and others which met together for instruction, confession, and like practices.[15]

God desires wholehearted love.

EVANGELISM AND GOOD WORKS

John Wesley not only insisted on holiness of life but felt that outreach and good deeds were essential elements of the church. *"What does it profit, my brethren, if someone says he has faith but does not have works? Can faith save him? ...Thus also faith by itself, if it does not have works, is dead"* (James 2:14,17 NKJV).

In addition to founding Methodist societies, Wesley embarked upon evangelistic work with great vigor. He is said to have preached 40,000 sermons and to have traveled 250,000 miles on horseback. As the doors of the Anglican Church closed for him, Wesley undertook open-air or field preaching. He also insisted on seeking out the poorest of the poor, former prison inmates, and the very dregs of society.

Wesley taught a practical faith that prepared people for everyday life. Not only did he teach holiness and theology, but how to handle finances, be a leader, and make a difference in society by demonstrating love wherever a need existed. *"Let us consider how to spur one another to love and to good works. Let us not forsake the assembling of ourselves together, as is the manner of some, but let us exhort one another, especially as you see the Day approaching"* (Heb. 10:24-25).

Because of Wesley's emphasis on discipleship, which led to action, lives were changed, holy living resulted, and good works were done such as the building of orphanages and schools, thereby transforming an entire nation in one generation. While the salvation of individuals is wonderful, Father God promised Jesus entire nations, saying, *"Ask of Me, and I will give you the nations for your inheritance, and the ends of the earth for your possession"* (Ps. 2:8).

Through Wesley, an entire nation was transformed in one generation.

DISCOVERING THE DIDACHE

Because John Wesley looked to the purity of the early church as his model, we began our own comprehensive study of the first- and second-century church as we began to plan a small group program following the Wesleyan model. (The *Didache* wasn't discovered until 1873, long after John Wesley passed away.)

Because of our own passion for discipleship, when we ran across the small training manual called the *Didache*, we were intrigued, and the more we learned, the more impressed we became. Immediately recognizing its potential, we studied it thoroughly then taught it in our own church.

We believe that the *Didache* is the most important training manual for believers you never read. Scholars say it is an extension of the Great Commission itself.

After extensive research, we made copies of the *Didache* available at our church and taught it to our congregation in a series of fourteen lessons then asked some mature believers in our congregation to share testimonies of what the *Didache* had meant to them personally.

> The *Didache* is an extension of the Great Commission.

THREE COMPONENTS OF DISCIPLESHIP

The primitive concept of discipleship was one of total immersion in a new way of life, much like learning a foreign language. To speak one, you must leave the other. Just as in the early church, the ideal discipleship program should include three main components.

Bible. First, they taught the Bible. However, it was taught according to the gospel of the kingdom, which was the gospel Jesus preached, and what He taught the disciples on the Emmaus Road when He opened up the Scriptures to them, revealing all things concerning Himself (see Luke 24:13-49).

Belief. Second, they taught what Christians should believe. The very first sermon preached by Peter covers the essentials of belief as found in the Apostles' Creed (and earlier Old Roman Creed).

A significant part of the responsibility of the church is preparing disciples to remain true to the faith. Many church fathers made apologetics (the intellectual defense of the truth of Messianic beliefs) their life's work. *"Beloved, while I diligently tried to write to you of the salvation we have in common, I found it necessary to write and appeal to you to contend for the faith which was once delivered to the saints"* (Jude 1:3).

Three types of sermons are found in the Book of Acts including edification of believers, evangelistic, and apologetic sermons, or those spoken in defense of the faith, or what followers of Jesus should believe. Almost half of the sermons found in Acts include apologetic, or creedal, aspects.

> *But there were also false prophets among the people, just as there will be false teachers among you, who will secretly bring in destructive heresies, even denying the Lord who bought them, bringing swift destruction upon themselves* (2 Peter 2:1).
>
> *For there are some men who secretly crept in, who were marked long ago for this condemnation. They are ungodly men, who pervert the grace of our God into immorality and deny the only Lord God and our Lord Jesus the Messiah* (Jude 1:4).

John Wesley said that, from the beginning, the Methodists were "orthodox in every point," the criterion of which was "firmly believing...the Three Creeds."[16,17] "Were you to recite the whole catalogue of heresies...it might be asked, 'Who can lay any one of these to their [the Methodists'] charge?'"[18] The teaching of the creeds had rendered early Methodism essentially heresy proof.

Life. Finally, last but not least, the early church taught believers how to *live.* Proper discipleship was at the heart of the Methodist movement. We can be certain that the apostles thoroughly *trained* novices how to live in the new way within the Messianic community, just as they themselves had been taught by Jesus. A failure to adequately equip believers to live like true disciples has been a great weakness in the church throughout the centuries.

To summarize, discipleship should include training in the Bible, what to believe, and how to behave. Bible, belief, and behavior. Like the early church, John Wesley addressed all three areas masterfully.

DISCIPLESHIP TODAY

The most pressing need of the church today is proper discipleship. The world is not impressed with believers who bear little resemblance to Jesus. The greatest concern of pastors and leaders in the church is the lack of passion for the Lord among believers and their lack of perseverance and progress as believers. Too many come to a standstill and don't advance beyond the rudiments of faith and practice. Many backslide and return to worldliness or indifference.

What do believers need to become true disciples of Jesus? First, they need to agree with God about morality, learn how to live in the Spirit, and surrender to the work of the Cross. Then, training about the Bible and other principles of a life of faith can rest upon a solid foundation.

John Hall, a member of one of Wesley's groups, wrote in his autobiography, "What greatly helped me forward in the ways of God, were our band meetings...it was our only desire to live to the glory of God, and to help each other forward. ...The Lord remarkably crowned our little meetings with His presence and blessing. Our souls increased daily in love and unity. We enjoyed a heaven upon earth!"[19]

The most pressing need of the church is proper discipleship.

Seasoned believers, who had been in the church for twenty or thirty years, who were profoundly affected when we taught the *Didache* to our congregation testified about the impact it had on them.

Be prepared to have your world rocked. When we started to put into practice the kingdom principles in the *Didache*, my heart was branded with fire. I was challenged to become that Bride Jesus wants. I learned practical ways to enter the fullness of the heart of Jesus to become the Bride He desires. Be prepared to have your world rocked!

The Didache raised my standards. Studying the *Didache* raised my standard as to what the lifestyle of a believer should look like in real, ordinary life. It also answered questions I've had regarding Holy Spirit power in the first-century church. They were given much because they loved Jesus wholeheartedly. I definitely had gotten casual about what is actually sin in my life. The *Didache* awakened me to take it seriously when I grieved the Lord seriously with certain thoughts and actions.

My compromised faith had seemed permissible. I mostly ignored heart attitudes that were nominally godly and my standards had been allowed to slip. I am humbled, broken, and longing again for my First Love while feeling His longing for me. I am believing once again that He still is who He says He is, and I am His and He is mine. Called, loved, and kept, forever.

ENDNOTES

1. Norman Grubb, *Rees Howells: Intercessor* (Fort Washington, PA: Christian Literature Crusade, 1987, first published 1952 by Lutterworth Press), 35.

2. John Wesley, *A Plain Account of Christian Perfection* (Columbia, SC: CreateSpace, 2013), 6-7.

3. Gerald Sittser, *Resilient Faith: How the Early Christian "Third Way" Changed the World* (Grand Rapids, MI: BrazosPress, 2019), 156-157.

4. John W. Ritenbaugh, "What the Bible Says about the Athlete Analogy," *Forerunner Commentary, Bible Tools*; retrieved April 18, 2020 from https://www.bibletools.org/index.cfm/fuseaction/Topical.show/RTD/CGG/ID/1572/Athlete-Analogy.htm.

5. Sittser, 157.

6. Debra Kelly, "10 Heartbreaking Stories from Britain's Workhouses," ListVerse, July 11, 2015; retrieved June 9, 2018 from https://listverse.com/2015/07/11/10-heartbreaking-stories-from-britains-workhouses.

    "The workhouses of Britain were a last resort. Getting yourself and your family admitted to one was something you only did if there was no other choice. It was submitting to a life of long days, mediocre meals, horrendous sanitation, separation from the rest of your family, and a high likelihood you wouldn't see your freedom again. Workhouses were dark, dismal places, and some heartbreaking stories came out of them."

7. Diane Severance, "Evangelical Revival in England," Christianity.com, April 28, 2010; retrieved June 6, 2018 from https://www.christianity.com/church/church-history/timeline/1701-1800/evangelical-revival-in-england-11630228.html.

8. Ibid.

9. Kevin Watson and Scott Sisker, *The Band Meeting: Rediscovering Relational Discipleship in Transformational Community* (Franklin, TN: Seedbed Publishing, 2017), 86.

10. Ibid., 87.

11. Ibid., 87-88.

12. Ibid., 94.

13. For teaching materials on the groups we established, *Small Groups that Go Deep*, visit our website at www.forgive123.com.

14. Andrew Dragos, "How John Wesley's class meetings serve as identity formation," Seedbed, June 7, 2012; retrieved June 6, 2018 from https://www.seedbed.com/how-john-wesleys-class-meetings-serve-as-identity-formation.

15. Michael Mack, "The pioneers of the small-group movement," *Christianity Today*, July 28, 2014; retrieved June 8, 2018 from https://www.smallgroups.com/articles/2014/pioneers-of-small-group-movement.html.

16. The Apostles', Nicene, and Athanasian Creeds.

17. John Wesley, *The Sermons of John Wesley*, Sermon 132, "On Laying the Foundation of the New Chapel," (Columbia, SC: CreateSpace Independent Publishing, 2013), 614-619.

18. Thomas Oden, *John Wesley's Scriptural Christianity: A Plain Exposition of His Teaching on Christian Doctrine* (Grand Rapids, MI: Zondervan Publishing House, 1994), 66; John Wesley, "A Farther Appeal to Men of Religion and Reason Pt. I," v. 16-22; II:155-163.

19. James Hall, "An Account of Mr. James Hall, Written by Himself," *Arminian Magazine* 16 (1793): 287.

CHAPTER 7

APPLYING THE POWER OF THE CROSS

GOD is opening ancient spiritual wells that have not only been capped for many years but are hardly even mentioned in a great many of our churches. The most important forgotten well is the deep work of the Cross available to us through identification with the death, resurrection, and ascension of Messiah. The enemy has plugged the wells of revival and awakening in the church, but God is directing His servants to uncap the wells and allow the fountain of the water of life to flow freely once again.

I will open rivers in desolate heights, and fountains in the midst of the valleys; I will make the wilderness a pool of water, and the dry land springs of water (Isaiah 41:18 NKJV).

John Wesley lived during the eighteenth century, but the Second Great Awakening in America, which began in the late eighteenth century and lasted until the middle of the nineteenth century, was marked by a rediscovery of Wesleyan truth. Charles Finney (1792–1875) taught Wesley's holiness theology at Oberlin College in Ohio for twelve years before he had an experience, and then he continued to preach the message.

Based on the truths expounded by Wesley, the Higher Christian Life (or Keswick) movement swept through America and Western Europe in the late nineteenth century, drawing multitudes into a life of holiness.

We can't experience holiness without a work of the Cross. The Cross is the narrow gate through which we must pass to enter resurrection life. The narrow gate is not the gate of salvation—it is the gate of the overcomer.

Enter at the narrow gate, for wide is the gate and broad is the way that leads to destruction, and there are many who are going through it, because small is the gate and narrow is the way which leads to life, and there are few who find it (Matthew 7:13-14 NKJV).

God is opening ancient spiritual wells.

In seeking the will of God, Jesus is our example. He lived on earth in complete dependence on His Father and did nothing apart from Him. His obedience was perfect. The Spirit of Holiness rested upon Him and remained. Father God pronounced His approval at both the beginning and end of Jesus's ministry by saying, *"This is My beloved Son, in whom I am well pleased"* (Matt. 3:17; 17:5).

When Jesus lived on earth, He was the perfect expression of His Father. *"He who has seen Me has seen the Father"* (John 14:9). We were created by God to be expressions of the Father—just like Jesus. God loves us unconditionally; even when we fail to appropriate all He has for us, He loves us. However, He rejoices when we choose His best. God's best is the ultimate intention He purposed in His heart for humankind—His eternal purpose. He created us to live by the life that is in Messiah, be conformed to His image, and enter into the glory of Messiah as co-heirs with Him as a real experience, not just doctrine (see Rom. 8:17,29).

> From eternity past up to the resurrection, the Lord is the only begotten Son. But after He is raised from the dead He becomes the firstborn Son. Accordingly, after the resurrection He says this to Mary Magdalene: "Go unto my brethren, and say to them, 'I ascend unto my Father and your Father'" (John 20:17).
>
> By the death of God's only begotten Son, many sons are born. ...God takes His Son as the mold or stamp, and in this stamp God impresses us many sons so that His Son might be the firstborn among many sons. He causes us to have the glory of His Son as well as the life [and nature] of His Son (Romans 8:29-30).[1]

We were created to be expressions of God.

CREATED AS CONTAINERS

We were created in God's image as vessels, or containers, of God's Spirit to walk as Jesus walked. Unlike animals, which only have biological life, we must have a spirit in us to live. *"The body without the spirit is dead"* (James 2:26). We are vessels, servants, branches, temples with no independent lives of our own. We were formed to be vessels, or containers, of an indwelling spirit.

We are a derivative life requiring a spirit to dwell in us. We merely express the nature, or spirit, filling us. A vessel is designed to be *filled* with something. Otherwise it serves no purpose. In our case, we are designed to contain *Someone* (see Eph. 3:19). The Scriptures call us vessels, branches of the vine, and temples of the Holy Spirit.

> These symbols used to describe us humans are all those which express no nature of their own but as means of expressing that to which they are attached. Vessels contain the liquid, but are not the liquid; the cup is not the coffee. We don't speak of a cup and coffee. So we are branches; but the branch is not the nature but the vine which reproduces itself in leaf and fruit form on the branch.[2]

We were made to be containers of an indwelling spirit.

> Spirit can mix with spirit, or *interpenetrate*, unlike physical matter. When a carpenter makes a chair, he does not become part of the chair. It is impossible. However, it *is* possible for us to be in union with God. We are spirit beings made *"in the image of God"* (Genesis 1:26-27). In receiving the Spirit of [Messiah], we are *"joined to the Lord"* and become *"one spirit with Him"* (1 Corinthians 6:17). Our spirit becomes one with His Spirit. "Our 'bodies are the temple of the Spirit,' and God is spoken of as 'dwelling in us and walking in us'" (2 Corinthians 6:16).[3]

A REPLACED LIFE

Prior to the Fall, Adam and Eve were faced with a choice. Would they eat of the Tree of Life and be filled with the Holy Spirit or eat from the Tree of the Knowledge of Good and Evil? They ate from the wrong tree. The devil stole

God's property and filled them with a sin spirit—the spirit of error. All people inherited a wrong nature and became *"sons of disobedience"* and *"children of wrath"* due to Adam's disobedience (Eph. 2:1-3).

From eternity past, God had a plan to reclaim what was His. In the fullness of time, God sent His Son to die for us that we might become sons and daughters restored to our Father! *"For God so loved the world that He gave His only begotten Son, that whoever believes in Him should not perish, but have eternal life"* (John 3:16). And: *"God demonstrates His own love toward us, in that while we were yet sinners, Messiah died for us"* (Rom. 5:8).

From eternity past, God had a plan to reclaim what was His.

How could fallen sinners be reconciled with a God who loves with holy love? God is love but He is also holy. He is *"of purer eyes than to behold evil"* (Hab. 1:13 KJV).

God is love. Love is the nature of God, not just something He has. From the very beginning, God loved with a perfect, unselfish love that exists to give. It is total self-giving love. With the Fall, human beings turned in on self and became self-loving selves. The nature of humanity apart from God is selfish and self-serving to the core. Love reached out to us fallen sinners and made a way to restore us to fellowship. Love seeks communion.

God is holy. Only God is holy. Holiness is not just one of God's divine attributes; it is the innermost essence of God. He doesn't have holiness as a "thing"—He is holy because it is His nature. In rescuing fallen humanity, God had to satisfy the tension between love and holiness. Holiness separates God from everything unholy. Love seeks communion, but holiness requires separation. Holiness is both separation from all sin and separation unto God. Holiness is separateness, glory, and blazing purity.

Love seeks communion.

When the prophet Isaiah encountered God in His holiness, the seraphs covered their faces and sang, *"Holy, holy, holy is the Lord of Hosts; the whole earth is full of His glory"* and Isaiah cried out, *"Woe is me, for I am undone! Because I am a man of unclean lips, and I dwell in the midst of a people of unclean lips; for my eyes have seen the King, the Lord of hosts*" (Isa. 6:3,5 NKJV). The prophet was dumbstruck by the contrast between his sinfulness and God's holiness.

How can a holy God meet unholy us? God's plan of redemption provides the solution. He made provision for communion with His created ones through the work of Jesus on the Cross. He satisfied His requirement for holiness through replacing our life with Messiah's life.

Holiness requires separation.

TWO-FOLD REDEMPTION

In Adam, we inherited two problems—*sins* committed and a *wrong spirit* filling us. In Messiah, God provides a two-fold redemption—the blood and the Cross. We receive forgiveness of our sins through His shed blood. *"In Him we have redemption through His blood and the forgiveness of sins"* (Eph. 1:7). Our second dilemma is the presence of a *wrong spirit* in us, or a sin nature, governed by the law of sin and death (see Rom. 8:2). Therefore, we need a *new Spirit!* That is also accomplished by the work of the Cross.

Jesus took all humanity with Him when He died on the Cross. We died when He died. Because our spirit leaves our body when we die, the sin spirit, or nature, left when we died with Messiah. *"The body without the spirit is dead"* (James 2:26). Because we died, we died to the infilling of the wrong spirit so we could be filled with another Spirit—the Spirit of God. When Messiah was raised from the dead, we were raised together with Him with a *new Spirit*. We received *"newness of life"* (Rom. 6:4). The indwelling sin spirit was *replaced* by the Spirit of Messiah!

The spirit of sin is replaced by the Spirit of Messiah!

Our life replaced by Messiah's life gives us:

- The Spirit of Life instead of a spirit of death
- The Spirit of Truth instead of a spirit of error
- The True Vine (source of living) instead of a false vine
- The Spirit of Holiness instead of a spirit of sin

God doesn't make *us* good, because there is no goodness in us. God doesn't make *us* loving, because human love falls short of God's love. God doesn't make *us* holy, because only He is holy.

For every need, God gives us Messiah. *"By His doing you are in* [Messiah] *Jesus, who became to us wisdom from God, and righteousness and sanctification* [holiness], *and redemption"* (1 Cor. 1:30 NASB). And: *"it is no longer I who live, but Messiah lives in me"* (Gal. 2:20 TLV).

It was impossible for us to live the believing lifestyle all along. "We are forced to admit that we cannot manifest godliness apart from God, or righteousness apart from the Righteous One, Jesus. ...The Christian life is [His] life lived out in us, as us, and through us, while we as dependent creatures derive [everything] from Him."[4] Through a replaced life, we no longer manifest a wrong spirit, but Messiah's Spirit.

> When Paul says we are raised with [Messiah], he is not speaking only of the resurrection. The resurrection was the beginning of Jesus's ascension, but Paul has more in mind than just the resurrection... Paul clearly has the result of the resurrection and the ascension of Jesus in mind because he is thinking of Jesus's exaltation to heavenly places. This is the result of both His resurrection and His ascension. What is even more shocking than Jesus's own ascension is that Paul tells us that we have been raised up with Him. In other words, when Jesus ascended, we ascended.
>
> Paul describes this reality by using the past tense. We *have* ascended. It has already been accomplished. Paul is describing a governmental reality, not a metaphysical one. He is not simply saying that we are raised up in our spirit. He is telling us that Jesus, as a man, has taken a governmental position and in doing so recovered the governmental position of man for all those who are in Jesus. We will be raised from the dead in the future, but we have already been raised positionally with Jesus. What man lost and forfeited in the garden in terms of his position and authority before God has been reclaimed.[5]

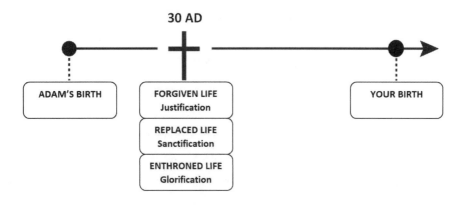

Our Inheritance in Messiah

When we were born again, most of us received forgiveness of sins alone because that's all we understood. Messiah becomes an influence in our lives, but we continue to struggle with sin by willpower as we *try* to live the life of faith (see Rom. 6 and 7). Later, another recognition comes. We not only need forgiveness but a *new* nature or new spirit!

> *I will give you a new heart and put a **new spirit** within you* (Ezekiel 36:26 NKJV).

For every need, God gives us Jesus.

Personal Pathway of the Cross

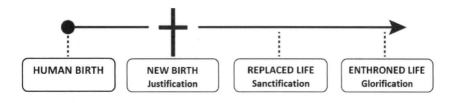

Because we are vessels, or containers, not independent "selves," we cannot have two natures or two spirits filling us. Only one spirit can fill our vessel. We cannot be filled with the Spirit of truth *and* the spirit of error at the same time (see 1 John 3:24; 4:6). Our "self" is expressed by the spirit filling us. It is not possible to "die to self" in the sense that our self actually *dies*. We will always be a self. We simply die to one spirit only to be instantly filled with another Spirit.

A STARTLING VISION

Almost 30 years ago, I (Jennifer) had a startling vision. I was a new believer who wanted to be transformed into a "child from another world" with all my heart. And yet, it was horrifying to me to discover that sin was still a struggle after salvation. How could I possibly be like Jesus? It seemed like the more I tried, the more I failed. Even when my outward behavior seemed commendable, my attitudes were often wrong.

My signpost individuals, even before I came to Jesus, were those saints who seemed ever unruffled by the circumstances of life and seemed to dwell in a heavenly realm inaccessible to ordinary people. Even in novels like *Jane Eyre*, Jane did not interest me so much as the orphan girl, Helen Burns, who lived and died in the love of Jesus.

One day, as a new believer, I found myself standing in the altar area after the church service. Suddenly Jesus appeared and we stood face to Face. As I gasped audibly, Jesus stepped toward me, put His hands on mine, and then, much to my amazement, He turned and stepped into me. His eyes were now my eyes and His heart my heart. I was overwhelmed with love at first, but the impression gradually faded away. Things went back to life as usual. Three decades afterward, my experience still fell far short of that vision.

In the summer of 2016, I finally understood the secret. It's not that I hadn't searched the Scriptures and pored over the many books written by saints of old. The Lord Himself must remove the veil that blinds our eyes, according to His timing. Discovering that I had been born a slave who needed a new Master was perhaps the most liberating revelation of my life next to the new birth. *"Having been set free from sin, and having become slaves of God, you have your fruit to holiness"* (Rom. 6:22 NKJV).

The Lord began to reveal the mystery of my life replaced by Messiah's life. His Spirit hovered over me for months and the word I wrote again and again in my journal was "overshadowed." I felt as though the Spirit of Holiness was hovering over me, as in Genesis, and that He was preparing to birth something, or Someone, new in me (see Gen. 1:2; Luke 1:35; 9:34). The following year a revival of holiness broke out in our church. And then just as in the vision, He came to live His life in me. The experience was mine. Now, we are seeking an even deeper experience of surrender individually and corporately.

> We are born slaves who need a new Master.

THE TWO-NATURE FALLACY

Before we discover the mystery of Messiah in us, we feel as though we have a bad dog and good dog constantly fighting within us. Many believers have believed this two-nature fallacy because this seemed true based on their experience. However, if it is true that we will forever have an internal battle, what do we do with the following Scriptures from Romans 6?

> *How shall we who died to sin live any longer in it?* (Romans 6:2)

> *Our old man has been crucified with Him, so that the body of sin might be destroyed, and we should no longer be slaves to sin* (Romans 6:6).

> *The one who has died is freed from sin* (Romans 6:7).

> *Sin shall not have dominion over you, for you are not under the law, but under grace* (Romans 6:14).

> *Having been freed from sin, you became the slaves of righteousness* (Romans 6:18).

> *But now, having been freed from sin and having become slaves of God, you have fruit unto holiness* (Romans 6:22).

What about Romans 7, we might ask? Is that the way we are doomed to live our lives? Doesn't the prospect of such bondage contradict the freedom promised in Romans 6? If true freedom is impossible to attain, why does Paul joyfully cry out in the final verse: *"I thank God—through Jesus...our Lord!"* (Rom. 7:25 NKJV)? That hardly seems like the wretched man of verse 24 who still needed deliverance: *"O wretched man that I am! Who will deliver me from this body of death?"* (NKJV). Notice that Paul's question asked, *"Who?"* The very next part of the verse tells us that the way of deliverance is the Deliverer: *"Jesus our Lord!"* We are rescued by the Person who takes our place!

Then what is Romans 7 really about? It's all about the "I" of self-effort. In Romans 6 we learn we've been delivered. In Romans 7 we see the futility of trying to live the life of faith through self-effort. We have been delivered from *trying* to keep the law by a Person who lives in us as the embodiment of the Law. *"It is God who works in you both to will and to do for His good pleasure"* (Phil. 2:13 NKJV). If it's Messiah in us willing and working, what is left for us to do? Thank Him and yield to Him!

We are rescued by the Person who takes our place!

WHAT IS GRACE?

What is grace? The definition of grace as the "unmerited favor of God toward man" is very shallow. That particular definition does apply to the initial conversion experience in the sense that God reaches out to fallen man with the provision of forgiveness through the blood of Jesus. But that is where it stops.

Other more complete definitions of grace include:

- Grace is the presence of Jesus within, working in us so we can obey God's commandments and meet His standards of holiness and love.

- Law demands of man what only "God is." Grace supplies man with what "God is" in order to meet God's demands.

- Grace is the personal presence of Jesus empowering us to be all that God calls us to be and do all that He calls us to do.

The *Merriam-Webster Online Dictionary* includes both conversion and the subsequent quality of life by defining *grace* as "unmerited divine assistance given to humans for their regeneration or sanctification [holiness]."

God meets us at our point of need then lifts us up to where He is...by grace. Therefore, you can define grace as a Person. God doesn't give us things. For every need, God gives us Messiah. God doesn't make *us* good, because there is no goodness in us. God doesn't make *us* loving, because human love falls short of God's love. God doesn't make *us* holy, because only He is holy. *"By His doing you are in...Jesus, who became to us wisdom from God, and righteousness and sanctification [holiness], and redemption"* (1 Cor. 1:30 NASB).

It is impossible for us to live the believing lifestyle through human effort. The most liberating discovery a believer can make is that only Jesus can meet the high standards of God. Therefore, grace is Jesus living His life in us: *"It is no longer I who live, but Messiah who lives in me"* (Gal. 2:20). I give up and Jesus takes over.

We must point out that serious divisions have occurred in our churches over some of these subjects. Do we have it all at the new birth? Is there a second work? Is there one baptism of the Spirit or are there many? Does sin get permanently destroyed in us? Do believers have two natures fighting within them until they get to heaven? How many works of grace are there?

> There are thousands, whole groups and denominations, whose beliefs on such points as these are diametrically opposed. Should that not be a warning to us not to be too fierce in our denunciations of others, nor too separate from them? Do we not get nearer the truth when we recognize that in all of us our hearts have gone farther than our heads? We can experience what we can only stumblingly expound. Once again, we come back to what? A Person—the Lord Jesus Himself.

> Around Him we unite in our hearts' love, when our heads would keep us far apart... Not with those who hold the same doctrines about Him, but those who love Him. There we unite... If there are so many convinced bodies of believers who hold passionately to their special viewpoints, it is because they each have something from God the whole body needs... All opposites meet in Him, and all opposites have truth.[6]

I give up and Jesus takes over.

Do we get all the riches of Messiah at our conversion? Yes! Do we grow in our faith progressively? Yes! Are there some things we will only understand in heaven? Yes! Does God want us to love our brothers and sisters in the Lord even if we disagree? Yes! Could it be that in the next Great Awakening some or all of this will become clear by increased revelation from our Lord? He will further enlighten His body to remove some walls of division and inspire us to spiritual heights we have not yet experienced in the fullness of Him and the blessing of unity as believers according to the prayer prayed by our Lord Jesus in John 17.

> *That they may all be one, as You, Father, are in Me, and I in You. May they also be one in Us, that the world may believe that You have sent Me. ...I in them and You in Me, that they may be perfect in unity* (John 17:21,23).

In light of this, our position emulates that of the Moravians in Germany during the 18th century who were known for their love and unity.[7] These believers who actually experienced the answer to the prayer of Jesus for unity took as their motto: "In essentials, unity; in nonessentials, liberty; in all things, love."

In all things, love.

Under Mosaic law, only the high priest could enter the Holy of Holies in the temple on one day of the year. However, the day of Pentecost ushered in a new era. The early church displayed God's rule and reign in and through individuals. Now God was not confined to living in the midst of His people; He made people His temples (see 1 Cor. 6:19)!

The three levels of the cross correspond to the three rooms of the Tabernacle of Moses and the Temple—outer court, Holy Place, and the Holy of Holies. The first room symbolizes living by human understanding, or the light of the sun. In the second room, we discover the light of revelation. Only in the third room does God Himself become our light: *"They need no lamp nor the light of the sun, for the Lord God will give them light. And they shall reign forever and ever"* (Rev. 22:5).

God's dwelling place multiplied from a physical location to the hearts of a multitude of believers. *"Your body is the temple of the Holy Spirit, who is in you"* (1 Cor. 6:19). Jesus no longer preached just in Israel, but His testimony would be preached and demonstrated through *believers* around the world through the power of the Holy Spirit.

CHILDREN, YOUNG MEN, FATHERS

In his first epistle, John the beloved likens the three great levels of our faith experience to *little children, young men,* and *fathers* (1 John 2:13-14). We inherit the fullness of all three levels at the time of initial salvation, but usually require further revelation to understand how to experience *"the glorious riches of this mystery...Messiah in you, the hope of glory"* (Col. 1:27).

What do these levels signify? Little children are those who are born again because they have received forgiveness for their sins. A child lives in dependence on his parents and knows them outwardly. Little children live in self-effort knowing God is for them externally rather than living by Messiah's life within. The second level is that of the young men who have *"overcome the wicked one"* and Messiah abides in them as the Living Word.

The third level, fathers, is those who know *"Him who is from the beginning"*—the Eternal One who now, as from the beginning, is completing His eternal purpose. Fathers are consumed by the eternal purpose of God in loving and redeeming others. Fathers volunteer to live sacrificial lives just as Paul did: *"If I am being poured out as a drink offering on the sacrifice and service of your faith, I am glad and rejoice with you all"* (Phil. 2:17 NKJV). The third level is summit living—the level of the overcomers who have seen the door still open in heaven and share the Throne (see Rev. 4:1; 3:21).

The entrance to each level is through the work of the cross and involves a counting of the cost. To those who would be His disciples, Jesus says, *"If anyone desires to come after Me, let him deny himself, and take up his cross, and follow Me. For whoever desires to save his life will lose it, but whoever loses his life for My sake will find it"* (Matt. 16:24-25 NKJV).

God made people His temples.

FIRST LEVEL FORGIVEN LIFE	SECOND LEVEL REPLACED LIFE	THIRD LEVEL ENTHRONED LIFE
"Little Children"	"Young Men"	"Fathers"
In Him we have redemption through His blood and the forgiveness of sins (Ephesians 1:7).	I have been crucified with Messiah. It is no longer I who live, but Messiah lives in me (Galatians 2:20).	I urge you therefore...that you present your bodies as a living sacrifice, holy, and acceptable to God, which is your reasonable service (Romans 12:1).

What about Temptation and Sin?

After coming into the experience of the replaced life, does sin go away forever? No. It simply loses its power over us. We must still deal with the duality of our humanity—Messiah within but the world, the flesh, and the devil without. When we know that temptation is not sin, we don't feel condemned when we are tempted! Temptation is merely an opportunity for Messiah to reveal His power working in us. *"My brothers, count it all joy when you fall into diverse temptations"* (James 1:2).

Temptation is inevitable.

We live in a sinful world filled with sinful people and every kind of sinful enticement imaginable, so temptation is an inevitable part of human living: *"Each man is tempted when he is drawn away by his own lust and enticed"* (James 1:14). We are tempted when our mind and body are stirred up by our flesh. We are delivered from indwelling sin, but we are not out of calling distance.

We are kept by the power of God.

Because we are now set free from the suspicion that temptation is sin *and* our response to it are both sin, we can relax in confidence that the power of God is strong enough to hold us close to Him. Temptation and sin *pull* on our flesh. However, the power of God has a *more powerful magnetic pull*. We are kept by *"the power of God"* indwelling us (1 Peter 1:5)!

Jesus was *"in every sense tempted like we are, yet without sin"* (Heb. 4:15). The truth you need to see is that anything Jesus did in His earth walk He can do *through you!* When tempted, simply yield to Jesus within and resist. *"Therefore submit yourselves to God. Resist the devil, and he will flee from you"* (James 4:7).

We are kept by the power of God.

Receive and Believe

Again, we will be a "self" for all eternity. We just change from one master, *satan*, to another Master—the Lord Jesus, expressing His life in us. In Him, we *replace* a wrong spirit, *sin and death*, with the right Spirit—the *"Spirit of life in Messiah Jesus"* (Rom. 8:2). "There is a great difference between realizing, 'On that Cross He was crucified *for me*,' and 'On that Cross I am crucified *with Him*.' The one aspect brings us deliverance from sin's *condemnation*, the other brings us deliverance from sin's *power*."[8]

> What is the normal Christian life? The Apostle Paul gives us his own definition...in Galatians 2:20. It is *"no longer I, but* [Messiah]." Here he is not stating something special or peculiar—a high level of Christianity. He is...presenting God's normal...which can be summarized in the words: I live no longer, but [Messiah] lives His life in me. God makes it quite clear in His Word that He has only one answer to every human need—His Son, Jesus... In all His dealings with us He works by taking us out of the way and substituting [Messiah] in our place. The Son of God died instead of us for our forgiveness: He lives instead of us for our deliverance.[9]

As this truth is quickened to us, we simply receive and believe. Faith reaches out and grasps truth, thus bringing it into our present reality. *"I have been crucified with Messiah. It is no longer I who live, but Messiah who lives in me. And the life I now live in the flesh, I live by faith in the Son of God, who loved me and gave Himself for me"* (Gal. 2:20). How do we receive the promises of God? We believe until the object of our faith becomes reality. Through *"faith and patience"* we *"inherit the promises"* (Heb. 6:12).

Through faith and patience, we inherit the promises!

- Be steadfast in believing and confessing it as truth (see Rom. 10:10).

- Hold on by faith until you receive the full reality (see Heb.10:23; 11:1).

- God will make it a real experience through a spiritual encounter.

ENDNOTES

1. Watchman Nee, *God's Plan and the Overcomers* (New York, NY: Christian Fellowship Publishers, 1977), 12-13.

2. Norman Grubb, *It's as Simple as This* (Blowing Rock, NC: Zerubbabel Press, 2005), 8-9.

3. Ibid.

4. James A. Fowler, "No Independent Self: An Attempt at Clarification," Christ in You Ministries 2005; retrieved May 8, 2017 from http://www.christinyou .net/pages/noindependentself.html.

5. Samuel Whitefield, "God's Eternal Purpose for Man," December 14, 2014; retrieved May 5, 2017 from https://samuelwhitefield.com/1519/ gods-eternal-purpose-for-man.

6. Norman Grubb, *The Liberating Secret* (Blowing Rock, NC: Zerubbabel Press, 2010), 114-115.

7. A group of Moravian families fleeing bitter persecution for their faith found refuge in 1722 in Saxony, Germany, on the estate of Count Nicholas von Zinzendorf (1700–1760), a pietist nobleman. They built the community of Herrnhut, which became a safe haven for many other persecuted Christians. The Moravians experienced a great outpouring of the Spirit in 1727 that was later called the Moravian Pentecost. They were known for Christian unity. On his deathbed, von Zinzendorf said with joy that he had seen the prayer of Jesus for unity in John 17 answered in his lifetime.

8. Gregory Mantle, *Beyond Humiliation: The Way of the Cross* (Minneapolis, MN: Bethany House Publishers, 1975), 64-65.

9. Watchman Nee, *The Normal Christian Life* (Fort Washington, PA: CLC Ministries International with permission of Tyndale House Publishers, Inc., 2009. Previously published 1957 and 1977), 9-10.

DEVELOPING
SPIRITUAL
PROWESS

CHAPTER 8

SPIRITUAL ANATOMY

by Jennifer

DENNIS and I have long been known as "the how-to couple." When we were first married, Dennis mentored me in simple but profound ways that enabled me to progress from being a *head* to a *heart* believer. Believing in Jesus is not a mental philosophy but an encounter with God Himself.

An African Anglican bishop attended one of our seminars and made the following comment based on what he observed: "From the initial encounter with Jesus and the subsequent process of relationship that follows, Drs. Dennis and Jen have documented a step-by-step explanation that combines God-encounter with process. It is a descriptive approach that demystifies how to live in the Spirit. It is based on the simplicity of a relationship with Jesus."

One of the most wonderful things Dennis taught me was how to yield to Jesus in my heart and experience the supernatural peace of His presence. Another example was learning how to forgive from the heart. I had struggled with "trying" to forgive from my head for years, but, when I learned how to forgive from my heart, I found it also washes pain and anger out quickly and completely. Moreover, it is as easy as receiving forgiveness was at the time of salvation by simply yielding to Jesus. As a result, when we were launched into a twelve-year period of itinerant ministry, we often found ourselves teaching the basics of what we now call using "the God-tools."

> *We use our powerful God-tools for smashing warped philosophies, tearing down barriers erected against the truth of God, fitting every loose thought and emotion and impulse into the structure of life shaped by Christ. Our tools are ready at hand for clearing the*

ground of every obstruction and building lives of obedience into maturity (2 Corinthians 10:5-6 MSG).

For a robust and healthy spiritual life, it is essential that we know what our God-tools are *and* how to use them. Many seasoned believers have said, "Here's someone telling us *how* to do what we already knew we were supposed to do!"

What are some of our God-tools?

- Forgiveness from the heart (Matt. 18:35; Acts 13:38; 1 John 1:9)
- Five functions of the human spirit (receiving, forgiving, loving, releasing, and resisting)
- Fruit of the Spirit (1 Cor. 13; Gal. 5:22-23). "The enemy can't touch the fruit of the Spirit."
- The armor of God (Eph. 6:10-18)
- Prayer (Matt. 6:9-13; Eph. 6:18)
- Fasting (Matt. 6:16-18; Matt. 17:21)
- The Bible (Matt. 4:1-4; Eph. 6:17)
- The believer's authority in Christ (Luke 9:1; 10:19; James 4:7)
- The name of Jesus (Matt. 18:20; Mark 16:17)
- The Holy Spirit (John 14:26; John 7:38-39)
- The blood of Jesus (Rev. 12:11)
- The work of the Cross (1 Cor. 1:18; 2 Cor. 4:11-12)
- Spiritual gifts (Rom. 12:3-8; 1 Cor. 12:1-28; Eph. 4:7-16)
- Spiritual discernment (Phil. 1:9; Heb. 5:14)
- Patterns and principles of God (explained in Christian literature and teachings, salvation tracts, the *Blue Card* prayer steps in chapter 9, and so forth)

The *Didache* presupposes that the Gentile believers being mentored are impacted by spiritual reality rather than mental assent. It is not hard to imagine the richness of experience the apostles enjoyed on the Day of Pentecost. We can be certain that their disciples similarly knew the power and presence of God more fully that most of us do today. It is as though they were mentored with the light of a thousand-watt lightbulb while we must get by with a candle. Much spiritual truth was lost over the centuries along with the *Didache*. Therefore, truths that the early believers seemed to know automatically may need to be explained more fully to modern-day believers.

LOCATION OF THE HEART

One of these recovered keys is the location of our spiritual heart. Many believers erroneously believe that the word *heart* in the Bible refers to the physical heart in the chest, especially because so many modern translations have substituted the generic word *heart* for the original Hebrew and Greek words. When the Bible talks about the heart of man, it refers to the "belly" or "bowels" (the actual words used in both the Hebrew Old Testament and the Greek New Testament). This doesn't mean your heart and spirit are in a physical organ of the body. It just means the belly area is the epicenter of spiritual and emotional activity.

> The belly is the epicenter of spiritual and emotional activity.

In the Old Testament, the word *bowels, me'ah* in Hebrew, is correctly translated in the King James Version of the Bible, but the less accurate word *heart* is substituted in later translations. The Hebrew word used for *heart* in Song of Solomon 5:4 is *me'ah,* meaning "inward parts, digestive organs, bowels, womb, or, figuratively, the place of emotions of distress or love." When the Shulamite's Beloved came to her, she says, *"My bowels were moved for Him"* (KJV), meaning that her heart was moved with affection.

In the New Testament, we find that the heart of man is also located in the belly. *"He that believeth on Me, as the scripture hath said, out of his belly shall flow rivers of living water"* (John 7:38 KJV). The words of Jesus indicate that the epicenter of spiritual activity is in the belly area. In the original Greek, the word used here is *koilia,* meaning "belly." Later translations use the English word *heart* instead of belly, but *belly* is the correct translation.

Only one verse in the New Testament refers to the physical heart, Luke 21:26: *"Men's hearts failing them from fear"* (KJV). The Greek word *apopsucho* is used for "hearts failing" meaning their physical hearts "breathe out life" or they "die." With this one exception, *heart* always refers to the innermost being. According to *Vine's Expository Dictionary of Old and New Testament Words*: "By easy transition the word [heart] came to stand for man's entire mental and moral activity, both the rational and emotional elements. In other words, the heart is used figuratively for the hidden springs of the personal life... Scripture regards the heart as the sphere of Divine influence."[1]

The heart is our innermost being.

What happens when Jesus rules our heart and takes the ascendancy over our thoughts, feelings, and will? *Revelation* rules our thoughts, *conscience* rules our will, and *communion* or *fellowship* with Jesus rules our emotions. Our heart must be open to both believe and receive. We must first *want* to receive. The second key to receiving is *belief.* Jesus tells us, *"If you can believe, all things are possible to him who believes"* (Mark 9:23). And, *"Whatever things you ask when you pray, believe that you receive them, and you will have them"* (Mark 11:24).

When Jesus rules, revelation rules our thoughts, conscience rules our will, and communion rules our emotions.

"BUCKET MAN"

To understand how we function spiritually, picture an old-fashioned well with a crank, bucket on a rope, and fresh, cool water deep down in the well. The crank is in your head and the water is deep within your heart—in your spirit being. The bucket is your awareness or focus.

Close your eyes and open your heart in prayer. In your imagination, crank the bucket all the way down to your spirit, to the living water in your heart. *"The water that I shall give* [you] *will become* [within you] *a fountain of water springing up into eternal life"* (John 4:14). Pay attention to your gut. (It's very subtle so don't expect fireworks or euphoria.) Maybe you'll feel something? Do you? Most people feel a mild sense of peace.

> *Counsel in the heart of man is like water in a deep well, but a man of understanding draws it out* (Proverbs 20:5 AMPC).

Just as we can open our heart to the Lord or shut Him out, our choices determine the course of our life decision by decision. Therefore, we can clearly see that our heart has a door. The door into our heart is governed by our *will*, our faculty of choosing. When we open the door of our heart to God in prayer, we touch Him spirit to Spirit. When we *keep* the door open in everyday life, we begin to abide in Him as a lifestyle. We stay connected with the Lord.

We touch the peace of His presence.

If you ever sat quietly in church with an attitude of reverence toward God, whether or not you were aware of it, you most likely "dropped down" to your spirit. You may know intellectually that God is omnipresent, but when you focus on the fact that He is always with you, even at this very moment, your perception shifts based on this awareness. He is not only our Savior but our Immanuel, or *"God with us"* (Matt. 1:23).

I will never leave you, nor forsake you (Hebrews 13:5).

God is our refuge and strength, a well-proven help in trouble (Psalm 46:1).

As soon as we open our heart to include the Lord, the peace we feel is a gentle sense that Someone else is with us. It is much the same as driving a car with a passenger in the back seat. You may not be able to see them, but you know they are there. When Dennis was teaching me about peace and the presence of God, he reminded me to "include God" in the moment. For example, when I became anxious about something, he would tell me, "Open your heart to God and include Him."

We begin to a*bide,* or remain, in God's presence when we stay connected to the Lord. As we learn to stay connected to Him in everyday life, we practice the presence of God. If you become distracted during the day and disconnect, don't become frustrated with yourself. Simply make the connection again. Drop down to your spirit. Remember, practice makes *permanent.*

Brother Lawrence was a seventeenth-century monk who lived in France. His godly character and deep relationship with the Lord attracted many visitors. With a reputation for experiencing profound peace, his way of life drew people seeking spiritual guidance to him. The wisdom he passed on in conversations and letters later became the basis for his book *The Practice of the Presence of God*. When we have Jesus in our heart, we can learn to be aware of Him all the time just like Brother Lawrence.

Learn to be aware of Jesus all the time.

If we focus on our head, the door of our heart closes and our bucket goes up. When we were teaching this concept at a Christian school, a small child commented, "There's no living water in your head!" That was a very perceptive statement. If we focus on our own thoughts apart from God, our bucket goes up where no living water can influence our thoughts. The children love the bucket man illustration, but we occasionally borrow him to teach adults as well.

The peace of God is the opposite of anxiety.

Proverbs 3:5-6 tells us, "*Trust in the Lord with all your heart, and lean not on your own understanding; in all your ways acknowledge Him, and He will direct your paths.*" Notice that we are instructed to trust the Lord in our heart rather than relying upon our mental reasoning. The word for *acknowledge* is *yâda* in Hebrew, meaning "to know" in a relational sense. It is often used for intimate union between husband and wife (see Gen. 4:1,17,25). As used here, *yâda* refers to divine intimate connection with the Lord. We make a heart connection with Jesus in us when we drop our bucket down to our heart.

LOCATION OF THE WILL

The belly or gut is not only the seat of our spirit and emotions, but also of our *conscience* and *will*, the faculties of choice and decision making. The word *will*, in some translations of the Old Testament, is translated *reins*, or literally our *kidneys*.

I the Lord search the heart, I try the reins [kidneys] (Jeremiah 17:10 KJV).

Door of the heart. The door of the heart is the *will*. It is in the belly. Scripture tells us that the door of the heart can either open or close, choose or refuse.

Jesus says in Revelation 3:20, *"Behold, I stand at the door and knock. If anyone hears My voice and opens the door, I will come in to him"* (NKJV).

Yielding. One of the most powerful lessons we can learn is how to *yield* our will. Unless this lesson is learned, believers will struggle in many areas of their life. Yielding instantly connects us to Messiah within. When we *don't* yield, we function by our own willpower! On the other hand, when we yield and connect with God, *God* works.

> *It is God who is at work in you, both to will and to work for His good pleasure* (Philippians 2:13 NASB).

TROUBLESHOOTING

Quite often, people who say they can't feel peace have an unrealistic expectation. Even an unbeliever knows if they're relaxed or stressed. As believers, however, relaxing allows *supernatural peace* to take the ascendancy and rule in our life in obedience to Scripture. Jesus has given us the gift of peace (see John 14:27). Peace should be the *starting place* for living the life of faith. The Scriptures command us to *"let the peace of God rule"* in our life (Col. 3:15 NKJV).

Children don't seem to have a problem feeling the peace of God's presence, although they sometimes use the word *good* instead of *peace*. However, adults often have difficulty when they have made a habitual practice of compartmentalizing, or living out of their head instead of their heart. Our expectations and habitual way of life can make a lifestyle of peace harder than it should be. We must first *learn* to be still then *practice* peace in everyday life.

> Most supernatural peace is too quiet for our flesh.

Psalm 46:10 tells us, *"Be still and know that I am God."* "Be still" comes from the stem of the verb *rapha,* meaning "let go, surrender, or release." This verse contains two imperatives. We are to first *be still* and then we can truly *know* the power of God in our life. We are not to intellectually understand the words but experience the reality of the kingdom of God at work in our heart.[2] In doing so, we are delivered from our fears and find supernatural peace: *"Surely I have calmed and quieted my soul, like a weaned child with his mother; like a weaned child is my soul within me"* (Ps. 131:2 NKJV).

But to what end are we to "be still," "let go," "surrender," and even to "die to ourselves"? ...We surrender *in order* to know that God is in control as *Ribbono Shel Olam*—the Master of the Universe. We "let go" in order to objectively know the saving power of God in our lives. We give up trusting in ourselves and our own designs in order to experience the glory of God's all-sufficiency.[3]

The Lord will fight for you, and you shall hold your peace and remain at rest (Exodus 14:14 AMPC).

Although some individuals may instantly feel the presence of God strongly when they drop down to their spirit, over time the sense of His presence will increase for all. The absence of turmoil is a good starting point, but your awareness of supernatural peace will grow when you continue yielding to Jesus within. The practice of *Christian meditation* is not merely thinking about God but surrendering our entire being to Him: "*I meditate in my heart; my spirit made a diligent search*" (Ps. 77:6). And: "*I will meditate on the glorious splendor of Your majesty, and on Your wondrous works*" (Ps. 145:5 NKJV).

The Bible does speak positively about meditation. In the Psalms, David sings of meditating on the Law of God day and night. The biblical concept of meditation is not without reference to thought and content. To the contrary, it is about thinking that is directed by the Word of God—scripturally saturated thought.

[Biblically based meditation] is almost the exact opposite of Eastern meditation, which sets the emptying of the mind as its goal. The Eastern concept of emptying the mind is just not anything close to the biblical vision of filling the mind with the Word of God. ...The biblical concept of meditation on the Word of God does involve an emptying, of course. We must empty our minds of ungodly and unbiblical thoughts, of desires for sin and resistance to the reign of God in our lives. But that emptying never involves an empty mind. Instead, it involves a mind in which unbiblical thoughts are replaced by the truth of Scripture—not a blank slate of meditation that revolves around the self.[4]

Blessed is the man who walks not in the counsel of the ungodly, nor stands in the path of sinners, nor sits in the seat of scoffers; but his delight is in the law of the Lord, and in His law he meditates day and night (Psalm 1:1-2).

PRACTICE

Yielding to Messiah Within

1. Sit down in a quiet room and close your eyes. Place your hand on your belly. Relax and yield to Messiah in you. Focus on your heart but notice that the atmosphere of the room also feels more peaceful. You become more aware of the Lord when you focus on Him.

2. Honor God by acknowledging the fact that He is with you. The Lord is not only omnipresent but you are also God indwelt. When you invite Him into your heart, He never leaves you.

3. Spend a few minutes waiting in the presence of God. Often, as we become more relaxed, our awareness of peace increases.

4. We should never attempt to make our mind go blank, but simply become aware that the Lord is with us by paying attention to Him. Focus is the opposite of "blank." We don't "empty our mind." We fill our mind and heart with God.[5]

ENDNOTES

1. William E. Vine, *Vine's Expository Dictionary of Old and New Testament Words*, Vol. 2 (Old Tappan, NJ: Fleming H. Revell Company, 1981), 206-207.

2. John J. Parsons, "Surrender: God's Irrepressible Care of the World," Hebrew for Christians; https://www.hebrew4christians.com/Meditations/Be_Still/be_still.html.

3. Ibid.

4. Albert Mohler, "The Empty Promise of [Eastern] Meditation," *Albert Mohler,* November 20, 2008; Retrieved September 11, 2014 from https://albertmohler.com/2008/11/20/the-empty-promise-of-meditation.

5. The Christian approach to prayer and seeking God is an active pursuit with the intention of quieting the soul (the carnal mind, will, and emotions) while focusing intently on Jesus. *"Let us go right into the presence of God with sincere hearts fully trusting him"* (Heb. 10:22 NLT). Thoughts, emotions, and perceptions are brought under the control of the Holy Spirit and yielded to the Lord. The goal is drawing closer to God.

> *If a son asks for bread from any father among you, will he give him a stone? Or if he asks for a fish, will he give him a serpent instead of a fish? Or if he asks for an egg, will he offer him a scorpion? If you then, being evil, know how to give good gifts to your children, how much more will your heavenly Father give the Holy Spirit to those who ask Him!* (Luke 11:11-13 NKJV)

CHAPTER 9

EMOTIONS
AND PEACE

OURemotions were created to be channels of the love of God. They were intended to be transmitters of the fruit of the Spirit (see Gal. 5:22-23). However, as soon as sin entered the world, Adam and Eve were taken hostage by the enemy and felt toxic emotions for the first time. Adam began to feel unpleasant emotions like fear, lust, anger, guilt, and shame. Eve no longer enjoyed the tranquil paradise she had known because her once peaceful heart became polluted with negative emotions. They suddenly felt the need to run from God when He came to talk with them, and they made some bad choices. The enemy had hijacked their emotional pipelines!

> Our emotions should be channels of the love of God.

At the time of salvation, God rescued us from the enemy's kingdom. He *"delivered us from the power of darkness and conveyed us into the kingdom of the Son of His love"* (Col. 1:13 NKJV). We instantly received forgiveness and experienced peace with God. Kingdom emotions were restored to us and are tangible evidence that the kingdom of God is at hand: *"The kingdom of God is...righteousness and peace and joy in the Holy Spirit"* (Rom. 14:17 NKJV). And: *"the kingdom of God is within you"* (Luke 17:21).

EMOTIONS ARE FRIENDS

Toxic emotions don't come from God's kingdom. They come from the wrong kingdom. We don't lose our salvation when we feel a negative emotion, but we take a temporary detour into enemy territory. The same answer that gave us peace with God in the first place—forgiveness—will keep us in peace when we live a forgiveness lifestyle. When we forgive, our emotions are instantly restored to the supernatural peace of God. As you received Messiah, so walk (see Col. 2:6). Peace is the evidence that nothing is separating us from the presence of God. Emotions are friends that let us know what kingdom is in operation at any given time—the kingdom of God or the kingdom of the enemy.

> When we forgive, we are instantly restored to the supernatural peace of God.

Earth is our battleground (see 1 Pet. 5:8; Eph. 6:11). Believers are the property of God. However, negative emotions always give the enemy permission to attack us. The only way evil spirits can torment us is for us to give them permission. As long as demons have legal ground in us, they can harass us. When we remove negative emotions, we take back the ground. The enemy can't touch the fruit of the Spirit.

> *Like a flitting sparrow, like a flying swallow, so a curse without cause shall not alight* (Proverbs 26:2 NKJV).

> The enemy can't touch the fruit of the Spirit.

BITTER ROOTS

A bitter root is a personality structure that forms when a toxic emotion is planted in the heart. It takes root and grows up like a weed and produces poisonous fruit. Over time, sinful judgments form a root system that takes on a life of its own and operates automatically, coloring our perceptions, driving behavior, and causing cycles of trouble. As long as a bitter root remains, it continues to grow and inject poison into our life.

> *Pursue peace with all men, and the sanctification without which no one will see the Lord. See to it that no one comes short of the grace of God; that no root of bitterness springing up causes trouble, and by it many be defiled* (Hebrews 12:14-15 NASB).

> *And judgment sprouts like poisonous weeds in the furrows of the field* (Hosea 10:4 NASB).

A root transmits either a flow of life or death, producing good or bad fruit. Your root system either draws nourishment or poison into your life and relationships. We can be rooted in God and life or rooted in bitterness producing death. You can identify a root by its fruit. A root always produces fruit. Bad fruit comes from a bad root. Good fruit comes from a good root.

> *A tree is identified by its fruit. If a tree is good, its fruit will be good. If a tree is bad, its fruit will be bad* (Matthew 12:33 NLT).

Toxic emotions are not sin; unforgiveness is sin.

BITTER ROOTS AND UNFORGIVENESS

Bitter roots cause trouble.

Because many roots form in early childhood, we may forget about them as we grow older. Nevertheless, they still produce harvests of trouble in adulthood.

Bitter roots disrupt relationships.

They distort how we see and understand God as well as how we see others and ourselves. *"Pursue peace* [forgiveness] *with all men"* (Heb. 12:14) to be able to know and understand (see) the Lord. God ties forgiving people to knowing Him.

Bitter roots rob us of God's presence and power.

Bitter roots cause believers to forfeit the grace of God that could have been theirs. See to it that no one comes short of the grace of God (see Heb. 12:15). Grace is the personal presence of God enabling you to be who He called you to be and do what He called you to do. Grace is not just favor; it is power to live the believing lifestyle. When you don't forgive, bitter roots block the presence of God from working in your life.

Bitter roots cause us to reap bitter harvests.

They result in repetitive cycles of trouble and destruction. They also defile others, pushing them to sin against us. An individual who has been abused attracts abusers—until the root is removed. Any "root of bitterness springing up" has a life of its own, causing all sorts of trouble in unpleasant repetitive cycles (see Heb. 12:15). Although it is not always obvious, one sure way to identify a bitter root is to pay attention to the bad things that happen again and again. We may even say, "Oh no! Here it goes again!" or, "Why do I always get a difficult boss at every job?"

Bitter roots push others to sin against us.

Individuals with a bitter root have something in them that causes others to react negatively toward them. Abused children often behave in ways that cause people to become irritated when they are with them. People who are wounded by rejection often have a "shell" around them that causes others to reject them or makes them difficult to talk to.

Bitter roots cause repetitive cycles of trouble and destruction.

Roots Can Drive Habits

Although roots are often hidden or forgotten, God will reveal the entry points in prayer when we ask. Sin and toxic emotions give the enemy legal ground to harass us. Old-time believers used to call these repetitive sinful behaviors *besetting sins*.

David provides an excellent example of how to seek the Lord's help for cleansing the heart and removing barriers. He allowed the Lord to have full access to his heart. However, Psalm 19 illustrates David's process of approaching the Lord for healing and deliverance. He didn't try to figure himself out. David also admitted to God that he knew that the *unknown things lodged in his heart* could lead to very serious consequences.

> *Who can understand his errors? Cleanse me from secret faults. Keep back Your servant also from presumptuous sins; may they not rule over me. Then I will be upright, and innocent from great transgression* (Psalm 19:12-13).

Jesus the Forgiver

Jesus in us does the forgiving through us. Through grace we become believers, and by grace we live in the Spirit. "*I have been crucified with Messiah. It is no longer I who live, but Messiah who lives in me*" (Gal. 2:20). Therefore, it is no longer I who love, but Jesus who loves in me. It is no longer I who forgive, but Jesus who forgives through me!

The Forgiver in us does all the work. And everything He does is easy for Him! All we have to do is yield and allow Him to work: *"God is the One working in you, both to will and to do His good pleasure"* (Phil. 2:13). What do *we* do then? We surrender our will to God's will and He does the work.

> Jesus in us does the forgiving through us.

WHO DOES THE FORGIVING?

The Bible clearly says that only God can forgive sins (see Mark 2:7). However, Jesus tells us that we must forgive or our heavenly Father won't forgive us (see Matt. 18:35). So, which is it? Does God forgive or do I forgive? The answer lies in the fact that we become a new creation when we are born again: *"Therefore, if any man is in Messiah, he is a new creature. Old things have passed away. Look, all things have become new"* (2 Cor. 5:17).

The new creation is our identity when we are born again—us fused together with Jesus. The new creation yields and allows forgiveness to flow from our heart. The one who does the forgiving is not *me* but *we*. *"But he who is joined to the Lord becomes one spirit with Him"* (1 Cor. 6:17).

THE PEACE OF GOD

Let's take a closer look at the *supernatural peace* Jesus has given to us as a gift: *"Peace I leave with you. My peace I give to you"* (John 14:27). Jesus makes His peace available for *us* to enjoy! In English, the word *peace* is usually understood as tranquility or a lack of conflict. The peace of God, however, is so much more than that. When His peace rules our heart, we know Jesus is ruling in our life at that moment. He never withdraws His gift of peace, so it is always available.

In *shalom,* Hebrew for *peace,* we find completeness, wholeness, health, peace, welfare, safety, soundness, tranquility, prosperity, perfectness, fullness, rest, harmony, and the absence of agitation or discord. There is much more to biblical peace than tranquility or lack of conflict. Peace is the power that establishes the government of the Prince of Peace in our life. Peace is authority. Peace is power! When peace rules, Jesus rules.

Peace, be still. From the place of peace, Jesus could sleep in the boat in the middle of a terrible storm, then stand and command the wind and waves, saying, *"Peace, be still!"* The same Prince of Peace who took authority over a storm on the Sea of Galilee also has authority over the storms of life.

When we walk in the peace that God gives, people and circumstances can't control us. Was Jesus ever frazzled or anxious? Of course not! He is the Prince of Peace. He has perfect peace, has authority to give us peace, and is the Commander of peace.

Romans 16:20 assures us, *"The God of peace will soon crush Satan under your feet."* Peace is living in the presence of the Prince of Peace, for *"He is our peace"* (Eph. 2:14). When we are in peace, we are in the presence of God.

Forgiveness restores peace. If we happen to lose our peace temporarily, how do we return to peace? Forgiveness! Forgiveness always gets us right back into the atmosphere of the kingdom of God (see Col. 1:13). When you became a believer, did you have to wait to receive God's forgiveness? No, it happened instantly. Forgiveness is always available and forgiveness never fails.

We should let our emotions be our *friends.* They confirm the presence of peace and the absence of negative emotions. Once we know a toxic emotion is present, we can make a *supernatural exchange.* Any toxic emotion is a signal that the application of forgiveness is needed. When we present our negative emotions to God, He *transforms* them into Spirit-born emotions.

When we present our negative emotions to God, He transforms them into Spirit-born emotions.

HOW TO FORGIVE

Important keys for prayer. Forgiveness is the answer for dealing with conflict and offenses in the moment as well as the baggage of the past. Jesus is the Forgiver, so forgiveness works every time! It is instant, not a process, just like when you were born again. Deal with whatever God shows you, even if you think it is unimportant. There is no "big or little." If you think it is too traumatic to face, you only have to feel the pain momentarily to present it to Jesus for healing. It's all easy for Jesus! Finally, sequence is important, so always go in God's order. Pray through one thing at a time until you get peace.

Forgiveness brings roots to death. Jesus provided a solution through forgiveness. It brings bitter roots to death and replaces toxic emotions in our heart with supernatural peace.

Forgiveness is instant. When we are born again, we experienced instant forgiveness. Forgiveness is still instant in our walk afterward when we present our heart for Jesus to heal.

WHO TO FORGIVE

Forgive in Three Directions. Forgiveness goes in three directions—toward God, self, and others. Sometimes we must forgive in two or more directions. If in doubt, forgive. You can't love or forgive too much!

1. **God.** God didn't do anything wrong, but people get angry at Him anyway. Sometimes people feel hurt that God didn't do what they wanted Him to do or become angry that God didn't *stop* something from happening. Forgiving God gets *your* heart right by releasing your judgments toward Him.

2. **Self.** If you are angry, disappointed with, or ashamed of yourself, you need to receive forgiveness for judging yourself so harshly. Frequently people are much harder on themselves than others!

3. **Others.** Release forgiveness to other people. It sets you free!

REMOVING ROOTS

Forgiveness removes the negative emotion revealing the presence of a root issue and replaces it with peace in a supernatural transaction. Negative emotions are barriers to healing. If you are angry at God, start by forgiving Him. Most root healings require only the steps of *first, feel, forgive.* We have the following prayer steps on a blue index sized card we call the *Blue Card.* It is a tool those attending our seminars use when they practice praying for one another. The person praying reads off the card while the other person closes their eyes and cooperates internally.

PUT ON THE NEW MAN

The Bible uses many metaphors that describe God as the defender and protector of His people. He is our Rock, Fortress, High Tower, Hiding Place, Shield, and Dwelling Place. Psalm 91 is perhaps the most well-known hymn celebrating God as our Protector and Deliverer.

> *He who dwells in the shelter of the Most High shall abide under the shadow of the Almighty. I will say of the Lord, "He is my refuge and my fortress, my God in whom I trust"* (Psalm 91:1-2).

Although we have little need for mountain fortresses to survive during an enemy siege today, in Old Testament days having a refuge to flee from enemies was a very real need. Stronghold cities, high towers, and ramparts allowed residents of regions to escape and gain a strategic advantage when defending themselves from enemy forces. Rocks and caves provided personal safety for

David during the many years he ran from Saul: *"David remained in the wilderness in strongholds...Saul sought him every day, but God did not give him into his hand"* (1 Sam. 23:14).

> *God is our refuge and strength, a well-proven help in trouble* (Psalm 46:1).

We find our own place of safety when we "hide" in the presence of God. When we stay in peace, God Himself guards us and delivers us from the enemy. The enemy can't touch us when we are kept by the power of God! Rather than running to a stronghold in the hills, God has established Himself a fortress in our own heart. When we drop down to our spirit, we enter His presence, our Hiding Place. God keeps us safe. God delivers us from the snare of the enemy.

When we stay in peace, God guards us.

Let's look more closely at the great deliverance the Lord has provided for us. When we get born again, much is provided for us, but we are responsible for appropriating our inheritance and equipment. Therefore, when we are told to "put off" the old man and his deeds and "put on" the new man, we need to know how to do that (see Eph. 4:22-24). Of course, at the time of our salvation we *began* the process of putting off and putting on and were made a new creation in our spirit. However, we must continue the procedure in our daily walk.

Whether or not we are aware of it, we have enlisted in God's army. Every soldier must go to boot camp and be trained before entering into battle. Training includes wearing the right uniform, learning how to use weapons, and obeying the commander's orders. We have been issued spiritual clothing for warfare, but we are responsible for wearing it. Using the metaphor of soldiers engaging in warfare, we are told to:

- Put on the whole armor of God (Eph. 6:11).
- Put on the breastplate of righteousness (Eph. 6:14).
- Put on the armor of light (Rom. 13:12).
- Put on the Lord Jesus Messiah (Rom. 13:14).

How do we do that? We drop down to our spirit and become immersed in the presence of God. The Greek word for *put on* is *enduo,* which means "to sink into as being clothed." When we drop down to our spirit, we put off carnality and put on supernatural clothing. We can liken it to baptism in water. We sink into the water and it completely surrounds us. When we sink into Messiah within, He surrounds us. He is both within us and around us.

Enduo is used in another Scripture verse that sheds even more light on the subject. Jesus told His disciples: *"Behold, I send the Promise of My Father upon you; but tarry in the city of Jerusalem until you are endued with power from on high"* (Luke 24:49 NKJV). Only when we tap into the power of God in our heart can we obey the command to be *"strong in the Lord and in the power of His might"* (Eph. 6:10).

With God as our fortress, how can the enemy get to us? He can't. We only become vulnerable when we allow the enemy to cause us to lose our peace. The *"peace of God, which surpasses all understanding, will protect* [our] *hearts and minds through Messiah Jesus"* (Phil. 4:7). No foe can get past God. We can make ourselves vulnerable, however, if we fail to guard our emotions, thoughts, and choices.

Be flooded with God.

CHAPTER 10

TAKING THOUGHTS CAPTIVE

AS soon as we are born again and receive forgiveness, God instantly cleans up many aspects of our life. However, we don't know what He dealt with or what remains. Moreover, most of us spend years accumulating emotional baggage even after we become believers. It is a sad truth that most believers leave their church due to unresolved offenses. It is our responsibility to use what God has given us and cooperate with Him as we grow spiritually. We first know Jesus as Savior, but He wants us to surrender our thoughts, emotions, and will to His Lordship.

Too many believers know Jesus as their Savior, but not their Lord. When Jesus is Lord, He is ruling. When Jesus is Lord, we sense the peace of His presence. Our thoughts are conquered by taking them captive *"to the obedience of Messiah"* (2 Cor. 10:5). We vanquish negative emotions by applying forgiveness. Our will submits when we yield to Messiah within.

> When Jesus is Lord, we sense the peace of His presence.

PUT THOUGHTS TO THE TEST

Both negative emotions and upsetting thoughts can trigger sinful behavior. A thought that upsets us has emotional power over us. Therefore, when we deal with thoughts, we must first deal with the *power* behind the thought—the toxic emotion.

Thoughts have two *tracks* through which they influence us. One track is the line of *communication* (hearing), and the other is the line of *authority*. We can't *silence* all the different "voices," but we can break their *power* in our life.

The anointing breaks the line of authority but not the line of communication. Voices—the past, the world, the flesh, and the devil—do not stop speaking, but the anointing nullifies their *power* over us. Even though we may still hear a voice, when it has no authority, or power, we can ignore it.

We can't stop a thought from coming into our head, but we can defuse its power over our life. Take responsibility for your thought life. Refuse to listen to wrong voices. Test voices according to the Word, the Spirit, and the fruit.

> *Beloved, do not believe every spirit, but test the spirits to see whether they are from God* (1 John 4:1).

Refuse to listen to the wrong voices.

Test by the Word. Does the voice line up with God's Word? God will never violate His written Word—the Bible. Everything you hear from God will agree with the Bible. Obviously, the more Bible you know, the more you can recognize as scriptural or not scriptural. God will never encourage sin or violate a teaching in His Word. Does the thought line up with Scripture? Is the thought scriptural or something God would say?

> *All Scripture is given by inspiration of God and is profitable for doctrine, for reproof, for correction, for instruction in righteousness* (2 Timothy 3:16 NKJV).

Test by the Spirit. Does your spirit bear witness with God's Spirit? Any word from God has His nature attached! When you spend time with the Lord in prayer, you become familiar with His presence. His presence is pure, holy, and full of love. Even a corrective word from God has all the love of heaven behind it. When God speaks, His voice imparts life. When the enemy speaks, it is intrusive, negative, or seducing. The voice of the enemy releases poison or death.

> *The [Holy] Spirit distinctly and expressly declares that in latter times some will turn away from the faith, giving attention to deluding and seducing spirits and doctrines that demons teach* (1 Timothy 4:1 AMPC).

Test by the Fruit. God's voice produces good fruit. Can you bear witness that the voice produces the fruit of the Spirit? If you listen to the voice, will it ultimately produce good or bad fruit?

> *You will know them by their fruit. Do men gather grapes from thorns, or figs from thistles? Even so, every good tree bears good fruit. But a corrupt tree bears evil fruit. A good tree cannot bear evil fruit, nor can a corrupt tree bear good fruit* (Matthew 7:16-18).

TAKING THOUGHTS CAPTIVE

We must take responsibility for our thoughts to walk in true freedom. We should bring *"every thought into captivity to the obedience of Messiah"* (2 Cor. 10:5). How do we take thoughts captive and make them obedient to Jesus in a practical way? We make distinctions.

1. Make a distinction: the new creation.

The real you is a new creation who loves God and loves His Word. The new creation always agrees with God. *"Therefore, if any man is in Messiah, he is a new creature. Old things have passed away. Look, all things have become new"* (2 Cor. 5:17). The new creation always agrees with God and His Word. If a thought doesn't sound like something God would say, don't accept it.

2. Make a distinction: inside or outside.

Differentiate between your flesh and demonic influence.

Check inside. When we feel something negative, we should first check inside. We feel our emotions *inside* us, in the gut. When we feel a negative emotion inside, we should deal with our emotions first through forgiveness until we feel peace.

Check outside. When we have peace inside but feel *external* oppression, the pressure is outside us. When we have peace inside, we have the spiritual authority and strength to resist anything negative in the atmosphere. If you accidently "own" a bad atmosphere outside of you, receive forgiveness and you will feel peace again.

Submit to God. Resist the devil and he will flee from you.

Categories of Thoughts

- *Simple distractions.* We give power to what we give attention to. When we lose our peace due to a mild distraction or fleeting worry, we should renounce it (silently or aloud). Release the thought into the hands of God from the gut until you feel peace again. When we *"take a thought captive,"* we give it to God.

- *Repetitive thoughts.* A repetitive thought with a corresponding negative emotion is a *mental stronghold.* If a lie comes in, it always comes in at the time of emotional wounding. (Most of the time, emotional wounds do *not* have a lie, or mental stronghold, attached to them.) When a lie *is* believed, it blocks the truth from being received. A lie becomes a repetitive thought that we hear repeatedly. A negative emotion is always attached to a lie.

Examples of Mental Strongholds

- "I'm unworthy." What does God say?

- "I can't do anything right." What does God say?

- "I never belong." What does God say?

- "I'm a failure." What does God say?

- "I have to have everyone's approval to be happy." What does God say?

Pulling Down Strongholds

Start with the emotion. To deal with a mental stronghold, always deal with the emotion first through forgiveness. When we have a negative emotion fortifying the stronghold, we don't have power to dislodge the lie. When we have peace, we have access to supernatural power over any lie. Always start with the emotion. When you have peace, you have spiritual authority.

Always start with the emotion.

In approximately one out of 30 or 40 emotional woundings, a repetitive negative thought is connected, such as, "I don't belong," "I'm a failure," or "I'll always be alone." Assess the thought. Is it something God would say? Does it have the love of God attached to it? If not, don't receive it. Remember, if God didn't give it to you, you don't want it. If there *is* a repetitive thought, deal with the emotion first and get peace. Then, you have power to renounce the thought.

DISLODGING DEMONIC HITCHHIKERS

Demons can't remain in an area ruled by God. We can't stab demons with a sword so they bleed and die. The enemy is *displaced* by the presence of God when He comes in. Light overcomes darkness. Unforgiveness gives the enemy legal ground, but repentance takes back that ground. Holiness purges out the unclean.

God's presence evicts evil and occupies the territory. When God cleanses an area in our life, His presence takes up residence. He occupies the territory. Demonic hitchhikers are evicted when God enters.

> *When the enemy shall come in like a flood, the Spirit of the Lord will lift up a standard against him and put him to flight* (Isaiah 59:19 AMPC).

Demonic hitchhikers are evicted when God enters.

WEAPONS OF WARFARE

To mature spiritually, we must learn how to use our "God-tools," also known as *"the weapons of our warfare"* (2 Cor. 10:4), and be diligent in applying them to transform our thoughts, emotions, and impulses (choices) *"into the structure of life shaped by"* Jesus by *"building lives of obedience into maturity"* (2 Cor. 10:6 MSG).

> *We use our powerful God-tools for smashing warped philosophies, tearing down barriers erected against the truth of God, fitting every loose thought and emotion and impulse into the structure of*

life shaped by [Jesus]. *Our tools are ready at hand for clearing the ground of every obstruction and building lives of obedience into maturity* (2 Corinthians 10:5-6 MSG).

We gain clarity of thought as our hearts turn toward God. Many things that we could not understand before now become clear. Our preferences and actions begin to reflect our desire to love and serve God. We experience supernatural peace with God in our emotions. We are introduced to the fruit of the Spirit at conversion when we have peace with God for the first time.

The good news is that each time we cooperate with God in the ongoing process of sanctification, more and more of our heart is set apart for Him. In every area that comes under the authority of God, evil spirits lose their foothold in our life.

At the time of our initial salvation experience, we gain a great deal of freedom. However, many areas of our heart remain "un-evangelized" and don't yet submit to the Lordship of Jesus. If you suspect that the enemy has some legal ground in your life or you feel like you are being attacked by the enemy, close your eyes in prayer and let the Lord show you the entry point for that attack. Pray the first-feel-forgive prayer steps until you feel peace. Let the peace of God rule!

As you have therefore received [Messiah], [even] Jesus the Lord, [so] walk (regulate your lives and conduct yourselves) in union with and conformity to Him (Colossians 2:6 AMPC).

CHAPTER 11

PRACTICING THE FUNCTIONS OF THE HUMAN SPIRIT

FOR a number of years, we did a lot of traveling ministry. It was very eye-opening because we learned that many believers seemed to struggle because they don't understand the functions of their human spirit. They prayed in tongues at altar calls, not understanding that we can't give and receive at the same time. To receive altar ministry, drink in, don't pour out.

As soon as we pointed this out and showed the location for receiving, they were instantly able to drink in the anointing that was on the minister's words. We also did exercises such as asking the congregation to close their eyes and worship without words. When we do this, we let love flow from our heart to God. It became very clear that believers could certainly use some instruction in this area.

> Many believers struggle because they don't understand the functions of their human spirit.

The first loving function of the human spirit the Lord taught me (Dennis) was receiving. If you're reading this and saying, "I've never done this kind of thing before," we want you to stop trying and simply open your heart to experience and receive all God has for you. Opening the heart and yielding to the presence of Messiah within is the way we get filled with more of God.

RECEIVING

Receiving is your God-tool for spiritual nourishment and receiving impartation. Receiving is absorbing, drinking in, taking into your spirit. We receive in our heart by drinking in just like we welcomed Jesus into our heart at the time of salvation. Everything of the anointing you receive, you can then pour out on behalf of others. We can only receive what we are open to and we can only give what we have received.

When we read Scriptures like First John 3:1, *"Behold what manner of love the Father has bestowed on us, that we should be called children of God! Therefore the world does not know us, because it did not know Him"* (NKJV), how do we receive that Scripture? Do we think about it or memorize it, or should something deeper be experienced?

> We can only receive what we are open to and we can only give what we have received.

Many of us have had experiences where we have heard messages, closed our eyes, and received the content and the anointing on the message more than the actual descriptive words that were used in the sermon. What were we doing? We were drinking it in and welcoming it into our heart rather than listening to mere information. When we spend time in prayer, we give God time to saturate us with His presence.

Seeking God. I (Dennis) was a young Catholic at the time I was born again. I knew little about prayer and how other people prayed, but when I closed my eyes in prayer I *felt* the supernatural peace of God. Now, I had always been somewhat hyperactive, so peace of any kind was a new experience for me, much less the gift of supernatural peace Jesus gives to believers (see John 14:27).

Whenever something interrupted this peace (such as a negative emotion), I wanted to return as quickly as possible. I became acclimated to "touching" His peace and living in that atmosphere. Because peace is a gift given to believers by Jesus Himself, I understood that it was always available. All disruptions, therefore, were caused by me breaking my connection with Him.

My times of prayer did not consist of talking to God. Instead, I enjoyed His presence, touching His divine nature. Later, I read many books on prayer, but by that time I was so addicted to just being *with* the Lord that I only had one petition and that was for more of Him. As a matter of fact, I discovered that in seeking God Himself alone, He always gave me what I needed so I never needed to pray for "things." The Lord became my *"exceeding great reward"* (see Gen. 15:1).

My guiding scripture verse was Philippians 3:10 from the Amplified translation of the Bible: *"that I may know Him."* Years later I began to read books on prayer and was confused because there was so much talking involved. Later, I became convinced that my first approach, simply enjoying being with the Lord, was so much more satisfying; that settled the question for me.

Simple Prayer. Simple prayer is prayer focused on loving God and spending time in His presence. It is based in the simplicity of a life-giving relationship with the Lord. We enjoy being with Him and He imparts life to us. Paul tells us to remain fixed upon *"the simplicity and purity of devotion to Christ"* (see 2 Cor. 11:2-4). Simple prayer, therefore, is simply being in the presence of Jesus—no more, no less.

Come into the presence of God *expecting* to meet with Him spirit to Spirit. Present your time as an offering to Him. Offer yourself to Him and yield your will. Drop down to your spirit and open the door to your heart to welcome His Spirit. Seek God for Himself alone, and make relationship with Him your top priority!

Perhaps the way to describe *simple prayer* would be communing with God. We touch Him spirit to Spirit. Prayer is a relationship with a Person. The communion we experience in our time of prayer doesn't have to end as though we go in and out of prayer. We can learn to maintain our connection with the Lord throughout the day. It may take some effort at first to learn a new way of living, but the reward of a life lived in peace is priceless.

When we practice the presence of God as a lifestyle, we begin to *abide* in Him. In John 15, Jesus tells us to abide in Him, using the metaphor of a branch connected to a vine. A branch must be attached to its life source to flourish and produce fruit.

> *Abide in Me, and I in you. As the branch cannot bear fruit of itself, unless it abides in the vine, neither can you, unless you abide in Me. I am the vine, you are the branches. He who abides in Me, and I in him, bears much fruit; for without Me you can do nothing* (John 15:4-5).

Waiting in God's presence. As you wait silently, without speaking, simply become aware of the presence of the Lord in your heart. This way of prayer is both a relationship with God and a discipline that encourages growth of the relationship. *Simple prayer* is not intended to replace other types of prayer. However, it does bring deeper meaning to all prayer and leads you from more active kinds of prayer into prayer in which you wait in God's presence.

The two necessary ingredients of abiding prayer are silence and stillness. If you have ever stilled your thoughts in your prayer time or church to quietly enjoy God's presence, you have already experienced silent prayer. The mind does not become blank, but awareness of God increases.

GETTING STARTED

1. Decide on a time. My prayer time is: _____.
   If you don't devote a specific prayer time into your schedule, it is too easy to skip.

2. Choose a quiet place with a comfortable chair in which to sit. My quiet place is: _____

3. Get your Bible, a pen or pencil, and your journal so that you can keep a written record.

___ Bible	___ Pen	___ Journal

4. How long should I spend in prayer? We suggest a minimum of 20 or 30 minutes at a time.

5. If possible, ask someone to be your prayer partner.

PRACTICE

Simple Prayer

In an attitude of prayer, silently focus on Messiah within.

1. **Honor:** Begin by presenting yourself to the Lord in humility and adoration as His child. Honor God as a real Person who is

right there with you, not far away. Yield to His presence and desire God's will, His thoughts (revelation), and His emotions (the fruit of the Spirit).

2. **Awareness:** As you sense the presence of God, pay attention to the atmosphere. What facet of His nature is the Lord revealing to you? Love, comfort, peace, refreshing, holy anticipation? What words come to mind that describe the atmosphere? Pay attention to scriptures or pictures that corroborate what you feel. Don't just think about it, but receive, absorb, drink in. Allow it to be written on your heart. Later, take some action by writing it down, cherishing it, speaking of it, and living it!

3. **Time:** How long should you spend in prayer? Enough time for your flesh to become still in the presence of God. How can you tell? Your thoughts will cease to wander, you will feel peace, and you will lose the urge to go do something rather than pray (see Ps. 131:2; Isa. 40:31).

4. **Five Loving Functions:** Your human spirit cooperates with the Holy Spirit in:
   a. *Receiving*
   b. *Forgiving*
   c. *Loving*
   d. *Releasing* (people and circumstances)
   e. *Resisting*

FORGIVING

The second function of the human spirit is forgiving. Forgiveness provides cleansing for our heart and sets us free from negative emotions. Anytime we lose our peace, forgiveness will restore our peace. Negative emotions create barriers in our heart that separate us from God and others. God conveys us into His kingdom when we become believers. Any area with a negative emotion is back under enemy control. Forgiveness removes toxic emotions in our heart. Forgiveness always transports us back into God's territory.

He [God] *has delivered us from the power of darkness and has transferred us into the kingdom of His dear Son, in whom we have redemption through His blood, the forgiveness of sins* (Colossians 1:13-14).

Forgiveness removes toxic emotions in our heart.

INTERRUPTIONS IN PEACE

When we begin to practice connecting with Jesus through dropping down, we will sometimes experience interruptions in our connection. If we feel any negative emotion, we have lost our peace. When we lose our peace, we can no longer feel the presence of God. But don't be worried. The antidote for any toxic emotion is forgiveness and/or release. Occasionally we simply need to release a person or situation into the hands of God.

If the interruption was just a mere temptation that briefly distracted us, causing us to lose a sense of God's presence, we can simply release it from the gut and we'll instantly get our peace back.

For example, if your spouse forgets to pick up the dry cleaning and you feel irritated, you can release it to God right away and get your peace back immediately. If you get angry and dwell on it for even a few minutes, you need to release forgiveness. If we behave badly, we need to receive forgiveness. If we ever wonder whether it is a mere temptation or a sin, we should forgive. We can never forgive too much. If in doubt, forgive. As soon as we drop down and let Jesus the Forgiver cleanse us, our peace comes back every time.

Forgiveness is not a principle but an encounter with the Prince of Peace Himself, Jesus the Forgiver within you. God is the One who forgives and He lives and abides within each of us. When we need to extend or receive forgiveness, we simply allow Him to go to any toxic emotion that resides within us.

Forgiveness is not a principle but an encounter with the Prince of Peace.

The internal evidence that forgiveness has taken place is that the negative emotion changes to peace. Forgiveness is not complete if we still feel the unpleasant emotion. That is how we know we did it right. If in doubt, we only need to close our eyes and think of the person or event that was associated with the negative emotion. If we have peace where there was once pain, we did it right. If hurt, fear, lust, anger, guilt or shame is still there, we need to forgive. To experience forgiveness, we allow Jesus to go to the pain, anxiety, or the toxic emotion, and let Him wash it away. Forgiveness is like a beautiful love river that washes away pain and sorrow from our hearts and replaces it with peace.

> Forgiveness is like a river of love.

In watching Dennis minister, it didn't take too long for me (Jen) to see that the Holy Spirit worked according to certain patterns and similarities. I noticed first of all, God is quite capable of bringing to mind what need He wants to address, as well as the order or sequence He chooses each time. As I observed, I noticed that Dennis always followed the lead of the Holy Spirit, so when I made notes of the steps of ministry, I simply wrote down how the Holy Spirit was working. Neither Dennis nor I "came up with a method." We simply documented how God works. After all, the Holy Spirit is the minister. Our only job is to allow Him to do the work and be His facilitators, assisting those to whom He is ministering.

Remember, God will always hear a person who wants to become a follower of Jesus. In the same way, God is always present to forgive. He is always present to sanctify a heart presented to Him. Sanctification includes the removal of pain, anger, and fear in our heart through forgiveness. Jesus the Forgiver works in us and through us so He does the forgiving whenever we allow Him to do so. Any toxic emotion in our heart gives a foothold to the enemy.

> Any toxic emotion in our heart gives a foothold to the enemy.

REVIEW PRACTICE

Steps of Forgiveness

Prayer. Get in an attitude of prayer. Close your eyes and drop down.

First. First person or situation. What is the first person or situation God brings to mind—in an image or memory?

Feel. Feel the feeling. What is the emotion you feel in your gut?

Forgive. Yield your will and let Jesus the Forgiver flow out toward the person, yourself, or God. (You don't forgive a situation; you release it. If a situation came to mind such as a heavy workload at work, release it into the hands of God from the gut.)

Forgiveness can flow to others, ourselves, or to God. Let a river of forgiveness flow to others, drink forgiveness in for yourself (just like when you were born again), and let forgiveness flow out to God. (God didn't do anything wrong, but we must forgive Him when we are angry at Him to set ourselves free.)

Fact. Most emotional wounds do not have a lie attached. Occasionally a lie may be believed at the time of an emotional wounding and become a mental stronghold. Let forgiveness flow first until you have peace, then renounce the lie out loud. Ask the Holy Spirit for the truth (fact) and allow it to be written on your heart. Receive it and drink it in.

Fill. Then, if there was an emotional need that wasn't met, such as love or attention, forgive first, then release (use the God-tool of releasing) demands on people and receive filling from the Holy Spirit.

NOTE: Occasionally, you made need one or two additional steps of Fact and Fill, in perhaps one out of every 30 or 40 emotional healings.

- Jesus is the Forgiver, so forgiveness works every time.
- Forgiveness is instant, not a process.
- There is no "big or little" offense—forgiveness is all easy for Jesus.

LOVING

The third function of the human spirit is loving intercession. Simply picture somebody you love and then, down in your gut, release a river of love, allowing it to flow from your heart to them. We don't need words to release supernatural love to someone. However, when we add words, they will carry an anointing of love. Loving intercession should be an experience happening within us and flowing outward from our heart.

Love is released from the belly as loving intercession for people, worship to God, compassion for miracles, and motivation for righteous deeds.

Loving Intercession

Therefore I exhort first of all that supplications, prayers, intercessions, and giving of thanks be made for all men (1 Timothy 2:1 NKJV).

Worship from the Heart

For we are the circumcision, who worship God in the Spirit, rejoice in...Jesus, and have no confidence in the flesh (Philippians 3:3 NKJV).

Compassion for Miracles

And when Jesus went out He saw a great multitude; and He was moved with compassion for them, and healed their sick (Matthew 14:14 NKJV).

Righteousness (Obedience Motivated by the Love of God)

The marriage of the Lamb [at last] has come, and His bride has prepared herself. She has been permitted to dress in fine (radiant) linen, dazzling and white—for the fine linen is (signifies, represents) the righteousness (the upright, just, and godly living, deeds, and conduct, and right standing with God) of the saints (God's holy people) (Revelation 19:7-8 AMPC).

RELEASING

The fourth loving function is releasing, letting go, from our belly, and it is similar to forgiveness. When we release, we're not forgiving a person but releasing people and circumstances. Say that we have a workload piled up on our desk and we feel anxious about it. When we release it into the loving hands of God, the anxiety changes to peace. Why? It is because we have entrusted it to God so we are no longer carrying the burden ourselves. Jesus invites us to this place of rest:

> *Come to Me, all you who labor and are heavy laden, and I will give you rest* (Matthew 11:28 NKJV).

When we learn to release from our heart, we give people and circumstances to God. It is like an internal Jubilee takes place. We are placing our problems into the hands of a loving, capable God, who is able to do what He knows is best. He watches over them because we've entrusted them to Him. We are not being irresponsible; we are simply releasing into the realm of the kingdom. When we hang on to things, our willpower actually hinders God.

When we release, we place people and circumstances into the hands of God.

People

> *They are God's servants, not yours. They are responsible to him, not to you. Let him tell them whether they are right or wrong. And God is able to make them do as they should* (Romans 14:4 TLB).

Circumstances

> *He went a little farther, and falling on His face, He prayed, "O My Father, if it is possible, let this cup pass from Me. Nevertheless, not as I will, but as You will"* (Matthew 26:39).

> When we release from our heart, we place people and circumstances in God's hands.

RESISTING

The fifth loving function of the human spirit is resisting. There is a right way to resist and a wrong way. For example, the wrong way to resist, and many believers do this regularly, is to see someone we don't want to talk to and close the door of our heart. We become tense in our gut, which means we have put up a wall with our will. Sure, we can put on a smile and talk to them, but inwardly we are protecting ourselves.

There is a proper way to resist. God has given us a way to resist any negative atmosphere around us and guard our hearts with His peace. We can feel the atmosphere around us but experience peace in our heart. We bear witness to outside pressure but don't take it in.

In a hostile environment or when you are in the presence of an angry person, drop down and let the peace of God guard your heart and your mind. Remember, we don't open our heart to the person; we open our heart to Jesus in us. That way Jesus "stands" between us and any person who might confront us. Because Jesus is guarding us, we can resist attacks from both flesh and spirit.

> We can feel the outside atmosphere but experience peace in our heart.

AFTER OUR WILL

Both God and the devil want our will. Why is our will so important? In the Garden of Eden, Adam's thoughts, will, and emotions were in harmony with God's thoughts, will, and emotions. Yielding to God's will releases a flow of divine purpose. In heaven, God's will is always perfectly expressed. He wants His will done on earth through yielded vessels. When we yield our will to God's will, we allow heaven to be released on earth through us.

God and the devil want our will so they can express their nature through us. God and the devil want our will so their plans and purposes will be accomplished on earth. God's nature is love and He wants to bring redemption to humankind. God has a divine plan for earth and He needs people to cooperate with Him. The devil's nature is fear and hate, and he wants to bring destruction and death to us. The devil has an evil plan for earth and he ensnares people to cooperate with him (see John 10:9-10).

> Both God and the devil want our will.

Our behavior is determined by whatever controls our will. When a mother hears her child cry, she rushes to see what is wrong because her heart is moved by love and concern. Our will is motivated by emotions and thoughts, which are then expressed through our behavior. If our will is not engaged, we do nothing because we "don't want to." If we are thirsty, we choose to reach forth our hand and pick up a cup of water to drink. Our will has been "engaged" for action.

Consider the Gadarene demoniac. Jesus and His disciples crossed the Sea of Galilee and came to the region of Gadara. As soon as they got out of the boat, they encountered a demon-possessed man who appeared wildly insane:

> *When He had come out of the boat, immediately a man with an unclean spirit came out of the tombs and met Him. He lived among the tombs. And no one could constrain him, not even with chains, because he had often been bound with shackles and chains. But he had pulled the chains apart and broken the shackles to pieces. And no one could subdue him. Always, night and day, he was in the mountains and in the tombs, crying out and cutting himself with stones* (Mark 5:2-5).

If the demon-possessed man was not manifesting his human nature, who was being expressed through him? The Scriptures tell us that evil spirits were expressing themselves through this man. When Jesus commanded the evil spirits to come out of him, they spoke and said they were "legion." (A Roman legion consisted of an entire army of more than 5,000 soldiers.)

God desires to work in and through His people on earth. God wants to connect with us, own us, and express His nature through us. When we live a yielded life, we are transformed more and more into the image of Jesus. Peter reminds us:

> *But you are a chosen race, a royal priesthood, a dedicated nation, [God's] own purchased, special people, that you may set forth the wonderful deeds and display the virtues and perfections of Him Who called you out of darkness into His marvelous light* (1 Peter 2:9 AMPC).

God's Goal: Connect → Own → Express

The enemy also wants bodies in which to live. Evil spirits want to connect with us, own us, and express their nature through us. The devil wants to express his evil nature in thoughts, words, and actions. The Gadarene demoniac was demon-possessed. Evil spirits made a connection, owned his will, and began to express their personalities through him.

> The Enemy's Goal: Connect → Own → Express

RESISTING THE ENEMY

Submit yourselves to God. Resist the devil, and he will flee from you (James 4:7).

Start from the place of the new creation fused together with Jesus. Make a distinction between the new-creation you and the thoughts and impressions that the enemy wants to impose on you. We are already victorious. The battle has already been won by Jesus.

If you feel peace in your heart, the pressure is coming from the outside. Simply resist and don't give in. External pressure is demonic.

If you don't have peace in your heart, you may have to pray through an emotional healing, asking, "Where did that get started?" When you get peace but still feel pressure outside, you need to resist. If you accidently own a bad atmosphere, simply receive forgiveness and you will feel peace again.

SELF-DELIVERANCE

We don't have to go to an "expert" for deliverance. Through Jesus the Deliverer within we can do self-deliverance. When we submit to God and get peace inside, we have already won the victory. When we take back ground from the enemy, he has to flee from us. Self-deliverance involves three steps. First, get peace inside. In prayer, ask, "Where did this get started?" Forgive to wash out the negative and you will feel peace. You have taken back legal ground that had been given to the enemy. Deliverance is usually automatic when the enemy has no ground.

Second, resist the outside atmosphere. The enemy can't get through a door you won't open.

Yield to peace in your heart while resisting the outside atmosphere. It is like having a spiritual screen door. You can feel the breeze, but mosquitoes can't come in. If you have peace inside and feel a bad atmosphere outside—such as depression, fear, or anger—don't take it in. If you give in to it by accident, receive forgiveness and get your peace back.

Deliverance is automatic when the enemy has no ground.

Third, guard your doors. The enemy tries to connect with you through two doors—the mind door or the emotion door. Remember, the enemy works from the outside to get your will. If you have peace, you are safe. Don't own all the thoughts that you hear in your head. If you hear a thought that doesn't sound like something God would say, don't accept it. It doesn't matter if the devil or your flesh says it; don't take it if God doesn't give it.

When you have peace in your heart but still feel pressure, yield to Jesus the Deliverer in you and welcome Him to fill you from head to toe. As you yield to Him, allow His presence to radiate outwardly, pushing back anything oppressive in the atmosphere.

When we drop down and allow peace to guard our heart, we cultivate spiritual prowess, or strength and skill. You may fail at times, but what do you do when you fail? You forgive and receive forgiveness. Allow the Forgiver to restore your peace. When we allow the Lord to rule our heart, we cultivate patience and hope.

As you become more proficient in exercising the five functions of your spirit, you will notice your spiritual strength increases. Things that once made you have a meltdown or greatly irritated you will eventually be slight annoyances that you easily release. Ever-increasing peace will be a *way of life*.

THE *DIDACHE* AS THE WAY OF LIFE

INTRODUCTION TO THE *DIDACHE*

THE *Didache* is not a gospel, an epistle, or a theological treatise about religion. The *Didache* was framed by the twelve apostles to teach believers how to walk in the Way of Life. Designed to produce transformation of heart rather than teach mental information, it is a tool intended to be applied in the everyday ordinariness of life. It was originally designed as a training program for the spiritual transformation of a Gentile convert before they were baptized and became part of community of believers.

The apostles taught believers how to walk the Way of Life.

The *Didache* is not meant to be learned but absorbed. It can't be taught in a classroom but must be mastered in the crucible of life. It was designed to make authentic believers. And what is a real believer? A real believer is someone whose inward and outward lives have been transformed—that is, conformed to Jesus.

Daily life reveals our heart and character, strengths and weakness like nothing else can do. It reveals whether or not our faith is genuine and allows what is in our heart to manifest. The *Didache* is concerned with passing on the Way of Life revealed to the apostles by the Father through Jesus. Our daily lives should be a microcosm of the kingdom. Because God wants to bring His kingdom to earth through us, everything that happens in life provides an opportunity to manifest the kingdom (which is how Jesus lived) or to react with carnal emotions.

Paul likens our walk to running a race:

> *Therefore, since we are encompassed with such a great cloud of witnesses, let us also lay aside every weight and the sin that so easily*

entangles us, and let us run with endurance the race that is set before us (Hebrews 12:1).

Daily life reveals the reality of our faith.

Participating in the *Didache* training program prepares us to run the race of our life well.

It is believed that the apostle Paul referred to the *Didache* in the following verses:

> *But thanks be to God, for you were slaves of sin, but you have obeyed from the heart that form of teaching to which you were entrusted* (Romans 6:17).

> *Holding firmly* **the trustworthy word that is in accordance with the teaching***, that he may be able both to exhort with sound doctrine and to convince those who oppose it* (Titus 1:9).

"The layout of the *Didache* allows the new disciple to progress slowly from introductory material into the more complex rituals of daily living and community."[1] It is designed specifically to be used by a mentor-student pair. "The *Didache* offers evidence suggesting that each novice was paired off with a single spiritual master [one seasoned in the faith]. The principle clue for this is that the entire training program addresses a single novice using the second-person singular."[2]

> The *Didache* represents a bridge to the past. In the *Didache*, the centrality of Jesus is affirmed, but so are the election of Israel and the promises made to David. In the *Didache* one finds the first steps of a Jewish movement to define itself at the boundaries of Judaism as a legitimate expression of true religion bent on the inclusion of Gentiles in the promises made to Israel....
>
> Thus, the *Didache* represents a Christianity free of anti-Judaism, and for that reason, it bears an importance in our times to aid [believers] to arrive at self-definition that allows them to acknowledge that "Jews remain very dear to God, for the sake of the patriarchs, since

God does not take back the gifts He bestowed or the choice He made [of Israel]" (Vatican II, *Nostra Aetate* sec 4).[3]

At the time the *Didache* was written, there was no division between Judaism and what would later be called Christianity. There were simply Jews who were Messianic and those who were not within the fold.

> Because of its early date and inherent grounding in Judaism, it gives us a view unparalleled in any other non-canonical literature of what being a disciple of the Master was all about. It most certainly deserves to be treated as one of the greatest *Torah* works of the early Messianic community and should be studied by all followers of Messiah—both Jews and non-Jews. May the Lord of Legions be pleased to bless us through the holy vine of His servant David that He made known to us through His servant Yeshua as we study the wellspring of the *Didache*. To Him be glory forever.[4]

ENDNOTES

1. Janicki, *The Way of Life*, 23.
2. Milavec, *The Didache: Text, Translation, Analysis, and Commentary*, 48.
3. Milavec, *The Didache: Faith, Hope, and Life of the Earliest Christian Communities*, 562.
4. Janicki, *The Way of Life*, 24.

DIDACHE: CHAPTER SUMMARIES

CHAPTER ONE	There are two ways—life and death. Love God and man, love enemies with no retaliation, be a giver, have a right attitude.
CHAPTER TWO	Do not murder, do not commit adultery, and do not hate. Some people rebuke, some pray for, some love more than your own life.
CHAPTER THREE	"My Child": child and mentor relationship is introduced. Have fences against sin. Accept that all things, pleasant and unpleasant, work together for good, which is meekness.
CHAPTER FOUR	Honor mentors and preachers. Assemble with proper associations. Have humility with all. Confess sins both privately and publicly.
CHAPTER FIVE	The way of death is evil and greedy. This includes those who murder children, advocate on behalf of rich, lawless, judges, and so forth.
CHAPTER SIX	Beware of teachings contrary to what you have learned. Bear the yoke of the Lord, which is the will of God, as Jesus accepted the will of His Father. Guard yourself from food offered to idols.
CHAPTER SEVEN	Be baptized in the name of the Father, Son, and Holy Spirit after fasting.
CHAPTER EIGHT	Fast twice a week and pray three times a day with your community.
CHAPTER NINE	Partake of the cup and the bread to celebrate the kingdom. The broken bread of His body is gathered together. Eat and drink in His nature.
CHAPTER TEN	Thank the Father for the spiritual food and drink of His kingdom.
CHAPTERS ELEVEN-FIFTEEN	Honor true teachers and beware of false teachers.
CHAPTER SIXTEEN	Be watchful like the wise virgins, be ready like faithful servants, and be gathered together in unity.

DIDACHE: THE LORD'S TEACHING THROUGH THE TWELVE APOSTLES FOR THE GENTILES

The Didache is public domain.

Edited in 2019 for modern English readers by Drs. Dennis and Jennifer Clark.

PART ONE

TWO WAYS

CHAPTER 1

1:1 There are two ways, one of life and one of death, and there is a great difference between the two ways.

1:2 The Way of Life is this: First, you shall love the God who made you, and, second, your neighbor as yourself; and whatever you do not want to be done to you, do not do to someone else.

1:3 Now, the teaching of these words is this: Speak well of those who curse you by speaking evil words about you, pray for your enemies, and fast for those who persecute you. For what credit is it to you if you love those who love you? Don't even the heathen do the same? But, for your part, love those who hate you, and you will not have an enemy.

1:4 Abstain from fleshly and bodily lusts: If someone slaps you on the right cheek, turn to him the other cheek also, and you will be perfect; if anyone forces you to go with him one mile, go with him for two; if someone takes your coat, give him your shirt also; if someone wants to take something you own from you, don't refuse him.

1:5 Give to everyone who asks you, and do not ask for it back, for the Father's will is that we give to others from the gifts we have received. Blessed is he who gives according to the rule; for he will be blameless; but he who receives without need shall be judged as to why he took it and for what use, and, being in prison, he shall be questioned as to his deeds, and he shall not get out until he pays the last cent.

1:6 But concerning this rule it was also said, "Let your alms sweat in your hands until you know to whom you should give."

CHAPTER 2

2:1 But the second rule of the teaching is this:

2:2 You shall do no murder; you shall not commit adultery; you shall not commit pederasty to corrupt children; you shall not engage in sexual immorality; you shall not steal; you shall not use magic; you shall not use potions to cast spells; you shall not murder unborn children by having an abortion, or commit infanticide; you shall not covet your neighbor's possessions.

2:3 You shall not commit perjury, you shall not bear false witness, you shall not slander or gossip about others, you shall not hold grudges.

2:4 You shall not be double-minded nor double-tongued, for to be double-tongued is a deadly trap.

2:5 The words of your mouth shall not be false or empty, but fulfilled by action.

2:6 You shall not be covetous, greedy, hypocritical, malicious, nor proud. To sum it up, you shall not plot evil against others.

2:7 You shall not hate any person: But some you are to rebuke, for some you should pray, and some you should love more than your own life.

CHAPTER 3

3:1 My child, flee from all evil and everything like it.

3:2 Do not be angry, for anger leads to murder; nor envious, quarrelsome, or hot-tempered, for all these are sources of murder as well.

3:3 My child, do not be lustful, for lust leads to sexual immorality, nor a user of filthy speech, nor have roving eyes, for all these are sources of adultery.

3:4 My child, don't use divination to tell the future, for this leads to idolatry; neither be an enchanter who casts spells, nor an astrologer who tries to predict the future by using horoscopes or the alignment of planets and stars, nor a sorcerer, nor even desire to look into such things, for these all lead to idolatry.

3:5 My child, do not be a liar, for lying leads to theft; nor a lover of money, nor proud and boastful, for all these lead to theft.

3:6 My child, don't be a complainer, for this leads to blasphemy; nor self-pleasing, nor a thinker of evil, for all these lead to blasphemy.

3:7 But be meek and humble, for the meek shall inherit the earth.

3:8 Be patient and merciful, guileless, calm, and good-natured, and trembling all the time at the words which you have heard.

3:9 Do not exalt yourself or be presumptuous. Don't keep company with those who put on airs, but keep company with those who are righteous and lowly.

3:10 Accept the hardships that befall you as good, knowing that nothing ever happens apart from God.

Chapter 4

4:1 My child, always pay close attention to the one who speaks the word of God to you, and always remember to honor him just as you honor the Lord, for where Lordship is spoken of, the Lord is present.

4:2 And every day seek the presence of those who are righteous so that you may rest upon their words.

4:3 Do not be one who causes dissension, but you shall reconcile those who are quarreling to bring a peaceful resolution; you shall deliver righteous judgment; you shall not show partiality when reproving transgressions.

4:4 Do not be indecisive about whether or not your judgment is correct.

4:5 Do not be someone who stretches out his hands to receive, but shuts them when it comes to giving.

4:6 If you have the means, give offerings and alms as ransom for your sins.

4:7 Do not hesitate to give nor complain when you give, for you will be rewarded by your Father in heaven.

4:8 Do not turn away from someone in need but share with others. Do not insist on ownership, for if you are sharers in the imperishable, how much more in the things which perish?

4:9 Do not withhold discipline from your son or from your daughter, but teach them the fear of God from their youth.

4:10 Do not be harsh with your servant who hopes in the same God as you, so he ceases to fear the God who is over both of you. For He is not concerned with social status, but calls those whom the Spirit has prepared.

4:11 But you who are servants, submit to your masters, as they are examples of God's authority.

4:12 Hate all hypocrisy, and everything that is not pleasing to the Lord.

4:13 Don't forsake the commandments of the Lord, but guard what you received, adding nothing to it and taking nothing away.

4:14 Confess your transgressions when you assemble so you won't have a guilty conscience when you pray. This is the Way of Life.

CHAPTER 5

5:1 The way of death is this: First of all, it is wicked and full of cursing, murders, adulteries, lusts, illicit sexual acts, thefts, idolatries, witchcraft, magic, robberies, false witness, hypocrisy, duplicity, trickery, arrogance, malice, self-seeking, greed, foul speech, jealousy, overconfidence, haughtiness, and pretension.

5:2   It is the way of those who persecute good, hate truth, are lovers of lies, do not know the wages of justice, do not cleave to what is good, who stay awake at night for wicked things rather than good, are far from being considerate and patient, lovers of frivolous things, pursuers of recompense for everything they do, are unmerciful to the poor, fail to help the afflicted and over-burdened, those who do not know the God who made them, murderers of children, corrupters of what God has made; those who turn away the needy, oppress the distressed, advocate on behalf of the rich; those who are lawless judges of the poor; those who are altogether sinful. May you be delivered from all of these, my children.

Chapter 6

6:1   Let no one lead you away from this way of the teaching, for he does not teach you according to God.

6:2   For, if you can bear the whole yoke of the Lord, you will be perfect; but, if you cannot, do what you can.

6:3   And concerning food, bear what you can, but carefully stay away from food sacrificed to idols, for it is the worship of dead gods.

PART TWO

COMMUNITY AND CHURCH ORDER

CHAPTER 7

7:1 Concerning baptism, baptize in this way: Having first said all these things, immerse in the name of the Father and of the Son and of the Holy Spirit in flowing water.

7:2 But, if you have no flowing water, baptize in other water that is available; if you cannot baptize in cold water, then immerse in warm water.

7:3 But if you do not have either, pour water three times on the head in the name of the Father and the Son and Holy Spirit.

7:4 And, prior to baptism, let the baptizer and the one who is to be baptized fast, as well as any others who are able. Require the person who desires to be baptized to fast for one or two days before immersion.

CHAPTER 8

8:1 Do not let your days of fasting coincide with those of the hypocrites. They fast on Mondays and Thursdays, but you should fast on Wednesdays and Fridays.

8:2 And do not pray as the hypocrites, but as the Lord commanded in His gospel, pray in this way: "Our Father, who is in heaven, let Your name be venerated, let Your kingdom come, let Your will be done on earth as it is in heaven, give us this day our daily bread, and forgive us our debts as we now forgive our debtors, and do not lead us into that day of trial, but deliver us from evil, for Yours is the power and the glory forever."

8:3   Pray this way three times a day.

[Note: When praying, do not repeat memorized words but pray spontaneously for God's kingdom to be released and expanded on earth.]

Chapter 9

9:1   And concerning the eucharist, give thanks in this way:

9:2   First, concerning the cup: "We give thanks to You, our Father, for the holy vine of Your servant David which You made known to us through Your Servant Jesus; Yours is the glory forever."

9:3   And concerning the broken bread: "We give You thanks, our Father, for the life and knowledge which You revealed to us through Your Servant Jesus. Yours is the glory forever."

9:4   As this broken bread was scattered upon the mountains, but was brought together and became one, so let Your church be gathered together from the ends of the earth into Your kingdom, for Yours is the glory and the power through Jesus our Messiah forever.

9:5   But let no one eat or drink from your eucharist except those who have been baptized in the Lord's name. For the Lord said, "Do not give what is holy to the dogs."

Chapter 10

10:1   But after you are satisfied, give thanks in this way:

10:2   We give thanks to You, O holy Father, for Your holy name which You have caused to dwell in our hearts, and for the knowledge and faith and eternal life which You have made known to us through Your servant, Jesus Your Son. Yours is the glory forever.

10:3   You, Lord Almighty, created all things for Your name's sake, and gave food and drink to men for their enjoyment so that they might give thanks to You; but You have also blessed us with spiritual food and drink and eternal light through Your servant Jesus.

10:4   For all things we give thanks to You for You are mighty to save. Yours is the glory forever.

10:5 Remember, Lord, Your church, to deliver her from all evil and to make her perfect in Your love. Gather her together in holiness from the four winds to Your kingdom which You have prepared for her. For Yours is the kingdom of power and glory forever.

10:6 May grace of the kingdom come and may this world pass away. Hosanna to the God of David. Everyone who is holy, let him come! Everyone who is not, let him repent: Maranatha. Come, Lord! Amen.

10:7 Permit the prophets to lead the giving of thanks as often as they desire.

PART THREE

MINISTRY AND MINISTERS

CHAPTER 11

11:1 Receive whoever comes and teaches you truth according to all that has been taught to you before.

11:2 But if the teacher has turned aside and teaches another doctrine that undermines this teaching, do not listen to him. But if his teaching promotes righteousness and knowledge of the Lord, receive him as the Lord.

11:3 And concerning the apostles, prophets, according to the truth of the Gospel do this:

11:4 Let every emissary who comes be received as the Lord, but don't let him stay more than one day, or, at the most a second if necessary; but if he stays three days, he is a false prophet.

11:5 And, when an emissary leaves, let him accept nothing but bread for sustenance until he reaches his place of lodging for the night; but if he asks for money, he is a false prophet.

11:6 Do not test or pass judgment on any true prophet who is speaking in the Spirit: "For every sin shall be forgiven, but this sin shall not be forgiven."

11:7 But not everyone who speaks in the Spirit is a prophet, unless he behaves in a manner worthy of the Lord. From his conduct, then, the false prophet and the true prophet shall be recognized.

11:8 And no prophet who orders a eucharistic meal shall eat of it, otherwise he is a false prophet.

11:9 And if a prophet who teaches truth doesn't do what he teaches, he is a false prophet.

11:10 But every prophet who has been tried and is genuine, though he enact a worldly mystery of the Church, if he doesn't teach others to do what he does himself, shall be judged by you: for he has his judgment with God, for so also did the prophets of old.

11:11 But whoever shall say in the Spirit "Give me money, or any other thing for personal gain," you shall not listen to him; but if he tells you to give on behalf of others in need, let none judge him.

CHAPTER 12

12:1 Let everyone who comes in the name of the Lord be received; but when you have scrutinized him you will know him, for you shall have understanding of true and false.

12:2 If someone who comes is a traveler, however, help him as much as you can, but he shall not remain with you more than two days, or three if there is a necessity.

12:3 And if he wishes to settle among you and has a skill, let him work for a living.

12:4 But if he has no skill or way to provide for himself, according to your wisdom and understanding, plan in advance so that no follower of Jesus shall live among you in idleness.

12:5 However, if he will not conduct himself accordingly, he is making Messiah a commodity to serve his own interests. Beware of those who behave like this.

CHAPTER 13

13:1 But every true prophet who wishes to settle down among you and serve is worthy of his food.

13:2 Likewise a true teacher is also worthy, like the workman, of making a living.

13:3 Therefore, you shall take the first fruit of the produce of the wine-press and of the threshing floor and of oxen and sheep, and shall give them as the first fruits to the members of the prophets, for they serve as your high priests.

13:4 But if you don't have a prophet who serves among you, give to the poor.

13:5 If you make bread, take the first fruits, and give it according to the commandment.

13:6 Likewise when you open a jar of wine or oil [have an abundance, inheritance, or receive a gift], give the first fruits to the prophets.

13:7 Of money also and clothes, and of all your possessions, take the first fruits [of all sources of income], as it seems best to you, and give according to the commandment.

CHAPTER 14

14:1 On the day of the Lord, come together, break bread, and partake of the eucharist, after confessing your sins so your offering may be pure;

14:2 But let none who has an unresolved offense with someone join in your meeting until they are forgiven and also reconciled, if possible, so your sacrifice won't be defiled.

14:3 For this is that which was spoken by the Lord, "In every place and time offer me a pure sacrifice, for I am a great king," says the Lord, "and My name is wonderful among the heathen."

CHAPTER 15

15:1 Therefore, appoint for yourselves bishops and deacons worthy of the Lord, humble men, and not lovers of money, truthful, and proven, for they also perform the unpaid service of the prophets and teachers.

15:2 Therefore do not look down on them, for they are honored men along with the prophets and teachers.

15:3 Don't rebuke one another when angry but in peace with loving correction as you have been taught in the good news; and, if someone has done wrong to his neighbor, do not speak to him or let him hear from you as though you are not grieved but encourage him to repent.

15:4 But continue with your prayers and donations and all your good deeds and live as one who believes in the good news of our Lord.

PART FOUR

ESCHATOLOGY

CHAPTER 16

16:1 Be watchful over your life—do not let your lamps be snuffed out, and do not let your loins be ungirded—but be ready, for you do not know the hour in which our Lord is coming.

16:2 Gather together frequently, seeking those things appropriate for your soul, because a lifetime of faithfulness will not benefit you if you have not been perfected by the end.

16:3 For in the last days, false prophets and corrupters will increase in number, and the sheep will be changed into wolves, and love will be changed into hate.

16:4 Because of increasing lawlessness, those who have fallen away will hate one another, persecute one another, and also even betray one another. And then the deceiver of the world will appear as a false son of God, and he will do signs and wonders, and the earth will be delivered into his power, and he will commit repulsive acts that have never taken place since the beginning of time.

16:5 Then the whole human race will come into a burning trial by fire, and many will be entrapped and perish, but those who remain firm in their faith will be saved by the burning process itself.

16:6 Then the signs of the truth will appear: The first sign will be the unfurling [of a banner] in heaven, then the sign of a trumpet blast, and, finally, the resurrection of the dead.

16:7 However, not everyone will be resurrected but as it is said: "The Lord will come, and all the holy ones with Him."

16:8 Then the world will see the Lord returning upon the clouds of heaven.

The Lost Teaching of the Apostles

1. ***Personal study.*** Study *An Ancient Blueprint for the Supernatural* on your own, using the book, listening to the 14-CD set, or watching the *Lost Teaching* video course on the online school at training .teamembassy.com.

2. ***Family or homeschool.*** Use *An Ancient Blueprint for the Supernatural* as a family or for a homeschool course. Use this book, the *Didache* booklet, and 14-CD set. In addition, we suggest viewing the *Lost Teaching* video course on the online school at training.teamembassy.com.

3. ***Small group.*** Experience *An Ancient Blueprint for the Supernatural* as a church group or with friends, using this book, along with our 14-CD set or view the *Lost Teaching* as a video course via the online school at training.teamembassy.com. Include times of prayer and practice praying with one another.

4. ***Church seminar.*** Present *An Ancient Blueprint for the Supernatural* as a video seminar for a church congregation using the *Lost Teaching* video course on the online school at training. teamembassy.com.

5. ***Church leadership training.*** Study *An Ancient Blueprint for the Supernatural* with church leaders and staff. We also recommend viewing the *Lost Teaching* video course on the online school at training.teamembassy.com. Include prayer with one another.

6. ***Missionaries.*** Use for missionary training or with converts on the mission field. Materials include the *An Ancient Blueprint for the Supernatural* book, *Didache* booklet, and lessons in our 14-CD set. Or view the *Lost Teaching* video course at training .teamembassy.com. Include times of prayer and practice praying with one another.

DIDACHE: OVERVIEW AND COMMENTARY

PART ONE

TWO WAYS

THE Two Ways section of the *Didache* consists of the first six chapters, which contain practical instruction for living as a believer in Messiah. Chapters seven through fifteen of the *Didache* mostly focus on community living and church order. Chapter sixteen is the final chapter on eschatology, designed to comfort and protect them from falling prey to charlatans.

We will cover the Two Ways section extensively. The remaining chapters, seven through sixteen, are covered briefly.

DIDACHE ONE

1:1 There are two ways, one of life and one of death, and there is a great difference between the two ways.

1:2 The Way of Life is this: First, you shall love the God who made you, and, second, your neighbor as yourself; and whatever you do not want to be done to you, do not do to someone else.

1:3 Now, the teaching of these words is this: Speak well of those who curse you by speaking evil words about you, pray for your enemies, and fast for those who persecute you. For what credit is it to you if you love those who love you? Don't even the heathen do the same? But, for your part, love those who hate you, and you will not have an enemy.

1:4 Abstain from fleshly and bodily lusts: If someone slaps you on the right cheek, turn to him the other cheek also, and you will be perfect; if anyone forces you to go with him one mile, go with him for two; if someone takes your coat, give him your shirt also; if someone wants to take something you own from you, don't refuse him.

1:5 Give to everyone who asks you, and do not ask for it back, for the Father's will is that we give to others from the gifts we have received. Blessed is he who gives according to the rule; for he will be blameless; but he who receives without need shall be judged as to why he took it and for what use, and, being in prison, he shall be questioned as to his deeds, and he shall not get out until he pays the last cent.

1:6 But concerning this rule it was also said, "Let your alms sweat in your hands until you know to whom you should give."

OVERVIEW

The *Didache* begins with the teaching of two ways—the Way of Life and the way of death. The first section, *Didache* 1–6, is called the "Two Ways Section" of the document. Jewish believers understood the principle of God's way, the Way of Life, and its alternative, the way of death. Gentiles who joined a community of Messianic believers came directly out of a culture that followed the way of death. They needed instruction about what to avoid as well as encouragement to follow the new way. Chapter one describes how believers in Messiah should live. "You shall love the God who made you" and love "your neighbor as yourself."

The *Didache* is organized based on a distinction between the positive and negative commands in chapters one and two pertaining to the treatment of people: "You shall love your neighbor as yourself." Next, the teaching gives a prohibition, a negative version of the *golden rule*: "Whatever you do not want to happen to you, do not do to someone else."

For the survival of any community or group, their Way of Life and beliefs must be passed down to succeeding generations. If they are unable to accomplish this, they will perish as a people and be incorporated into the surrounding culture. The choice is separation or assimilation. If we don't pass our Way of Life down to our children, it will be forgotten. Parents quickly discover that their children pay more attention to what they do than what they say. Our Way of Life speaks louder than our words.

As its title states, *The Lord's Teaching through the Twelve Apostles to the Gentiles*, the *Didache* was framed by Jewish apostles as a training program for Gentiles. Its roots go deep into Jewish tradition, which is not surprising because Christianity itself has Jewish roots. Jesus was a Jewish rabbi and His disciples were Jewish disciples. Gentiles were grafted into the holy root of Israel (see Rom. 11:16-18).

> Reading the Two Ways we are forcefully struck by how embedded the life of the early Church was within Jewish life and practice at the time and within the vision of life that was the covenant of Israel. This covenant was not yet seen by followers of Jesus as an "old covenant" (or "old testament"), rather it was the same covenant, the same promise by God, and the same acceptance of being God's people that was continuing now in their following of Jesus.
>
> With Jesus that covenant had reached the new stage of the Messiah... having come among the people. ...The Way of Life required in

following the Messiah follows on from the Way of Life that the covenant with Israel demanded.[1]

The power and appeal of the apostles and early Messianic believers was that they were like Jesus. They were authentic and it showed individually and in community. *"A new commandment I give to you, that you love one another, even as I have loved you, that you also love one another. By this all men will know that you are My disciples, if you have love for one another"* (John 13:34-35). The importance of choosing the right way, or path, in life was reflected by the early believers in the name they chose for themselves—*The Way.*

> The *Didache* holds the secret as to how and why Jesus of Nazareth, a seemingly insignificant Galilean Jew executed as a Roman criminal, went on to attract and to convert the world. ...In truth, potential members assessed the movement not so much on the basis of claims made on behalf of Jesus who was absent, as on the basis of their experience of the Way of Life in members who were very much present to them.[2]

CHOOSING A WAY

As we learn in the *Didache*, there are two ways of life—the Way of Life and the way of death—and there is a great chasm between the two. There is no middle ground. One of two ways *must* be chosen. Life is about choices and the path we choose and our daily decisions determine our destiny. Every step leads somewhere. We must focus on how we live. Our believing means little if we don't live it. The mark of our faith is our daily walk. When Jesus calls us, He says, *"Follow Me."* When all is said and done, we will all give an account of how closely we followed Him.

> When we start thinking about our lives, where we are now with decisions we have to make, the past and how through various ups and downs we have arrived here, and then the future, our hopes and desires, we seem to adopt the image of walking along a path as if it were the most natural image in the world....
>
> The notion of life as walking along a path seems deeply embedded with us. ...But the image of walking along a "road" implies that we

are moving, looking forward, and can choose where our foot falls next. Not surprisingly, this notion had been in use for centuries (e.g. Jer. 6:16) before the time of Jesus and has played a key role in Christianity from the start.[3]

The concept of Two Ways is found in rabbinic writings. "Rabbi Yochanan questioned his disciples about what constituted 'the good way' and what constituted 'the evil way.' The sages state that 'the words of the Torah direct those who study them from the paths of death to the paths of life.'"[4]

Psalm 40:6 in the Amplified Bible, Classic Edition says, *"You have given me the capacity to hear and obey"* (Ps. 40:6 AMPC). We already have the ability to obey if we choose to do so.

> *Do not enter the path of the wicked, and do not walk in the way of evil. ...But the path of the just is like the shining sun, that shines ever brighter unto the perfect day* (Proverbs 4:14,18 NKJV).

> Faced with these harsh realities [of the hardships, persecution, and evil culture that surrounded the early believers], the first six chapters of the *Didache* unfold the training program calculated to alter irreversibly the habits of perception and standard of judgment of novices coming out of a pagan lifestyle. ...The *Didache* set about to form and transform the lives of Gentiles into that graced perfection demanded for ready inclusion into the anticipated Kingdom of God on earth.[5]

At the end of Deuteronomy, just before Israel was going to enter the promised land, God presented two choices to the Israelites:

> *I am giving you the choice between a blessing and a curse! You will be blessed if you obey the commands of the Lord your God that I am giving you today. But you will be cursed if you reject the commands of the Lord your God and turn away from him and worship gods you have not known before* (Deuteronomy 11:26-28, see also 30:19 NLT).

God even told them the answer, *"Choose life"* (Deut. 30:19). They could obey or disobey. They had freedom of choice. They could choose good or they could choose evil. The choice is white or black with no grey. You can take the good road or the evil road. However, it's not keeping a list of legalistic dos and don'ts but attitude of heart that leads to righteous actions. It's a matter of want to, not have to. We have the same freedom of choice. If we choose the correct path that leads to life, we draw ever closer to God.

> *Joyful are people of integrity, who follow the instructions of the Lord. Joyful are those who obey his laws and search for him with all their hearts. They do not compromise with evil, and they walk only in his paths* (Psalm 119:1-3 NLT).

LOVE OF GOD AND NEIGHBOR

Love of God and neighbor is the foundation of the *Didache*. In both the Old and New Testaments, the central truth is the holy love of God. Jesus tells us that love is the underlying basis of everything in the law of God. Love fulfills God's law (see Rom. 13:10). When we love God, we seek to please Him and He will be the delight of our heart. When we love our neighbor, we do that which is good for him and refrain from harm. Moreover, this love is resident in our heart. The *"love of God is shed abroad in our hearts by the Holy Spirit who has been given to us"* (Rom. 5:5).

"It was imperative for new Gentile believers and it is imperative for us as Yeshua's disciples today to write on our hearts these two great commandments and learn what it means to abound and walk in this Messianic community of love."[6] The *Didache* could be considered training for a life of love.

> *Love works no evil to a neighbor. Therefore love is the fulfillment of the law* (Romans 13:10).

ENDNOTES

1. O'Loughlin, *The Didache*, 40.
2. Milavec, *The Didache: Faith, Hope, and Life of the Earliest Christian Communities*, 48.
3. O'Loughlin, *The Didache*, 28-29.
4. Janicki, *The Way of Life*, 56-57.

5. Milavec, *The Didache: Faith, Hope, and Life of the Earliest Christian Communities,* 562.

6. Janicki, *The Way of Life,* 58.

COMMENTARY

DIDACHE 1:1

There are two ways, one of life and one of death, and there is a great difference between the two ways.

Enter at the narrow gate, for wide is the gate and broad is the way that leads to destruction, and there are many who are going through it, because small is the gate and narrow is the way which leads to life, and there are few who find it (Matthew 7:13-14).

The Way of Life is actually the way of the Cross by which we deny our self-life and enter into God's life. The life is resurrection life. Resurrection is that which passes through the death of the Cross yet lives. The narrow gate spoken of in Matthew 7:13-14 is the Cross and on the other side of the Cross is the highway of holiness, which is the Way of Life (see Isa. 35:7-9).

Then Jesus said to His disciples, "If anyone will come after Me, let him deny himself, and take up his cross, and follow Me" (Matthew 16:24).

SPIRITUAL PARENTS

The *Didache* implies that each novice was paired with a mentor based on the use of the second person singular verbs. Moreover, those who trained novices were not transmitting something of their own creation. Rather, such masters were "speaking to you the word of God (4:1)."[1]

Mentors did not merely teach information but would oversee a long-term apprenticeship during which the novice would undergo a transformation of heart and life. It has been estimated that such training lasted perhaps one to three years. Such mentoring would not be burdensome for the apprentice but a gentle yet firm "watching over" them in "love," and caring for the state of their souls. Confession and forgiveness played a large part in the mentoring process.

Confess your faults to one another and pray for one another, that you may be healed (James 5:16).

This "watching over" was practiced later in John Wesley's small groups to *"pursue peace with all people, and holiness, without which no one will see the Lord"* (Heb. 12:14 NKJV). Their efforts may be judged by the quality of believers produced by the apprenticeship.[2]

A QUIET REVOLUTION

Women were not excluded from a position of equality in either training or a participation in life and ministry within the Messianic community. Although men mentored men and women mentored women, that is as far as separation went.

> Care should be taken not to underestimate the significance of offering women training in the Way of Life. Having been so trained, a woman was not required to depend on her husband in order to learn from him whatever he thinks it is important for her to know. Trained by a competent woman, the female novice was on her way to becoming competent to discern for herself and for others what it meant to serve the Lord.
>
> Once a woman began to acquire the art of guiding her own life and trusting her own judgment in spiritual matters, she established herself as a disciple equal with the men... The Didache, therefore, was offering a quiet revolution when it came to training women along with the men to become active agents within the household churches.[3]

PRACTICE

Touching the Life of God

The life God gives us is tangible. We can touch His presence and, therefore, His life. Sit down in a quiet room and close your eyes. Place your hand on your belly to help you focus. Relax and yield to Messiah in you. Focus on your heart and notice a gentle sense of peace. *"He that believeth on me, as the scripture hath said, out of his belly shall flow rivers of living water"* (John 7:38 KJV). We become more aware of the Lord when we pay attention to Him.

Honoring God. Honor God by acknowledging the fact that His Spirit is within you: *"Messiah in you, the hope of glory"* (Col. 1:27 TLV). Spend a few minutes waiting in the presence of God. Often, as we become more relaxed, our awareness of peace increases.

Sensing peace. You are sensing the peace of His presence. When we touch the life of God, we always feel peace. Therefore, our goal in life should be to live in peace, the gift Yeshua gave us. He never takes it away, so when we "lose our peace," we have temporarily taken a detour away from His presence.

Note: We should never attempt to make our mind go "blank," but simply focus on Messiah within and be aware that He is with us. Focus is the opposite of blank.

DIDACHE 1:2

The Way of Life is this: First, you shall love the God who made you, and, second, your neighbor as yourself; and whatever you do not want to be done to you, do not do to someone else.

LOVE THE GOD WHO MADE YOU

God had not brought the Gentiles out of Egypt. However, He *is* the creator of all people. "Gentiles meet the Lord of Israel not as the 'God who brought you out of Egypt' (Exodus 20:2), but as 'the God who made you.'"[4] Not only did God make you, He ransomed you from death. The Master died for you; are you willing to die for Him? Being willing to die for the Lord's sake isn't the summit of discipleship, however. Being willing to die for Him is the *beginning* of our discipleship.

The Epistle of Barnabas expresses this thought in a slightly different way. What is called the Epistle of Barnabas was written at the end of the first or beginning of the second century. It is more a theological tract rather than a letter and discusses questions concerning Messianic believers at the time. It is not part of the canon of Scripture.

The Way of Light is this: If anyone intends to journey to the appointed place, he must hurry to arrive there through his deeds. Therefore, the knowledge given us in which to walk is this: You shall love the One who made you. You shall revere the One who formed you. You shall give glory to the One who ransomed you from death (Barnabas 19:1-2).

Didache 1:2 is similar to the Shema, the Jewish declaration of faith, which begins: *"You shall love the Lord your God"* (Deut. 6:5; see also 11:1). Our Master referred to the Shema when asked which was the greatest commandment:

"You shall love the Lord your God with all your heart, and with all your soul, and with all your mind." This is the first and great commandment. And the second is like it: "You shall love your neighbor as yourself." On these two commandments hang all the Law and the Prophets (Matthew 22:37-40).

The *Didache* was intended to be studied in pairs—a mentor and a student. It was said that we should honor our father who brought us into the world, but give even more honor to spiritual fathers or mothers who bring us into the life of the world to come.

In the case of Gentiles entering the Way of Life, they were often forced to leave their natural parents behind. The gospel can be like a sword that separates families when they can't tolerate a divergent belief system. There is often a price to pay for becoming a disciple of Jesus. Will you die for Him? Will you die daily to yourself? *"Then Jesus said to His disciples, 'If anyone will come after Me, let him deny himself, and take up his cross, and follow Me'"* (Matt. 16:24).

Even today, children of Jewish parents are sometimes declared dead by their parents who hold a mock funeral for them when they accept Jesus as their Messiah.

But whoever will deny Me before men, him will I also deny before My Father who is in heaven. Do not think that I have come to bring peace on earth. I did not come to bring peace, but a sword. For I have come to turn "a man against his father, a daughter against her mother, and a daughter-in-law against her mother-in-law" (Matthew 10:33-35).

The Messianic community had already seen Stephen stoned, so they understood what they were facing. The next challenge they faced was due to Saul of Tarsus before he was called Paul. Because of Saul, the first great persecution of the church took place.

> *And Saul was consenting to his [Stephen's] death. On that day a great persecution broke out against the church in Jerusalem. And they were all scattered throughout the regions of Judea and Samaria, except the apostles. Devout men carried Stephen to his burial and made great lamentation over him. But Saul ravaged the church, entering house by house and dragging out both men and women and committing them to prison (Acts 8:1-3).*

Overnight the believers in Jerusalem fled the city, many traveling south to Judea and some even reaching as far north as Antioch.

> *Saul, still breathing out threats and murder against the disciples of the Lord, went to the high priest, and requested letters from him to the synagogues of Damascus, so that if he found any there of the Way, either men or women, he might bring them bound to Jerusalem (Acts 9:1-2).*

LOVE YOUR NEIGHBOR AS YOURSELF

Jesus was asked the question, "Who is my neighbor?" Is our neighbor someone we like or identify with? Is our neighbor a fellow countryman? Is our neighbor a fellow believer? Just asking that question means that we don't give the word *neighbor* a very wide application.

> Jewish law defines "fellow," or "neighbor" (*rea*, רֵיעַ), as one's fellow Jew. This is not to say that traditional Judaism promotes unloving behavior to outsiders, but Jewish interpretation limits the definition of "your fellow" to "your fellow Jew."
>
> The Master addressed this interpretation with the parable of the Good Samaritan (Luke 10:29-37) and broadened the definition of one's fellow as one's fellow human being, regardless of a person's ethnic or religious background... Rabbi Ben Azzi states: "This is an even

greater principle." Ben Azzai argues that the overarching principle of the Torah is that we are all related to one man, that is, to Adam."[5]

But he, wanting to justify himself, said to Jesus, "And who is my neighbor?" Jesus answered… "Now which of these three do you think was neighbor to him who fell among the thieves?" He said, "The one who showed mercy on him." Then Jesus said to him, "Go and do likewise" (Luke 10:29-30,36-37).

THE NEGATIVE GOLDEN RULE

Didache 1:2b further cautions us, saying "whatever you do not want to be done to you, do not do to someone else." This a negative version of the Golden Rule. The commandment to "love your neighbor" was called the royal law by James, the brother of Yeshua: *"You shall love your neighbor as yourself"* (James 2:8). The *Didache* tells us not to do to others what we don't want done to ourselves. By stating it in this way, we become more sensitive because this brings the concept closer to home. Instead of a general concept, we must really consider what it means for us personally.

PRACTICE

Loving in the Spirit

Loving God

Pray. Close your eyes and pray. Focus on your heart and honor God.

Release love. Let a river of love flow out to God. This is a form of worship without words.

Loving People

Pray. Close your eyes and pray. Focus on your heart and pay attention to anyone who comes to mind.

Release love. Let a river of love flow out to that person. (When we forgive someone, after we forgive we can let the flow continue and it becomes a flowing river of love).

DIDACHE 1:3

Now, the teaching of these words is this: Speak well of those who curse you by speaking evil words about you, pray for your enemies, and fast for those who persecute you. For what credit is it to you if you love those who love you? Don't even the heathen do the same? But, for your part, love those who hate you, and you will not have an enemy.

First, the *Didache* says to love our neighbor. Now we are instructed to love our *enemies*. And who might our "enemies" have been at that time? Angry family members, disgruntled Jews, Roman authorities, and former friends.

It is common rabbinic practice to state the general concept first, then move to specifics. Not only are we supposed to love all people, we are told to *speak well* of those who say evil against us. We must refrain from evil speaking. We pronounce curses on people when we gossip by speaking evil of them. However, even more than biting our tongue, we are to let good words about them come from our lips. We are to love, bless, do good, and pray for them, and then rejoice when we are persecuted for the sake of Jesus.

In the words of the Master:

> But I say to you, love your enemies, bless those who curse you, do good to those who hate you, and pray for those who spitefully use you and persecute you (Matthew 5:44).

> Blessed are you when men hate you, and when they separate you from their company and insult you, and cast out your name as evil, on account of the Son of Man (Luke 6:22).

Didache 1:3 tells us not to speak ill of those who have wronged us because evil words reveal an evil heart: *"Out of the abundance of the heart the mouth speaks"* (Matt. 12:34).

The Talmud is a record of rabbinical discussions pertaining to Jewish law, biblical interpretation, ethics, customs, and history. In it we find "the story of Rabbi Meir as he lived near bandits who constantly troubled him. In desperation he prayed that they would die. His wife, Beruria, said to him, 'What makes you think a prayer like that is permissible? …Instead you should pray for them that they will repent.' ...So Rabbi Meir prayed for them and they repented. Acts of kindness toward our enemies bend our hearts toward them."[6]

LOVE YOUR ENEMIES

The apostle John tells us that love is the defining character of God. He does not just have love. He is love. *"Anyone who does not love does not know God, for God is love"* (1 John 4:8). To be disciples of the Master we should walk as He walked and love as He loved. "This teaching about loving and forgiving enemies is not some 'counsel of perfection' or some ideal: it is presented as the ordinary teaching that every [believer] had to take as part and parcel of following the Way of Life. Moreover, this was all seen as simply spelling out the... commandment: to love God."[7]

> *But I say to you, love your enemies, bless those who curse you, do good to those who hate you, and pray for those who spitefully use you and persecute you* (Matthew 5:44).

> *But love your enemies, and do good, and lend, hoping for nothing in return. Then your reward will be great, and you will be the sons of the Highest. For He is kind to the unthankful and the evil* (Luke 6:35).

PEOPLE ARE NOT ENEMIES

As we fast and pray for our enemies, our hearts are cleansed of toxic emotions and we begin to have compassion on those who oppose us and we begin to see their need. People are not our enemies. We are free and belong to God, but they are still in bondage to the enemy.

> *For our fight is not against flesh and blood, but against principalities, against powers, against the rulers of the darkness of this world, and against spiritual forces of evil in the heavenly places* (Ephesians 6:12).

> *And you were dead in your trespasses and sins, in which you formerly walked according to the age of this world and according to the prince of the power of the air, the spirit who now works in the sons of disobedience, among them we all also once lived in the lusts of our flesh, doing*

the desires of the flesh and of the mind, and we were by nature chil-
dren of wrath, even as the rest (Ephesians 2:1-3).

Our Master tells us that we are blessed when we bless those who persecute us. What is God after in all this? He wants us to have the same heart attitude that Jesus has for us. *"But God demonstrates His own love toward us, in that while we were yet sinners, Messiah died for us"* (Romans 5:8).

Blessed are those who are persecuted for righteousness' sake, for theirs is the kingdom of heaven (Matthew 5:10).

FASTING IS PRAYER THAT COSTS

Fasting is a particularly powerful addition to prayer. It is prayer that costs us something. When we sacrifice for someone, it changes our heart. When we fast and pray for our enemies, we begin to see them through the eyes of God who created all people. The one we once saw as a perpetrator is in need of the love of God. If we are truly at peace with a former enemy, he is no longer our enemy. We have no enemies at all.

When a man's ways please the Lord, He makes even his enemies to be at peace with him (Proverbs 16:7).

FASTING FOR HUMILITY

As we fast, we humble ourselves. We bring our human nature under submission and deflate our pride, which is the major taproot of sin. Pride produces self-sufficiency, which blinds people to their own and others' needs. Pride hardens the heart. Pride was involved in our separation from God at the Fall, but humility is the antidote for pride. Humility through fasting opens our eyes, tenderizes our heart, and heals our pride.

I wore sackcloth; I afflicted myself with fasting; I prayed with head bowed on my chest. I went about as though I grieved for my friend or my brother; as one who laments his mother, I bowed down in mourning (Psalm 35:13-14 ESV).

Forgiving Enemies

When we lose our peace, forgiveness removes any toxic emotion and our peace is restored.

Pray. With your eyes closed and in an attitude of prayer, allow the Lord to bring to your mind someone who has hurt you or wronged you in some way.

Feel. Feel the negative emotion.

Forgive and release. Allow a river of forgiveness to flow from your heart toward them until you feel peace. Next, receive forgiveness for allowing the poison of unforgiveness to even remain in your heart. (If someone has stolen something from you, release it as a gift to them from your heart into their hands. If you give something as a gift, no one can take it from you.)

Praying for Enemies

Pray. With your eyes closed and in an attitude of prayer, picture the person who wronged you.

Feel. Make sure you have already forgiven so you feel peace.

Release love. In an attitude of prayer, allow a river of loving compassion to flow to your enemy. After all, you are free and they are in the grip of our enemy, the devil.

DIDACHE 1:4

Abstain from fleshly and bodily lusts: If someone slaps you on the right cheek, turn to him the other cheek also, and you will be perfect; if anyone forces you to go with him one mile, go with him for two; if someone takes your coat, give him your shirt also; if someone wants to take something you own from you, don't refuse him.

Didache 1:4 begins, "Abstain from fleshly and bodily lusts." Most people think of lust only in connection to sexual appetites. However, lust is involved whenever we want any person, place, or thing more than God. Moreover, the emotion of lust is linked to seducing spirits. Lust is more powerful than our willpower.

> Disciples of the Master are exhorted to die to their own desires and earthly passions and instead seek to serve God alone. In this context the battle is with the ego: it is indeed a struggle to love one's enemies and suppress revenge and anger.[8]

Failing to accept the Bible as absolute truth and God's standard for humankind, have we just joined a religious club without rules? The standard in the Bible is the highest. We believers must be strict. We enter through a narrow gate and walk along a constricted way (see Matt. 7:14). *"Wide is the gate and broad is the way that leads to destruction, and there are many who are going through it"* (Matt. 7:13).

So much of what we hear in religious circles doesn't sound like the New Testament. Just reading what believers say on social media is shocking enough. Some say that because of grace, they can sin all they want because they are already forgiven. Others become angry when Bible truth is stated because, they say, the Bible is old-fashioned and must change with the culture.

Immediately after the Fall, God issued restrictions. Jesus Himself tells us we must be strict in our faith: *"For I say to you that unless your righteousness exceeds the righteousness of the scribes and Pharisees, you will in no way enter the kingdom of heaven"* (Matthew 5:20). And:

> Do not think that I have come to abolish the Law or the Prophets. I have not come to abolish, but to fulfill. For truly I say to you, until heaven and earth pass away, not one dot or one mark will pass from the law until all be fulfilled (Matthew 5:17-18).

We must stay far away from fleshly and bodily lusts. We should also refuse to retaliate or complain. To take the path of compromise is the way of death. May we be those who walk the Way of Life by taking the narrow gate and constricted way.

Turn the Other Cheek

Didache 1:4 tells us: "If someone slaps you on the right cheek, turn to him the other cheek also, and you will be perfect; if anyone forces you to go with him one mile, go with him for two; if someone takes your coat, give him your shirt also; if someone wants to take something you own from you, don't refuse him."

The *Didache* is written in an orderly progression based on what novices would be facing in real-life situations. The instructions to pray for enemies and turn the other cheek are quite timely. Turn the other cheek means, "Don't seek revenge when you have been wronged or insulted."

> *To him who strikes you on the one cheek, offer also the other. And from him who takes away your cloak, do not withhold your tunic as well* (Luke 6:29).
>
> *But I say to you, do not resist an evil person. But whoever strikes you on your right cheek, turn to him the other as well* (Matthew 5:39)

The phrase "if someone wants to take something you own from you, don't refuse him" is used in the sense of borrowing instead of keeping permanently. In the primitive church in Jerusalem during the time when everyone had all things in common, many believers were in need.

Be Perfect

Our word *perfect*, as derived from the Latin *perfectus*, means "complete and correct in every way, of the best possible type or without fault." However, the word used in the New Testament for "perfect" is the Greek word *téleios*, which does not mean absolute perfection. It refers to spiritual growth unto maturity, or becoming expressions of Jesus in the world. *"Therefore be perfect, even as your Father who is in heaven is perfect"* (Matt. 5:48). The aim of the *Didache* is to conform believers into expressions of Jesus in the Way of Life.

Go the Extra Mile

Few things were as difficult for the Jews in the first century than to be forced into servitude as pack animals for the Roman soldiers. Roman soldiers could force a man without Roman citizenship to carry a load for them one mile.

Jesus says, however, *"Whoever compels you to go a mile, go with him two"* (Matt. 5:41). Jesus tells His disciples to disarm their opponents by going an extra mile. Instead of complaining, a follower of the Master should submit without protest and do even more than was expected. This act of total love and submission would send an amazing message about the God of Israel and His love.

GIVE YOUR TUNIC

A "tunic" was a lightweight linen undergarment while the "cloak" was heavier outer wear usually made of wool, which provided protection from cold and rain. The *Torah* forbids creditors from taking a man's cloak because it provided protection from the elements. Amos chastises those who ignore this prohibition. The *Didache* instructs us to demonstrate our good faith by voluntarily setting aside our rights. Jesus is not telling us to be doormats. However, He does tell us to refuse to demand our rights. In choosing the Way of Life, we forsake self-dependence and know that our Father will take care of our needs.

> New recruits had to be immediately prepared to respond to abusive behavior by outsiders (1:3-4). When examined in detail...the enemies in this case were not highway robbers or Roman soldiers, but relatives and friends who had become "enemies" due to the candidate's new religious convictions. Thus praying and fasting...for such "enemies" provided the necessary orientation for sustaining a comprehensive nonviolent surrender to the abusive family situation hinted at in *Did.* 1:4.
>
> Among other things it was envisioned that the abusive family situation would lead to the forcible seizure of the novice's goods...and the candidate was instructed to yield completely to such hostile acts and, at the same time, to surrender his or her goods to... [those in need] (1:5), not because of any compulsion, but simply because the "Father" wished it. Implicit here is the contrast between a natural father who may be authorizing the tight-fisted seizure of his daughter's or son's assets with that "new Father" who generously gives to all and invites imitation.[9]

Receiving Forgiveness

Pray. In an attitude of prayer, let the Lord show you any area where you need to receive forgiveness for any wrong action or attitude.

Feel. Feel the negative emotion, such as guilt or shame.

Forgive. Receive forgiveness until the feeling changes to peace.

DIDACHE 1:5

Give to everyone who asks you, and do not ask for it back, for the Father's will is that we give to others from the gifts we have received. Blessed is he who gives according to the rule; for he will be blameless; but he who receives without need shall be judged as to why he took it and for what use, and, being in prison, he shall be questioned as to his deeds, and he shall not get out until he pays the last cent.

At the time the *Didache* was written, the entire church was in Jerusalem, comprised exclusively of Jewish believers, and the circumstances were unique. Later, when the church had moved into another phase, Paul wrote regarding free-loading believers, *"For when we were with you, we commanded you that if any will not work, neither shall he eat"* (2 Thess. 3:10).

GIVING IN JERUSALEM

To fully understand the teaching in the Didache about giving and sharing, we must look back to Passover and the Day of Pentecost when the church was born. At the time Jesus ascended, He had been with His disciples for 40 days following the resurrection. Before departing, Jesus directed His disciples to wait in Jerusalem until they were endued with power. Another ten days takes us to Pentecost—Sunday morning, AD 30.

Sunday morning started gloriously. The Holy Spirit fell upon those praying in the upper room, Peter preached his first sermon, and 3,000 were instantly added to the church. Now the church numbered 3,120. How awesome! But the apostles suddenly had some major problems to face. And this was only day one.

When Monday morning dawned, church life began in earnest and with immediate problems that needed to be solved. Things were messy.

Scores of out-of-towners had poured into Jerusalem for Passover and were still in Jerusalem for the Feast of Pentecost. Some had left, but most stayed. The city was packed with visitors. If it had been any other year, the celebrants would have begun returning to their homes in Judea, Galilee, and other countries on Monday.

Travelers had only packed for a short stay with some articles of clothing and a little money for the trip. Now what were they to do? Those who had suddenly been swept into the church were faced with a dilemma. They didn't want to leave, but how could they stay without food, houses, or jobs? Most new church members were broke and homeless. This was just the first day, and many more would soon be added to their number.

Where could that many people meet together? And where and how would they live? The solution to the first problem was relatively simple. The church could assemble at Solomon's porch outside the Temple. The second predicament was a bit more complex.

It is possible that having all things in common began here. They *had* to depend on one another simply to survive. Those who had homes in Jerusalem opened them to visitors and shared their food. Those who had material and financial resources helped those in need.

> *All who believed were together and had all things in common. They sold their property and goods and distributed them to all, according to their need. And continuing daily with one mind in the temple, and breaking bread from house to house, they ate their food with gladness and simplicity of heart, praising God and having favor with all the people. And the Lord added to the church daily those who were being saved* (Acts 2:44-47).

Look at the image of "church" through the eyes of a typical unbelieving Jerusalem citizen! To anyone on the outside looking in, to be a follower of [Jesus] meant the loss of all things: right down to the clothes you wore. ...Do you realize what this means? It means that during the first eight years of church history, to be "in the church" a man knew he would have to deliberately go out and sell everything on earth he had, even become penniless. This was the privilege (the *privilege* mind you) of being "in church." This is the image the church bore throughout the whole first century. …In the midst of tidal joy, men laid down all because of their simple, overwhelming love for [Jesus]. And the love grew out of their experience with Him.[10]

It was many years before any other churches were planted. Every member of the church stayed right there in Jerusalem at first. When the circumstances changed and churches were planted in other locations, believers were expected to get jobs and provide for themselves.

Giving Cheerfully

God our Father has given us everything we have. We can't say we "own" anything because God already owns it all. *"The earth is the Lord's, and all its fullness, the world and those who dwell therein"* (Ps. 24:1 NKJV). We are stewards, not owners, of everything lent to us from God. Therefore, when God lays it on our heart to give to others, we should be willing to release freely.

> *But this I say: He who sows sparingly will also reap sparingly, and he who sows bountifully will also reap bountifully. Let every man give according to the purposes in his heart, not grudgingly or out of necessity, for God loves a cheerful giver* (2 Corinthians 9:6-7).

The Scriptures also make it clear that we are not only supposed to give out of what God has given to us, but that we should have the proper attitude about giving.

Giving to Whoever Asks

In Matthew 5:42, Jesus says, *"Give to him who asks you, and from him who would borrow from you do not turn away."* In Luke 6:30, He speaks similarly, *"Give to everyone who asks of you. And of him who takes away your goods, do not ask for them back."*

At first glance, it appears that the *Didache* enjoins us to give anything to anyone who asks for it. However, the Greek word for "asks" is *aiteo* (αἰτέω), which is the equivalent in the Septuagint to the Hebrew word *sha'al* (שאל), in Mishnaic[11] Hebrew *sha'al* can be used in the sense of borrowing. The passage may be referring to someone who wants to borrow something rather than take it. This makes sense in light of the instructions not to ask for the item back; if it had been given, one would not want it to be returned.[12]

RECEIVING WITHOUT NEED

The Messianic believers had a high standard of morality, including honesty. To take something out of the general till without a need was stealing from God. The church had already witnessed the dire consequences of trying to deceive the Holy Spirit.

The story of Ananias and his wife, Sapphira, may be familiar to many believers (see Acts 5:1-11). During that time church members, under the inspiration of the Holy Spirit, were laying all they possessed at the feet of the apostles to the needs of the community. Ananias and his wife, Sapphira, sold some property and agreed together to keep some of the money for themselves while giving the rest to the church. Ananias only pretended to give it all. As soon as he laid the money at the apostles' feet, Peter reproached him for lying to the Holy Spirit and Ananias fell down dead.

When Sapphira arrived later, Peter questioned her about the amount of the sale. She was also deceitful, because Peter reproached her for putting "the Spirit of the Lord to the test," and she fell down dead as well. No wonder we are told, *"Great fear came on the entire church and on all those who heard these things"* (Acts 5:11). To receive without need, then, would be wicked in the eyes of God and the entire community.

DIDACHE 1:6

But concerning this rule it was also said, "Let your alms sweat in your hands until you know to whom you should give."

This somewhat unusual proverb to "let your alms sweat in your hand" appears to have been common in the early Messianic community. Augustine's commentary on Psalm 147:13 uses a variation of what we read in *Didache* 1:6: "Scripture says, 'Let alms sweat in your hand, till you find a righteous man to whom to give it.'"[13]

PRACTICE

Making Decisions

Decisions can require a simple "yes" or "no" or involve making a choice between two (or more) options. In the case of giving, we first need to know if God is prompting us to give.

"Yes" or "No" Decisions

Pray. Close your eyes and get in an attitude of prayer. You must be neutral and at peace before letting the Lord make the decision so you can hear clearly.

Inquire. "Should I give in this particular case?" You will probably sense and increase in anointing in your gut, which means "yes," or a check in your spirit, which means "no." If you can't tell any difference, God may be telling you to wait.

Making a Choice

Pray. Close your eyes and get in an attitude of prayer. Again, you must be comfortable and at peace with letting God choose.

Inquire. Let's say you have two options. Hold one choice before the Lord. Then hold the second choice before the Lord. Notice what you sense in your gut. Usually the anointing will increase on one of the choices or you will get a check on one. If you're not sure, wait.

ENDNOTES

1. Milavec, *The Didache: Text, Translation, Analysis, and Commentary*, 49.
2. When Christianity became the official state religion, as early as the fourth century, the training of disciples changed, but not without significant

reservations on the part of church leaders. Actual training was shortened to weeks so bishops had to teach much information in a short period of time.

"Cyril [331-386], bishop of Jerusalem, instructed catechumens [students] three hours a day during the entire season of Lent. It seems unlikely that catechumens could have absorbed and applied so much information. It was a matter of too little time and too much information... Monasteries preserved some features of the catechumenate [training program of the Didache] in the novitiate [the period of training and preparation that a Christian novice], a three-year process that prepared novices to take final vows and become permanent member of a monastic community"; Gerald Sittser, *A Resilient Faith: How the Early Christian "Third Way" Changed the World*, [Grand Rapids, MI: Brazos Press, 2019], 169-171.

3. Milavec, *The Didache: Faith, Hope, and Life of the Earliest Christian Communities*, 81.

4. Janicki, *The Way of Life*, 65-66.

5. Ibid., 70-71.

6. O'Loughlin, *The Didache*, 35.

7. Janicki, *The Way of Life*, 75.

8. Ibid., 77.

9. Milavec, *The Didache: Text, Translation, Analysis, and Commentary*, 49-50.

10. Gene Edwards, *Revolution: The Story of the Early Church* (Auburn, ME: Christian Books Publishing House, 1974), 35.

11. The Mishnah or Mishna is the first major written collection of the Jewish oral traditions known as the oral *Torah*. *Mishnaic* means of or relating to the Mishna (the first part of the Talmud).

12. Janicki, *The Way of Life*, 80.

13. Augustine, "Exposition on the Psalms"; retrieved March 4, 2020 from http://www.newadvent.org/fathers/1801147.htm.

DIDACHE TWO

2:1 But the second rule of the teaching is this:

2:2 You shall do no murder; you shall not commit adultery; you shall not commit pederasty to corrupt children; you shall not engage in sexual immorality; you shall not steal; you shall not use magic; you shall not use potions to cast spells; you shall not murder unborn children by having an abortion, or commit infanticide; you shall not covet your neighbor's possessions.

2:3 You shall not commit perjury, you shall not bear false witness, you shall not slander or gossip about others, you shall not hold grudges.

2:4 You shall not be double-minded nor double-tongued, for to be double-tongued is a deadly trap.

2:5 The words of your mouth shall not be false or empty, but fulfilled by action.

2:6 You shall not be covetous, greedy, predatory, hypocritical, malicious, or proud. To sum it up, you shall not plot evil against others.

2:7 You shall not hate any person: But some you are to rebuke, for some you should pray, and some you should love more than your own life.

OVERVIEW

Didache 2 continues teaching of the Two Ways. This chapter continues the negative commandment: "Whatever you do not want to happen to you, do not do to someone else." Verse 2 contains commands to avoid ten behaviors: murder, adultery, pederasty, sexual immorality, stealing, the use of magic, the use of potions, abortion, infanticide, and coveting.

Next, *Didache* 2 specifies five evil character traits to avoid: do not be greedy, predatory, hypocritical, malicious, or proud.

Finally, we are told not to hate anyone, after which three categories of people are described along with appropriate behavior toward each: "some you are to rebuke, for some you should pray, and some you should love more than your own life."

While it's true that Gentiles were brought into the Messianic fold when Peter was sent to the house of Cornelius in AD 39, it was nothing compared to the Gentile problem that was encountered by the apostles when they ventured farther abroad. The Jewish disciples who had fled to Antioch to escape the persecution of Saul "weren't in Kansas"—that is, Jerusalem—"anymore."

The Gentile believers from Israel after Peter's revelation were one thing. They were at least acquainted with Jewish life and many of them were "God-fearers."[1] However, the Antiochians were as pagan as they could be. When the disciples began to share the good news of Jesus with them, these Gentiles enthusiastically began to become followers of the Messiah and then learned how to live it out.

They were altogether ignorant of Jewish life and religious heritage. Their moral code was almost non-existent. They knew nothing of Jewish ethical and social discipline and they outnumbered the Jewish disciples by a whopping percentage. Something had to be done and it had to be done quickly. These Antioch believers desperately needed to be discipled, so an urgent letter was sent back to Jerusalem asking for a worker who could come help them.

Barnabas was the man appointed for the job. But Barnabas was prepared. He probably brought copies of the *Didache* with him.

"Such were some of you."

We have to know what sin is so we can know what we must avoid. *Didache* 2 amplifies the original commandments by targeting behaviors common in the Greco-Roman world of the day. While the vices range from murder to magic, there is a specific reason for every item included in the list. "The very fact that these prohibitions had to be listed is evidence that those reading the *Didache* had struggled with these very sins before coming to faith in Messiah."[2]

WHAT DOES JESUS SAY?

Jesus says that the commandments of the Old Testament are still valid. Rather than doing away with or relaxing the requirements of God, Jesus raises the standards even higher under the New Covenant. Jesus was even stricter than the Pharisees. If we wish to be like Jesus, then we must respond in love, but also teach repentance and obedience to the commandments of God. He not only condemns sexual immorality and all sexual activity outside of traditional marriage (between one woman and one man), He raises the standard to include holiness of heart.

> Do not think that I came to destroy the Law or the Prophets. I did not come to destroy but to fulfill. For assuredly, I say to you, till heaven and earth pass away, one jot or one tittle will by no means pass from the law till all is fulfilled. Whoever therefore breaks one of the least of these commandments, and teaches men so, shall be called least in the kingdom of heaven; but whoever does and teaches them, he shall be called great in the kingdom of heaven. For I say to you, that unless your righteousness exceeds the righteousness of the scribes and Pharisees, you will by no means enter the kingdom of heaven (Matthew 5:17-20 NKJV).

> You have heard that it was said by the ancients, "You shall not commit adultery." But I say to you that whoever looks on a woman to lust after her has committed adultery with her already in his heart (Matthew 5:27-28).

What Does the Apostle John Say?

The apostle John, the Apostle of Love, concluded the Book of Revelation by repeating Jesus' requirement for holiness and the forsaking of sexual immorality or any sexual activity outside of biblical marriage (see Matt. 19:4-5). Because sexuality is designed by God, only He can define its proper use. The Bible clearly says sex was designed by God for one man and one woman in marriage covenant sanctioned by God.

> He who wins the victory will receive these things, and I will be his God, and he will be my son. But as for the cowardly, the untrustworthy, the vile, the murderers, the sexually immoral, those involved with the occult and with drugs, idol-worshippers, and all liars—their

destiny is the lake burning with fire and sulfur, the second death (Revelation 21:7-8 CJB).

In First and Second Corinthians, we read about the apostle Paul wrestling against the vices common to the Gentile world that were being tolerated in the Corinthian church. When the apostle Paul receives the report of a man living with his stepmother, he insists that the Corinthians exclude those who persist in such practices as sexual immorality and greed from their fellowship. Paul points out that believers are set free from these sins by the power of Messiah when he says, *"Such were some of you."*

> *Do you not know that the unrighteous will not inherit the kingdom of God? Do not be deceived. Neither the sexually immoral, nor idolaters, nor adulterers, nor male prostitutes, nor homosexuals, nor thieves, nor covetous, nor drunkards, nor revilers, nor extortioners will inherit the kingdom of God. Such were some of you. But you were washed, you were sanctified, and you were justified in the name of the Lord Jesus by the Spirit of our God* (1 Corinthians 6:9-11).

TRAINING GENTILES

The early church was never without a Bible. Believers studied the Old Testament. Later, as the gospels and epistles were written, they were copied, circulated, and read in local church fellowships. Texts considered to be sacred were bound in book form rather than copied on scrolls.

You may have noticed that the *Didache* adds additional details and prohibitions especially tailored for Gentile disciples to help them walk out their faith in the midst of Greco-Roman society. Several specific prohibitions against certain practices are added in the *Didache*. These include pederasty (the corruption of young boys), sexual immorality, the use of magic and potions, and murdering infants by abortion or infanticide.

Most Evil Sins

Didache 2:2 lists the most evil of sins:

> You shall do no murder; you shall not commit adultery; you shall not commit pederasty to corrupt children; you shall not engage in

sexual immorality; you shall not steal; you shall not use magic; you shall not use potions to cast spells; you shall not murder unborn children by having an abortion, or commit infanticide; you shall not covet your neighbor's possessions.

Five Speech Prohibitions

Didache 2:3-5 list five speech prohibitions:

1. Do not swear falsely.
2. Do not bear false witness.
3. Do not slander or gossip about anyone.
4. Do not hold grudges.
5. The words of your mouth shall not be false or empty, but fulfilled by action.

Five Evil Character Traits

Didache 2:6-7 lists five evil character traits:

1. Do not be greedy.
2. Do not be predatory.
3. Do not be hypocritical.
4. Do not be malicious.
5. Do not be arrogant.

Three Categories of People

Didache 2:7 separates people into three categories. Do not hate any human being but:

1. Some you are to rebuke.
2. Some you are to pray for.
3. Some you are to love more than your own life.

Didache 2 contains three sections. The first section, *Didache* 2:2, lists particularly heinous sins. The second section, *Didache* 2:3–2:5, specifies speech that is prohibited. The third section, *Didache* 2:7, divides people into three categories—those we are to rebuke, those for whom we are to pray, and those we should love more than our own life.

It was important to address proper speech and character traits up front for the new Gentile believers. The focus...is on actions and not doctrine or a list of what to believe. As James, the brother of the Master says, "A person is justified by works and not by faith alone" (James 2:24). To demonstrate our repentance and faith in Messiah Yeshua, we need to display a lifestyle that is consistent with Torah and the Way of Life.[3]

ENDNOTES

1. New testament scholars, both Jewish and Christian, have for years accepted the existence of a group of Gentiles known as God-fearers. They were thought to be closely associated with the synagogue in the Book of Acts. Although they did not convert to Judaism, they were an integral part of the synagogue and provided fertile ground for early Christian missionary activity. As pious Gentiles, the God-fearers stood somewhere between Greco-Roman piety and Jewish piety in the synagogue (Mary Jane Chaignot, "God-Fearers," Bible Wise; retrieved March 4, 202 from https://www.biblewise.com/bible_study/questions/god-fearers.php).

2. Janicki, *The Way of Life*, 89-90.

3. Ibid., 96.

COMMENTARY

DIDACHE 2:1

But the second rule of the teaching is this:

As mentioned in the overview, the second commandment of the teaching focuses on the negative command: "Whatever you do not want to happen to you, do not do to one another." *Didache* 2 "brings ethical injunctions on word and deed specifically tailored for its Gentile audience and the issues that non-Jewish believers faced in their Greco-Roman pagan cultural context."[1]

DIDACHE 2:2

You shall do no murder; you shall not commit adultery; you shall not commit pederasty to corrupt children; you shall not engage in sexual immorality; you shall not steal; you shall not use magic; you shall not use potions to cast spells; you shall not murder unborn children by having an abortion, or commit infanticide; you shall not covet your neighbor's possessions.

At the time of salvation, we are forgiven much. However, we don't know how much was washed out and what remains. When we turn to the Lord, He can show us any current or past issues. It is common for God to reveal a hidden root at the time we have an emotional overreaction. Forgiving and receiving forgiveness should become a regular part of our lives as we walk in the Way of Life. It is wise to take a few minutes on a daily basis and allow the Holy Spirit to check our heart.

> *Therefore, my beloved, as you have always obeyed, not only in my presence, but so much more in my absence, work out your own salvation with fear and trembling. for God is the One working in you, both to will and to do His good pleasure* (Philippians 2:12-13).

DO NOT MURDER

In the sixth commandment, "you shall not kill," the word *kill* is rendered "murder" in Hebrew, meaning *unlawful killing*. War, capital punishment, and self-defense, therefore, are not considered murder. Both murder and adultery were classic prohibitions in Judaism. Because human beings are made in the image of God, murder is a particularly horrid crime that is rebellion against God. Taking an innocent life is also murder, including abortion and infanticide, as well as euthanasia and assisted suicide.

> *Whoever sheds man's blood, by man his blood shall be shed; for in the image of God He made man* (Genesis 9:6 NKJV).

DO NOT COMMIT ADULTERY

The seventh commandment in the Decalogue prohibits adultery. In the Old Testament, adultery only involved an unfaithful wife or betrothed woman and was punished by stoning to death. Jesus, however, raised the standard to include men as well as women. He then included matters of the heart: "*I say to you that whoever looks on a woman to lust after her has committed adultery with her already in his heart*" (Matt. 5:28).

DO NOT PRACTICE PEDERASTY

Our word *pedophilia* is related to the Greek word for *pederasty*. To the Jews, pedophilia was so clearly seen as wrong that it isn't alluded to in the *Torah*. In the Greco-Roman society, on the other hand, homosexual relations were socially acceptable, even those involving young boys. "For the first twelve years of their lives, boys were solely under the care of women (nurses and mothers), but when boys turned twelve, they were initiated in values and virtues from a masculine perspective, which often included sexual experiences."[2] This violates the *Torah's* prohibition against homosexuality.

> *You shall not lie with a man as one does with a woman. It is an abomination* (Leviticus 18:22)

> *If a man lies with another man as with a woman, both of them have committed an abomination. They shall surely be put to death. Their blood guilt shall be upon them* (Leviticus 20:13).

DO NOT COMMIT SEXUAL IMMORALITY

The Greek word *porneuo*, sexual immorality, is the word from which our word *pornography* is derived. It covers all types of sexual activity outside of marriage, including bestiality, homosexuality, and incest. *Porneuo* is sometimes translated "fornication."

The Apostolic Constitutions says about sexual immorality:

> You shall not commit adultery: for you divide one flesh into two. They two shall be one flesh: Genesis 2:24 for the husband and wife are one in nature, in consent, in union, in disposition, and the conduct of life; but they are separated in sex and number. You shall not corrupt boys: Leviticus 18:22 for this wickedness is contrary to nature, and arose from Sodom, which was therefore entirely consumed with fire sent from God. Genesis 19 Let such a one be accursed: and all the people shall say, So be it. Deuteronomy 26 You shall not commit fornication: for says He, There shall not be a fornicator among the children of Israel. Deuteronomy 23:17.[3]

> *But the cowardly, the unbelieving, the abominable, the murderers, the sexually immoral, the sorcerers, the idolaters, and all liars shall have their portion in the lake which burns with fire and brimstone. This is the second death* (Revelation 21:8).

Do Not Steal

"Do not steal" is the eighth commandment from the Decalogue. The apostle Paul says of former thieves who joined the Messianic community, *"Let him who steals steal no more. Instead, let him labor, working with his hands things which are good, that he may have something to share with him who is in need"* (Eph. 4:28). The word for "steal" also applies to the use of false weights and measures. *"A false balance is an abomination to the Lord, but a just weight is His delight"* (Prov. 11:1). And: *"Diverse weights are an abomination to the Lord, and a false balance is not good"* (Prov. 20:23).

> Rabbi Yohanan said: When a person robs his fellow even the value of a *perutah* [penny], it is as though he had taken his life away from him, as it is said, "So are the ways of everyone that is greedy of gain, which takes away the life of the owners thereof" (Proverbs 1:19). ... [This] instructs us not to steal or deal dishonestly (Leviticus 19:35-36). Most people would affirm that not stealing and not cheating are important moral principles and, if asked, would deny engaging in such practices. Yet the tradition realizes that it is not grand theft but the category of petty theft that involves the average person. As Rabbi Yohanan says above, in the eyes of the tradition there is no such thing as petty theft.[4]

All theft is wicked. Kidnapping is also considered theft in Judaism. Therefore, human trafficking would be considered stealing.

Do Not Practice Magic

Magic, sorcery, and all types of occult arts were widely practiced in the Greco-Roman world. "Magic and astrology were practiced widely amongst the populations of the Hellenistic world, at all levels of society. From ancient times the Greeks had consulted oracles, used charms and cast spells, but close contact with the complex system of astrology developed by the priests of ancient Mesopotamia had a powerful effect in them, and deeply penetrated their thinking."[5]

> Sorcery, the practice of malevolent magic, derived from casting lots as a means of divining the future in the ancient Mediterranean

world. Some scholars distinguish sorcery from witchcraft by noting that it is learned rather than intrinsic. Other scholars, noting that modern witches claim to learn their craft, suggest that sorcery's intent is always evil.[6]

Then Pharaoh called for the wise men [skilled in magic and omens] and the sorcerers [skilled in witchcraft], and they also, these magicians (soothsayer-priests) of Egypt, did the same with their secret arts and enchantments (Exodus 7:11 AMP).

When they say to you, "Consult the mediums and the spiritists who whisper and mutter," should not a people consult their God? Should they consult the dead on behalf of the living? (Isaiah 8:19 NASB)

But there was a certain man called Simon, who previously practiced sorcery in the city and astonished the people of Samaria, claiming that he was someone great, to whom they all gave heed, from the least to the greatest, saying, "This man is the great power of God." And they heeded him because he had astonished them with his sorceries for a long time (Acts 8:9-11 NKJV).

You shall not permit a sorceress to live (Exodus 22:18 NKJV).

Participating in occult practices was forbidden and the penalty for involvement was death. Occult practices involve incantations, spells, sorcery, fortune telling, mediums, necromancers (those who practice communication with the dead), the use of potions, infant sacrifice, tarot cards, Ouija boards, Halloween, and so forth. According to former satanic high priest John Ramirez, even if someone, including a child, participates "innocently" it opens a door to demonic activity.

Do Not Use Potions

Potions are drugs or compounds used when practicing magic and sorcery and include seeking spiritual power through incantations. Sometimes this practice was just called sorcery. (See the previous prohibition.)

Do Not Murder Children through Abortion

In the ancient world, it was common for unborn infants to be killed by abortion, usually induced by poison or potions. Because of the use of potions, abortion was closely connected with sorcery and magic. Some scholars believe that, because fewer women died due to complications from abortions and more babies were born, this prohibition contributed to the growth of the Jesus movement.

> *For You formed my inward parts; You covered me in my mother's womb. I will praise You, for I am fearfully and wonderfully made; marvelous are Your works, and that my soul knows very well. My frame was not hidden from You, when I was made in secret, and skillfully wrought in the lowest parts of the earth* (Psalm 139:13-15 NKJV).

Do Not Kill Babies after They Have Been Born

From the dawn of human civilization babies have been discarded because they were inconvenient, unwanted, or female rather than male. In the ancient world, it was common for children to be killed by strangulation or exposure—the intentional killing of infants by leaving them outside to be killed by the cold, starvation, or wild animals. Such practices were a form of birth control in the Greco-Roman culture. The early Messianic believers rescued babies who had been abandoned and raised them as their own. Some scholars believe that this contributed to the numerical growth of the Messianic movement.

The early believers took God at His word when He said in His Word: *"Behold, children are a heritage from the Lord, the fruit of the womb is a reward"* (Ps. 127:3 NKJV). Consider this verse from the sense that children are God's children first. They are lent to parents but ultimately belong to the Lord. Human beings are not animals because they have spirits and were created in the image of God. *"So God created man in His own image; in the image of God He created him; male and female He created them"* (Gen. 1:27).

"Regardless of what anyone may personally think about him, Jesus of Nazareth has been the dominant figure in the history of Western Culture for...

twenty centuries."[7] If we could remove every trace of the light and influence of Jesus in our culture, how dark would be the darkness.

The impact of Jesus on the world is immense. Before Jesus, life was cheap. After Jesus, human life was seen as sacred. Moreover, *all* human life is precious in the eyes of God. Even the handicapped, deformed, and elderly have great value. Martin Luther King, Jr. said, "There are no gradations of the image of God." People aren't accidents; they are created.

> Children would be thought of differently because of Jesus. Historian O.M. Bakke wrote a study called *When Children Became People: The Birth of Childhood in Early Christianity*, in which he noted that, in the ancient world, children usually didn't get named until the eighth day or so. Up until then there was a chance that the infant would be killed by strangulation or left to die of exposure—particularly if he or she was deformed or of the wrong sex. The custom changed because of a group of people who remembered that they were followers of a Man who said, *"Let the little children come to Me."*[8]

Do Not Covet Things that Belong to Your Neighbor

The *Didache* concludes its version of the Decalogue with the tenth commandment: "You shall not covet." Coveting is wanting something that belongs to someone else and/or the active pursuit of the object of desire. Worry is connected to coveting.

> *If God gives such attention to the appearance of wildflowers—most of which are never even seen—don't you think he'll attend to you, take pride in you, do his best for you? What I'm trying to do here is to get you to relax, to not be so preoccupied with getting, so you can respond to God's giving. People who don't know God and the way he works fuss over* [worry about] *these things, but you know both God and how he works. Steep your life in God-reality, God-initiative, God-provisions. Don't worry about missing out. You'll find all your everyday human concerns will be met* (Matthew 6:30-33 MSG).

When we covet the possessions of others, we show that we are not happy with what God has given us. Ibn Ezra [says], "Everyone should rejoice in their lot and try not to covet something that is not theirs because coveting demonstrates a lack of faith in God... Everyone must trust that their Creator will sustain them." His comment connects coveting to worrying. In a similar manner, our Master instructs us, *"Do not be anxious about your life, what you will eat or what you will drink, not about your body, what you will put on... Your heavenly Father knows that you need them all"* (Matthew 6:25, 32). While our heavenly Father will not always give us what we want, He will always provide us with what we need.[9]

You shall not covet your neighbor's house; you shall not covet your neighbor's wife, or his manservant, or his maidservant, or his ox, or his donkey, or anything that is your neighbor's (Exodus 20:17).

Then it happened one evening that David arose from his bed and walked on the roof of the king's house. And from the roof he saw a woman bathing, and the woman was very beautiful to behold. So David sent and inquired about the woman. And someone said, "Is this not Bathsheba...the wife of Uriah the Hittite?" Then David sent messengers, and took her (2 Samuel 11:2-4 NKJV).

DIDACHE 2:3

You shall not commit perjury, you shall not bear false witness, you shall not slander or gossip about others, you shall not hold grudges.

The next section of the *Didache* covers five restrictions on speech. It is the beginning of five commands concerning sins of the tongue. If our heart is right, our words will be right. Lies, gossip, and grudges are products of the wrong kingdom.

You Shall Not Commit Perjury

Our Master says, *"But let your 'Yes' mean 'Yes,' and 'No,' mean 'No.' For whatever is more than these comes from the evil one"* (Matt. 5:37). It is important to remember that there are no grey areas between the Way of Life and the way of death.

Perjury is the sin of lying under oath. An oath is regarded as a sacred obligation and making a false oath is more serious than simply telling a life. Leviticus 19:12 says, *"You shall not swear falsely by My name, and so defile the name of your God: I am the Lord."* "The Torah states that when a false oath is made in God's name, it is *chillul HaShem* ('profanation of the Name,' (חילול השם) because it makes God out to be a liar. The *Didache's* omission of 'by My name' universalizes this commandment, making it applicable to all oaths, not just those made in God's name."[10]

YOU SHALL NOT BEAR FALSE WITNESS

The prohibition against bearing false witness refers mainly to testimony in a court of law but has been expanded to include all deceit. As disciples of Jesus, the Truth Himself, we should represent Him by speaking truth with our words and being honest and forthright in our actions. *"You shall not steal, nor deal falsely, nor lie to one another"* (Lev. 19:11).

> *But those things which proceed out of the mouth come from the heart, and they defile the man. For out of the heart proceed evil thoughts, murders, adulteries, sexual immorality, thefts, false witness, and blasphemies* (Matthew 15:18-19).

YOU SHALL NOT SLANDER OR GOSSIP

Gossip and slander are called "character assassination" because we kill people with our words if we speak evil about them. To speak ill of someone is the same thing as pronouncing a curse over them. We can gossip with truthful facts that would be embarrassing or harmful to an individual if known by others. If someone starts to gossip in your presence, you can say something like, "Have you told this to that person?" "May I quote you on that?" "Why are you telling me this?" It's a sin to say it; it's a sin to listen.

> *And besides they learn to be idle, wandering about from house to house, and not only idle but also gossips and busybodies, saying things which they ought not* (1 Timothy 5:13 NKJV).

Leviticus 25:17 (AMPC), *"You shall not wrong one another"* is interpreted by the rabbis as referring to sinful words that would cause another person pain, embarrassment, anger, or fear if they knew you had said it about them. Three levels of gossip include: 1) minor gossip about true details of someone's life; 2) negative but true gossip; and 3) slander, or purposeful lies equivalent to murdering someone.

> *Speak evil of no one...be peaceable, gentle, showing all humility to all men* (Titus 3:2 NKJV).

> *Keep your tongue from evil, and your lips from speaking deceit* (Psalm 34:13).

Slander is malicious gossip intended to destroy someone's reputation. The Greek word used in the Septuagint for "slander" has the connotation "to pronounce a curse." If we speak evil words about an individual, we are cursing them. No disciple of the Master should speak evil about anyone.

You Shall Not Hold Grudges

A grudge is holding bitterness in the heart and releases poison into the life of the one who refuses to forgive.

> Many of the new Gentile believers would experience persecution and abuse from their family and friends for their newfound faith. They were not permitted to hold onto these evils and let them fester inside. Instead, they were to turn the other cheek...and love their enemies...exercising the utmost humility. While not specifically a verbal sin, holding grudges can indeed be brought on by speaking or listening to evil speech.[11]

> *Let all bitterness, wrath, anger, outbursts, and blasphemies, with all malice, be taken away from you* (Ephesians 4:31).

Forgiving Enemies

Bitterness can always be cleansed from our heart by forgiveness. If we lose our peace, forgiveness removes any toxic emotion and our peace is restored.

Pray. With your eyes closed and in an attitude of prayer, allow the Lord to bring to your mind someone who has hurt you or wronged you in some way.

Feel. Feel the negative emotion.

Forgive and release. Allow a river of forgiveness to flow from your heart toward them until you feel peace. Next, receive forgiveness that you have allowed the poison of unforgiveness to even remain in your heart. (If someone has stolen something from you, release it as a gift to them from your heart into their hands. If you give something as a gift, no one can take it from you.)

Praying for Enemies

Pray. With your eyes closed and in an attitude of prayer, picture the person who wronged you.

Feel. Make sure you have already forgiven so you feel peace.

Release love. In an attitude of prayer, allow a river of loving compassion to flow to your enemy. After all, you are free and they are in the grip of our enemy, the devil.

Receiving Forgiveness

When we hold a toxic emotion in our heart, it is the sin of unforgiveness. After forgiving perpetrators, receive forgiveness for allowing bitterness to take root in our heart. Also, if we have spoken evil about anyone, we need forgiveness for committing that sin.

Pray. In an attitude of prayer, let the Lord show you any area where you need to receive forgiveness for any wrong action or attitude.

Feel. Feel the negative emotion, such as guilt or shame.

Forgive. Receive forgiveness until the feeling changes to peace.

> ## DIDACHE 2:4
>
> You shall not be double-minded nor double-tongued, for to be double-tongued is a deadly trap.

DO NOT BE DOUBLE-MINDED

The apostle James uses the term *double-minded* in his letter in the New Testament.

A double-minded man is unstable in all his ways (James 1:8).

Draw near to God, and He will draw near to you. Cleanse your hands, you sinners, and purify your hearts, you double-minded (James 4:8).

Double-mindedness is damaging to our walk and can involve a number of areas in our lives. The Greek word for "double-minded" is *dipsuchos*. It is derived from *dis*, meaning "twice," and *psuche*, meaning "mind." It is used to describe an individual who is divided in his interests or loyalties, wavering, uncertain, two-faced, half-hearted. We will see double-mindedness as a theme throughout his letter.

James addresses several specific areas in regard to double-mindedness:

- Praying with doubt. Solution: Pray according to God's will, make sure your attitudes and Way of Life are godly, and release selfish desires.

- Hearing without doing. Solution: What was the last thing God asked you to do? Did you do it? Did you do part of what God told you but not all? If not, obey now.

- Giving preferential treatment. Solution: Ask the Lord to show you anywhere you have not been fair in attitude or action.

Do Not Be Double-Tongued

The prohibition against speaking with a double-tongue is the fifth speech prohibition. To be double-tongued is to say one thing to one person and something else to another. A double-tongued person is untrustworthy because they will say whatever necessary to get a wanted response. A double-tongued person is often a people pleaser because they have a strong desire to say what someone wants them to say in the moment. A person who is double-tongued lacks integrity. Titus 1:6-9 tells us that integrity is essential for godly leaders.

Not only is being double-tongued a sin and character flaw, it is evidence of an unmet emotional need for approval. If you are concerned about this issue in your own life, God can fill any "holes" in your heart by meeting your emotional needs.

PRACTICE

Prayer Steps

Pray. Get in an attitude of prayer. Close your eyes and pray, placing your hand on your belly.

First. First person or situation. What is the first person or situation that comes to mind—in an image or memory?

Feel the feeling. What is the emotion you feel in your gut?

Forgive. Yield to Jesus the Forgiver within and allow a river of forgiveness to flow from the belly until the emotion changes to peace.

Fact. After forgiving and getting peace, if there is a lie, renounce the lie out loud. Next, ask the Lord for the truth (scriptural fact) and receive it.

Fill. If there was an unmet emotional need: 1) forgive first; 2) release demands on people to give you what you needed; then, 3) receive filling from Jesus within.

DIDACHE 2:5

The words of your mouth shall not be false or empty, but fulfilled by action.

The fifth speech prohibition is continued in *Didache* 2:5. A false word is a lie and an empty word is one that is not followed up by action. If we speak a false word, we are deceitful, but an empty word manifests lack of commitment. We should receive forgiveness and repent for speaking idle words. If our word can't be trusted, we are not only committing sin but fail to reflect the character of Jesus as we should.

> *If a man vows a vow to the Lord, or swears an oath to bind himself with a bond, he will not break his word. He will do according to all that proceeds out of his mouth* (Numbers 30:2).

> *But I say to you that for every idle word that men speak, they will give an account on the Day of Judgment* (Matthew 12:36).

> *My little children, let us love not in word and speech, but in action and truth* (1 John 3:18).

DIDACHE 2:6

You shall not be covetous, greedy, hypocritical, malicious, nor proud. To sum it up, you shall not plot evil against others.

Didache 2:6 makes a shift from sins committed to five evil character traits. If we persist in sin, it becomes part of our character. For example, we no longer covet occasionally, but we become a covetous person. We don't give in to pride once in a while; we become a proud person.

Do Not Be Covetous

To be covetous is to want it and to be jealous of anyone else who has it.

> The opposite of covetousness is contentment in God. When contentment in God decreases, covetousness for gain increases. That's why Paul says in Colossians 3:5 that covetousness is idolatry. "Put to death what is earthly in you: immorality, impurity, passion, evil desire, and covetousness which is idolatry." It's idolatry because the contentment that the heart should be getting from God, it starts to get from something else.[12]

Then He said to them, "Take heed and beware of covetousness. For a man's life does not consist in the abundance of his possessions" (Luke 12:15).

Let your conduct be without covetousness; be content with such things as you have. For He Himself has said, "I will never leave you nor forsake you" (Hebrews 13:5 NKJV).

DO NOT BE GREEDY

To be greedy implies a strong desire to possess or acquire something beyond what is needed or deserved.

For this you know, that no sexually immoral or impure person, or one who is greedy, who is an idolater, has any inheritance in the kingdom of Messiah and of God (Ephesians 5:5).

For an overseer must be blameless, as a steward of God, not self-willed, not easily angered, not given to drunkenness, not violent, not greedy for dishonest gain (Titus 1:7).

DO NOT BE HYPOCRITICAL

When someone pretends to be different or better than they really are, they are being hypocritical. The word *hypocrite* comes from the Greek word *hypokritēs*, which means actor.

Therefore, when you do your charitable deeds, do not sound a trumpet before you as the hypocrites do in the synagogues and in the streets, that they may be honored by men. Truly I say to you, they have their reward (Matthew 6:2).

Hypocrite! First remove the plank from your own eye, and then you will see clearly to remove the speck from your brother's eye (Matthew 7:5 NKJV).

DO NOT BE MALICIOUS

A malicious person has cruel, vicious, or spiteful motives leading to behavior that is intended to hurt or harm someone.

But now you yourselves are to put off all these: anger, wrath, malice, blasphemy, filthy language out of your mouth (Colossians 3:8 NKJV).

Therefore let us keep the feast, not with old leaven, nor with the leaven of malice and wickedness, but with the unleavened bread of sincerity and truth (1 Corinthians 5:8 NKJV).

DO NOT BE PROUD

Pride that comes from self-righteousness or conceit is sinful. Psalm 10:4 tells us that those who are proud are so self-centered that their hearts are far from God. *"In his pride the wicked man does not seek him; in all his thoughts there is no room for God"* (NIV). Such pride is the direct opposite of the spirit of humility that is so pleasing to the Lord.

Pride goes before destruction, and a haughty spirit before a fall (Proverbs 16:18).

For all that is in the world—the lust of the flesh, the lust of the eyes, and the pride of life—is not of the Father, but is of the world (1 John 2:16).

PRACTICE

Receiving Forgiveness

We need to receive forgiveness for wrong attitudes and motives in addition to sins committed.

Pray. In an attitude of prayer, let the Lord show you any area where you need to receive forgiveness for any wrong action or attitude.

Feel. Feel the negative emotion, such as guilt or shame.

Forgive. Receive forgiveness until the feeling changes to peace.

DIDACHE 2:7

You shall not hate any person: But some you are to rebuke, for some you should pray, and some you should love more than your own life.

After telling us to not to hate anybody, *Didache* 2:7 describes three categories of people. Verse 7, which is the summary of chapter 2, has been called the "cornerstone verse" of the entire *Didache*.

> It is reminiscent of a passage by Jude, our Master's brother: "Have mercy on those who doubt; save others by snatching them out of the fire; to others show mercy with fear, hating even the garment stained by the flesh" (Jude 22-23). The verse reflects the message of love that our Master Yeshua taught: a love that results in challenging some; praying for others, and giving up our lives for others. The Apostolic Constitutions cites two proof texts: Do not hate any human being; you are to rebuke "your brother," and not "incur sin because of him" [Leviticus 19:17]; and "Reprove a wise man and he will love you" [Proverbs 9:8].[13]

The *Didache* is concerned here with believers within a Messianic community.

1. **Some you are to rebuke.** The purpose of rebuke is so that someone will turn from a wrong way to the right way. We should only rebuke an individual who will listen.

   When I say to the wicked, "O wicked man, you shall surely die," and you do not speak to warn the wicked from his way, that wicked man shall die in his iniquity. But his blood I will require from your hand (Ezekiel 33:8).

2. **For some you should pray.** If someone isn't willing to accept a reprimand, you should pray that they will come to repentance.

3. **Some you are to love even more than your own life.** This applies to members who are walking the Way of Life within a believer's own fellowship.

   Greater love has no man than this: that a man lay down his life for his friends (John 15:13).

ENDNOTES

1. Janicki, *The Way of Life*, 97.

2. Ibid., 100-101.

3. *Constitutions of the Holy Apostles* or, *The Apostolic Constitutions* (Columbia, SC: A Codex Spiritualis Publication), 110-111.

4. Rabbi Michael Strassfeld, "Jews and Stealing," My Jewish Learning; retrieved March 4, 2020 from https://www.myjewishlearning.com/article/jews-and-stealing.

5. "The Hellenistic World," TimeMaps, retrieved March 4, 2020 from https://www.timemaps.com/civilizations/hellenistic-world/.

6. J. Gordon Melton, "Sorcery," *Encyclopedia Britannica,* retrieved March 4, 2020 from https://www.britannica.com/topic/sorcery.

7. Jaroslav Pelican, *Jesus through the Centuries: His Place in the History of Culture* (New Haven, CT: Yale University Press), 1.

8. John Ortberg, *Who Is This Man? The Unpredictable Impact of the Inescapable Jesus* (Grand Rapids, MI: Zondervan, 2012), 15.

9. Rabbi A.J. Rosenberg, 1:318) *Shemoth: A New English Translation, Two Volumes* (New York, NY: Judaica, 195), 1:318.

10. Janicki, *The Way of Life*, 112.

11. Ibid., 116.

12. John Piper, "Battling the Unbelief of Covetousness," Desiring God, October 30, 1988; retrieved March, 5, 2020 from https://www.desiringgod.org/messages/battling-the-unbelief-of-covetousness.

13. Janicki, *The Way of Life*, 126.

DIDACHE THREE

3:1 My child, flee from all evil and everything like it.

3:2 Do not be angry, for anger leads to murder; nor envious, quarrelsome, or hot-tempered, for all these are sources of murder as well.

3:3 My child, do not be lustful, for lust leads to sexual immorality, nor a user of filthy speech, nor have roving eyes, for all these are sources of adultery.

3:4 My child, don't use divination to tell the future, for this leads to idolatry; neither be an enchanter who casts spells, nor an astrologer who tries to predict the future by using horoscopes or the alignment of planets and stars, nor a sorcerer, nor even desire to look into such things, for these all lead to idolatry.

3:5 My child, do not be a liar, for lying leads to theft; nor a lover of money, nor proud and boastful, for all these lead to theft.

3:6 My child, don't be a complainer, for this leads to blasphemy; nor self-pleasing, nor a thinker of evil, for all these lead to blasphemy.

3:7 But be meek and humble, for the meek shall inherit the earth.

3:8 Be patient and merciful, guileless, calm, and good-natured, and trembling all the time at the words which you have heard.

3:9 Do not exalt yourself or be presumptuous. Don't keep company with those who put on airs, but keep company with those who are righteous and lowly.

3:10 Accept the hardships that befall you as good, knowing that nothing ever happens apart from God.

OVERVIEW

Didache 3 cautions the novice to avoid evil of any kind. It lists five evil character traits to avoid along with explanations. Don't be angry, lustful, a seeker of omens, a liar, or a complainer. We are next instructed to adopt humility, after which six characteristics of the humble are specified: patient, merciful, guileless, quiet, good-natured, and trembling at the words you have heard. Finally, we must accept whatever befalls us in life because it comes from God.

Choosing to follow the Way of Life was a deliberate choice to flee from sin and follow Jesus, as described in detail to the novice in *Didache* chapters one and two. The student is prepared for a transition in *Didache* 2.7 beginning with "you shall not hate any person" and concludes by saying "some you should love more than your own life."

> Once the negative prohibitions are accounted for, the training moves on to delineate how one must cultivate the discipline to act and think in such a way as to remain far from any of the grievous infractions named. At the same time, there is a transition in mood signaled by the fact that the novice is now, for the first time, to be routinely addressed as "my child."[1]

Those who take the words of their spiritual parent seriously will have hearts that tremble at the word of God spoken through them.

> *For My hand made all those things, thus all those things have come to be, says the Lord. But to this man I will look, even to him who is poor and of a contrite spirit, and trembles at My word* (Isaiah 66:2).

"My child" is the Greek expression *teknon*, plural *tekna*, literally meaning "my offspring," referring to either men or women. "In the *Didache*, teknon may be used precisely because initiation into this community pertains to both men and women."[2] Although some portions of the training are oriented toward men, others specifically concern women. However, most instructions apply equally to both.

> *We were gentle among you, just as a nursing mother cherishes her own children* (1 Thessalonians 2:7 NKJV).

> *You know how we exhorted, and comforted, and charged every one of you, as a father does his own children, that you would walk worthy of God who calls you into His own kingdom and glory* (1 Thessalonians 2:11-12 NKJV).

Calling the novice "my child" reveals that a special relationship is developing in which the instructor is acting as a "father" or "mother" to their disciple. A well-known example of such a parent-child relationship is that of Elisha with the prophet Elijah, who addressed Elijah as "my father." (See 1 Kings 19:19-21; 2 Kings 2:1-15.) The apostle Paul "does not hesitate to liken himself" to both "a [female] nurse taking care of her children (*tekna*)" and "a father with his children (*tekna*)."

> In rabbinic literature the sage at the head of an academy of Torah is referred to as the father and his disciples are called his family; hence terms such as the "House of Hillel" (*Beit Hillel*) and the "House of Shammai" (*Beit Shammai*). ...The Master alluded to this relationship when he said to the Pharisees, "By whom do your sons [i.e. your disciples] cast them out?" (Matthew 23:8-9).[3]

According to the mentor-child principle, we should honor a spiritual father even more than a natural father. The rabbinic tradition is permeated with the notion of spiritual fatherhood. The Mishna explains:

> For his father brought him into the world, But his master, who taught him wisdom, will bring him into the life of the world to come (*m. Baba Mesia,* 2:11).

The sage, therefore, who gives wisdom which opens up "the life of the world to come" is to be esteemed over one's father who brought him into this world. The notion of spiritual fatherhood extended to God as well. In the Jewish tradition God was honored as the "Father of Israel. ...This fatherhood was not based upon God's activity in creating—a trait shared by the Gentiles—upon His election, His caring for them, His training them in Torah. ...Applying this to the *Didache*, it is no surprise that the 'one speaking to you the word of God' is honored 'as the Lord.'"[4]

FENCES

The railing on a high deck is a fence. It doesn't restrict us; it keeps us safe. *Didache* 3:1 instructs the novice to be watchful because minor sins can lead to worse sins. When you have a fence, you are within a safety zone. "My child, flee from all evil and everything like it." "The *Didache* did not randomly choose these prohibitions but rather drew upon the didactic models of Jewish tradition, in which these five are considered among the gravest transgressions and... universally applicable."[5]

The organization of *Didache* 3 follows this pattern: Flee from evil and everything like it because (3:1) anger leads to murder (3:2), lust leads to sexual immorality (3:3), magic leads to idolatry (3:4), lying leads to theft (3:5), and complaining leads to blasphemy (3:6). The main point of this teaching is to catch the seeds of evil before they put down roots. For example, giving tithes to God forms a fence around greed, being grateful is a fence around complaining, and remaining silent is a fence around wisdom when you are tempted to speak impetuously.

Within the *teknon* section of the *Didache* we find an "affirmation of the Torah, ensuring the fulfillment of the major precepts by avoiding the minor infringements... [which] also lies behind the 'greater righteousness' of... Mathew 5:17-18 rather than a rejection of the Torah in favor of the Gospel."[6]

HUMILITY

Following the warnings against negative character traits, *Didache* 3:7-10 extolls the trait of humility. "But be meek and humble, for the meek shall inherit the earth" (*Didache* 3:7). The Master says: *"God blesses those who are humble, for they will inherit the whole earth"* (Matt. 5:5 NLT). Clement of Rome (AD 35-99) wrote in his letter to the Corinthians: "So let us be humble, casting away all pride, foolishness, and wrath. Let us do what is written" (Clement 13:1-3).[7]

> Among pagan authors, "humility" had almost never been a term of commendation. It belonged to ignoble and abject [below the normal standards for decency and dignity] characters. Men were born "sons of god," said the Stoics, and thus they should cherish no "humble or ignoble" thoughts about their nature. The humble belonged to the abject, the mean [lacking dignity or honor], the unworthy.[8]

In Greece and Rome, status was everything. Romans and Greeks pursued greatness and acclaim. "Humility was not considered a virtue in that world."[9] In that day, being proud was a good thing.

> You and I are not morally superior to members of the ancient world. We are no better because we live later. But we live in a world where the lowliest of the low are seen differently than they were two thousand years ago. ...[Our Master] entered the world wearing swaddling clothes and exited it in the towel of a slave. ...Greatness looks different now.[10]

Jesus introduced a new way of thinking into the world and redefined "greatness" by the way that He lived. He showed us a better way to live—living seen from God's perspective. If you desire to be great, serve others.

> *Whoever desires to become great among you, let him be your servant. And whoever desires to be first among you, let him be your slave—just as the Son of Man did not come to be served, but to serve, and to give His life a ransom for many* (Matthew 20:26-28 NKJV).

PRACTICE

Repentance for Pride

Pray. Get in an attitude of prayer and become neutral so you are willing to deal with anything God reveals to you. (Even being willing to yield in this way is an act of humility.)

First. Focus on the first thing that comes to mind.

Feel. Allow yourself to feel the feeling in the gut.

Forgive. You may need to receive forgiveness for stubbornness or rebellion as well as for pride. Allow forgiveness to flow until you sense peace.

Release. Release any person or situation you're holding on to into the hands of God.

ENDNOTES

1. Milavec, *The Didache: Faith, Hope, and Life of the Earliest Christian Communities,* 147.

2. Ibid.

3. Janicki, *The Way of Life,* 132.

4. Milavec, *The Didache: Faith, Hope, and Life of the Earliest Christian Communities,* 148-149.

5. Janicki, *The Way of Life,* 132-133.

6. Jonathan Draper, "The Holy Vine of David Made Known to the Gentiles through God's Servant Jesus: 'Christian Judaism' in the Didache," in Matt Jackson-McCabe, ed., *Christian Judaism Reconsidered: Rethinking Ancient Groups and Texts* (Minneapolis, MN: Fortress Press, 2007), 267.

7. Kenneth Howell, *Clement of Rome and the Didache* (Zanesville, OH: The Coming Home Network, 2012).

8. Robin Land Fox, *Pagans and Christians* (New York, NY: Alfred A. Knopf, 1987), 324.

9. Ortberg, *Who Is This Man?* 74.

10. Ibid., 86.

COMMENTARY

My child, flee from all evil and everything like it.

MY CHILD

Didache 3:1 opens with a change in the relationship of novice and teacher. The student is not just a seeker now, but a beloved child with a spiritual parent. "When the *Didache* uses the expressions 'my child' and 'my children,' it taps into the rich culture of discipleship within the Jewish tradition."[1] Learning to be a believer by becoming an apprentice was considered to be a holy endeavor that brought mentor and student into the divine presence of God.

FLEE FROM ALL EVIL

The first two chapters of the *Didache* defined evil thoroughly. Beginning a new Way of Life in a new family, the disciple is now instructed to "flee from all evil." The word for "flee" in Greek is *phĕugō*, meaning "escape, flee away." It conveys the idea of being saved by flight or escaping safely out of grave danger.

> *But you, O man of God, flee these things and pursue righteousness, godliness, faith, love, patience, gentleness* (1 Timothy 6:11 NKJV).

> *So flee youthful desires and pursue righteousness, faith, love, and peace, with those who call on the Lord out of a pure heart* (2 Timothy 2:22).

AND EVERYTHING LIKE IT

Following rabbinic style, chapter three begins with the general then moves to the specific. Participation in small sins leads to greater sins.

> *Who can understand his errors? Cleanse me from secret faults. Keep back Your servant also from presumptuous sins; may they not rule over me. Then I will be upright and innocent from great transgression* (Psalm 19:12-13).

Rebbe Nachman of Breslov taught: When a person does one sin, it causes him to commit related offenses. ...The later sins are then responsible for still more related wrongs. ...The first sin along with the related ones following it, forms one package.[2]

Jesus, our Master, also cautions us to pay attention to the "little" things.

Whoever, therefore, breaks one of the least of these commandments and teaches others to do likewise shall be called the least in the kingdom of heaven. But whoever does and teaches them shall be called great in the kingdom of heaven (Matthew 5:19).

PRACTICE

Secret Faults

Pray. Get in an attitude of prayer. Adopt David's attitude of opening his heart to the eyes of God.

Who can understand his errors? Cleanse me from secret faults. Keep back Your servant also from presumptuous sins; may they not rule over me. Then I will be upright and innocent from great transgression (Psalm 19:12-13).

First. Focus on the first thing that comes to mind.

Feel. Allow yourself to feel the negative emotion in the gut.

Forgive. Receive forgiveness until you get peace.

Release. Release yourself into the hands of God.

DIDACHE 3:2

Do not be angry, for anger leads to murder; nor envious, quarrelsome, or hot-tempered, for all these are sources of murder as well.

The *Didache* 3:2-6 now specifies five major sins and the minor infractions that lead up to them. The first warning is against anger, which leads to murder. Also leading to murder are envy, being quarrelsome, and having a hot temper. The first murder in the Bible was due to the anger of Cain:

Cain was very angry and his countenance fell. The Lord said to Cain, "Why are you angry? Why is your countenance fallen? If you do well, shall you not be accepted? But if you do not do well, sin is crouching at the door. It desires to dominate you, but you must rule over it." Cain told Abel his brother. And it came about, when they were in the field, that Cain rose up against his brother Abel and killed him (Genesis 4:5-8).

You have heard that our ancestors were told, "You must not murder. If you commit murder, you are subject to judgment." But I say, if you are even angry with someone, you are subject to judgment! If you call someone an idiot, you are in danger of being brought before the court. And if you curse someone, you are in danger of the fires of hell (Matthew 5:21-22 NLT).

Warnings about anger are found in Jewish ethical teaching. "Anger is an evil trait. Just as scurvy is a disease of the body, so anger is a disease of the soul. ... For anger deprives a man from reasoning. ...Therefore, it is impossible for the angry man to escape great sins."[3]

On the other hand, patience is a great virtue because it forestalls anger. "*He who is slow to anger is better than the mighty, and he who rules his spirit than he who takes a city*" (Prov. 16:32). And: "*Therefore, my beloved brothers, let every man be swift to hear, slow to speak, and slow to anger*" (James 1:19).

PRACTICE

Forgiveness for Anger

Pray. Close your eyes and get in an attitude of prayer.

First. Focus on the first person or situation that comes to mind.

Feel. Feel the emotion in your gut.

Forgive. Receive forgiveness for your anger, then release forgiveness to whoever or whatever made you angry until your feel peace. If you are angry at another person, forgive them. If you are angry at circumstances, you are actually angry at God (like the children of Israel in the wilderness). If you are angry at yourself, receive forgiveness.

Break the tie. As an act of your will, break the soul tie. Then, from your gut, release your emotions back to God. Our emotions are designed to be conduits of the fruit of the Spirit, not ungodly soul ties.

DIDACHE 3:3

My child, do not be lustful, for lust leads to sexual immorality, nor a user of filthy speech, nor have roving eyes, for all these are sources of adultery.

Didache 3:3 addresses the second major sin, which is sexual immorality. Lust in the heart is an intense craving for someone or something. Sins that are like the evil lead to greater evil. Lust for another person can also be spiritual adultery. If spiritual adultery is not checked, it will lead to physical adultery.

While other toxic emotions may not immediately involve demonic activity, lust always attracts the presence of seducing spirits. Furthermore, a "soul tie," or emotional and spiritual attachment, forms with the object of desire (which may be a person, place, or thing). An unclean attachment to a "thing" is idolatry.

Didache 3:3 focuses specifically on a forbidden desire for a person. The presence of a soul tie can be felt in the gut as a sensation of "titillation." "*But I say, anyone who even looks at a woman with lust has already committed adultery with her in his heart*" (Matt. 5:28 NLT).

> *Let there be no sexual immorality, impurity, or greed among you. Such sins have no place among God's people* (Ephesians 5:3 NLT).

A man and his wife who had been arguing about his "friendship" with a female coworker asked for an appointment. When they arrived, we told them that it was possible to find out immediately. We asked him to close his eyes and think about the women. A seducing spirit manifested so strongly that not only could he feel the excitement in his gut, but everyone in the room could feel it.

FILTHY SPEECH

"In rabbinic literature this kind of talk is known as obscene speech...and the prohibition against it is taken quite seriously. The Talmud teaches that for the one who speaks obscenely, 'Gehenna is made deep for him' [*bShabbat* 33a]." Based upon Isaiah 9:16, it is said that "as a punishment for obscenity, troubles multiply, cruel decrees are proclaimed afresh...and the fatherless and widows cry out and are not answered."[4]

> *But fornication and all uncleanness or covetousness, let it not even be named among you, as is fitting for saints; neither filthiness, nor foolish talking, nor coarse jesting, which are not fitting, but rather giving of thanks* (Ephesians 5:3-4 NKJV).

ROVING EYES

"Roving eyes" literally means "one who looks up," or gazing upon someone with lustful eyes. Joseph had been sold by his brothers and sent to Egypt. The traders in the caravan purchased Joseph, took him to Egypt, then sold him as a slave to a man called Potiphar. Although Joseph was a faithful servant, Potiphar's wife tried to seduce him. However, when Joseph refused her advances, she told her husband that he had made improper advances toward her. Potiphar then had Joseph thrown into prison.

> *And it came to pass after these things that his master's wife cast longing eyes on Joseph, and she said, "Lie with me." But he refused* (Genesis 39:7-8 NKJV).

> *Having eyes full of adultery and that cannot cease from sin, enticing unstable souls. They have a heart trained in covetous practices, and are accursed children* (2 Peter 2:14 NKJV).

> The simple-hearted man...averts his eyes from a woman's beauty, so as not to mislead or corrupt his mind... I [the patriarch Issachar] have not committed fornication through a lustful eye (*Testament of Issachar* 4:4; 7:3).

DIDACHE 3:4

My child, don't use divination to tell the future, for this leads to idolatry; neither be an enchanter who casts spells, nor an astrologer who tries to predict the future by using horoscopes or the alignment of planets and stars, nor a sorcerer, nor even desire to look into such things, for these all lead to idolatry.

Didache 3:4 cautions against engaging in divination, magic, or sorcery, which always come directly from the kingdom of darkness. There are only two sources for the supernatural. If the source is not the kingdom of God then the source is evil. "This is the first and only mention of idolatry in the training program. Divination is specified as the leading inducement to idolatry."[5] In the first centuries, magic and occult practices of all kinds were extremely prevalent.[6]

> The author of the Didache undoubtedly wished to warn novices against any practice calculated to gain privileged information regarding the future through omens attributed to this or that pagan god. Later on, the novice will be trained to yield to the future assured that "apart from God, nothing happens" (3:10).[7]

In addition to divination and fortune-telling, novices are warned against enchanters using incantations and astrology as particularly dangerous.[8]

> ## DIDACHE 3:5
>
> My child, do not be a liar, for lying leads to theft; nor a lover of money, nor proud and boastful, for all these lead to theft.

Didache 3:5 says that lying leads to theft. We can "lie" in a number of ways: telling a half-truth, making false promises, using flattery, omitting facts, and so forth. The point is that deceit is wrong and leads to greater transgressions. *"He who walks uprightly, and does righteousness, and speaks truth in his heart"* (Ps. 15:2).

Although, we might think that theft leads to lying to cover up the wrongdoing, *Didache* 3:5 reverses the sequence. It is possible that "lying" is used here in the broader sense of deception, betrayal, and treachery.[9] If lying is viewed as general dishonesty, small sins of deceit lead to more serious sins such as theft.

> *For out of the abundance of the heart the mouth speaks. A good man out of the good treasure of his heart brings forth good things. And an evil man out of the evil treasure brings forth evil things* (Matthew 12:34-35).
>
> *Finally, brethren, whatever things are true...meditate on these things* (Philippians 4:8 NKJV).
>
> *You desire truth in the inward parts, and in the hidden part You make me to know wisdom* (Psalm 51:6).

> ## DIDACHE 3:6
>
> My child, don't be a complainer, for this leads to blasphemy; nor self-pleasing, nor a thinker of evil, for all these lead to blasphemy.

Didache 3:6 specifies the final major sin as complaining. When we complain, the underlying emotion is anger. Anger toward circumstances is anger at God. When we are angry at God, we are accusing Him of treating us badly.

In the Septuagint, the term *blasphemy* is used almost exclusively complaints against God. Epictetus, a first century Greek philosopher, asked his disciples to take an oath "never to distrust, nor accuse, nor murmur at any of the things allowed by God" (*Discourses* 1:14).[10] Epictetus gave the following illustration as an admonition against complaining. The point is, we can't control life!

> How do we act in a voyage? What is in my power? To choose the pilot, the sailors, the day, the hour [to cast off]. Afterwards comes a storm. What have I to care for? My part is [already] performed. That matter belongs to another, the pilot. But [suppose] the ship is sinking; what then have I to do? That which alone I can do; I submit to being drowned, without fear, without crying out, accusing God, but as one who knows that what is born must likewise die. ... What signifies it whether by drowning, or by a fever? For, in some way or other, pass I must (*Discourses* 2:5).[11]

We can't control life!

PRACTICE

Forgiving God

Although God never does anything wrong, we can be angry at Him when we are unhappy with His choices. Being angry at God is sinful. Complaining is not always obvious anger, but it is anger nonetheless and we must repent. When we forgive God, we cleanse our heart of toxic emotions.

Pray. Close your eyes and get in an attitude of prayer.

First. Focus on God.

Feel. Feel the negative emotion in your gut.

Forgive. Receive forgiveness for your anger then release forgiveness to God.

DIDACHE 3:7

But be meek and humble, for the meek shall inherit the earth.

Didache 3:7 marks a transition to a final section about humility as a lifestyle. In the Sermon on the Mount, the first characteristic of a citizen of the kingdom is: *"Blessed are the poor in spirit* [those who are humble], *for theirs is the kingdom of heaven"* (Matt. 5:3).

POOR IN SPIRIT

When we are born, we are completely self-centered. We were born in the family line of Adam. At the time of salvation, we are transplanted into another life—that of Jesus. Before our salvation, we were "in Adam." Because we have inherited a new life, the life of Jesus, we are now "in Him."

We were created as vessels, or containers, of a spirit. In our lost condition, we lived by the spirit that controlled Adam. We can't live without a spirit in us: *"the body without the spirit is dead"* (James 2:26). When Adam sinned, his spirit, which was made to be filled with God's Spirit, was taken over by a wrong spirit. Spiritual death ruled. When we are born again, we become partakers of Messiah's Spirit. Now we are filled with another Spirit.

We will always be a "self." It is just a question of which spirit is the master of our "self-vessel."

> *Do you not know that to whom you yield yourselves as slaves to obey, you are slaves of the one whom you obey, whether of sin leading to death, or of obedience leading to righteousness?* (Romans 6:16)

RAISED TOGETHER

When Jesus died, we died. When Jesus was raised from the dead, we were raised together with Him.

> *Therefore we were buried with Him by baptism into death, that just as Messiah was raised up from the dead by the glory of the Father, even so we also should walk in newness of life* (Romans 6:4).

Moreover, when Jesus ascended on high, Father God *"raised us up and seated us together in the heavenly places in Messiah Jesus"* (Eph. 2:6).

> *And you He made alive, who were dead in trespasses and sins, in which you once walked according to the course of this world, according to the prince of the power of the air, the spirit who now works in the sons of disobedience, among whom also we all once conducted*

ourselves in the lusts of our flesh, fulfilling the desires of the flesh and of the mind, and were by nature children of wrath, just as the others (Ephesians 2:1-3 NKJV).

"JESUS LIVES IN ME"

Many believers don't understand that we have inherited a new Spirit, the Spirit by which Jesus is Lord in us, and they continue to try to live out their faith through the power of the flesh, or willpower. Our flesh can never be pleasing to God. *"For I know that in me (that is, in my flesh) nothing good dwells"* (Rom. 7:18). When we come to the realization that we can't live our faith in the flesh, we can stop "trying" and start trusting Jesus. We can't try and trust at the same time. In Galatians 2:19-20, we read, *"I have been crucified with Messiah; and it is no longer I who live, but Messiah lives in me"* (TLV).

Ultimately, we come to the realization that, apart from Messiah who dwells in us, we can do nothing good. *"For I know that in me (that is, in my flesh) dwells no good thing"* (Rom. 7:18). It doesn't matter if your flesh is quiet and gentle or loud and contentious, it is still flesh that is operated by the wrong spirit. Only the Spirit of Messiah is good enough to meet the standards of Father God. *"I am the vine, you are the branches. He who remains in Me, and I in him, bears much fruit. For without Me you can do nothing"* (John 15:5). How does Jesus live His life in us and through us? We yield to Him and allow Him to do it.

We no longer expect anything worthwhile to come out of our flesh, so we no longer think highly of ourselves nor do we despise ourselves. Only God is good (see Matt. 19:17). When we come to that realization and let Jesus live His life through us, we are *"poor in spirit"* (Matt. 5:3).

How do we become humble? We accept our dependence upon Jesus with joy and let Him be Lord. We can receive Jesus as our Savior, but it takes humility to submit to His Lordship. Submitting to Him is a daily dying and yielding process. When we are humble, or meek (*prautes* in Greek), we stop struggling with God about the decisions He makes as far as the circumstances of life.

Humility does not consist of just outward behavior, but our heart attitude mainly toward God. A humble person accepts all God's dealings in our life as good because they come from Him. We stop fighting against God. A humble person also ceases to struggle against people, knowing that God controls everything that happens to us. Humility is the opposite of self-centeredness because our allegiance has been transferred from self to God.

> ### DIDACHE 3:8
>
> Be patient and merciful, guileless, calm, and good-natured, and trembling all the time at the words which you have heard.

The humble person exhibits the fruit of the Spirit in their daily walk:

But the fruit of the Spirit is love, joy, peace, patience, gentleness, goodness, faith, meekness, and self-control; against such there is no law. Those who are Messiah's have crucified the flesh with its passions and lusts. If we live in the Spirit, let us also walk in the Spirit (Galatians 5:22-25).

Notice that the word *fruit* is singular. Love is *one fruit* with various expressions (see Gal. 5:22-23).

- Joy is love rejoicing.
- Peace is love ruling/resting.
- Patience is love enduring.
- Kindness is love caring.
- Goodness is love motivating.
- Faithfulness is love trusting.
- Meekness is love esteeming others.

In humility let each esteem the other better than himself (Philippians 1:3).

- Self-control is love restraining.

Love does not demand its own way (1 Corinthians 13:5 TLB).

The love of Messiah compels us (2 Corinthians 5:14 TLV).

At the time of salvation, we become citizens in the kingdom of God. We have access to a new Way of Life. God *"delivered us from the power of darkness and has transferred us into the kingdom of His dear Son"* (Col. 1:13). When we turn to Jesus, we make our peace with God and Jesus gives us His peace as a gift (see John 14:27).

God is love and He has deposited His love in our heart: *"The love of God has been poured out in our hearts by the Holy Spirit who was given to us"* (Rom. 5:5 NKJV). And Paul commands us to be joyful and *"rejoice in the Lord always"* (Phil. 4:4). We can't access something we don't have. Therefore, we already have the joy of the Lord in us. Emotions are meant to be conduits of supernatural emotions—God's emotions.

The fruit of the Spirit is evidence of the kingdom of God: *"For the kingdom of God is...righteousness and peace and joy in the Holy Spirit"* (Rom. 14:17 NKJV). When Jesus rules, righteousness, peace, and joy are evidence His kingdom has come. We know that peace and joy are emotional, but what about righteousness? It is emotional too, because righteousness may be defined as "the love of God in action." When we experience love, peace, and joy in our heart, therefore, we know we're operating out of the right kingdom: *"The kingdom of God is within"* (Luke 17:21). The love chapter of the Bible, 1 Corinthians 13, describes how we should allow God's love to work through us: *"Love is patient, love is kind"* (1 Cor. 13:4 NIV). Because Jesus is our peace, when peace rules, He rules (see Eph. 2:14; Col. 3:15).

Peace is evidence of the Lordship of Jesus at any given moment. If we lose our peace, a negative emotion is ruling. When we sense His peace, He is on the throne of our life. When peace rules, we know God is in control. If we lose our peace, we need to either deal with an attitude in our heart or make a course correction in our life to have peace again. It's that simple. We walk in "shoes of peace" (see Eph. 6:15).

DIDACHE 3:9

Do not exalt yourself or be presumptuous. Don't keep company with those who put on airs, but keep company with those who are righteous and lowly.

In *Didache* 3:9, we are instructed further about our lifestyle as followers of Jesus. We are also cautioned about the company we keep. *"Do not be deceived: 'Bad company corrupts good morals'"* (1 Cor. 15:33 NASB). The *Apostolic Constitutions* states:

> Do not go along with the foolish, but with the wise and righteous; for "Whoever walks with the wise becomes wise, but the companion of fools will suffer harm" (*Apostolic Constitutions* 7:8).

DIDACHE 3:10

Accept the hardships that befall you as good, knowing that nothing ever happens apart from God.

Didache 3:10 continues the theme of accepting everything that happens as coming from the hand of God. *"We know that all things work together for good to those who love God, to those who are called according to His purpose"* (Rom. 8:28). Acceptance of hardships is closely tied with humility.

> *But seek first the kingdom of God and His righteousness, and all these things shall be given to you. Therefore, take no thought about tomorrow, for tomorrow will take thought about the things of itself. Sufficient to the day is the trouble thereof* (Matthew 6:33-34).

ENDNOTES

1. Janicki, *The Way of Life*, 132.
2. Ibid., 141-142.
3. Rabbi Gavriel Zaloshinsky, *The Ways of the Tzaddikim* (trans. Rabbi Shraga Silverstein, 2 vols. (New York, NY: Feldheim, 1996), 1:237; Janicki, *The Way of Life*, 173.
4. Janicki, *The Way of Life*, 146-147.
5. Milavec, *The Didache: Faith, Hope, and Life of the Earliest Christian Communities*, 150.
6. Fox, *Pagans and Christians*, 215.
7. Milavec, *The Didache: Faith, Hope, and Life of the Earliest Christian Communities*, 151.
8. Ibid.

9. Kurt Niederwimmer, *The Didache: A Commentary* (Minneapolis, MN: Fortress Press, 1998), 98.

10. Epictetus, *The Complete Works of Epictetus* (Cambridge, MA: Little, Brown, and Company, 1865), 66-67.

11. Ibid., 124.

DIDACHE FOUR

4:1 My child, always pay close attention to the one who speaks the word of God to you, and always remember to honor him just as you honor the Lord, for where Lordship is spoken of, the Lord is present.

4:2 And every day seek the presence of those who are righteous so that you may rest upon their words.

4:3 Do not be one who causes dissension, but you shall reconcile those who are quarreling to bring a peaceful resolution; you shall deliver righteous judgment; you shall not show partiality when reproving transgressions.

4:4 Do not be indecisive about whether or not your judgment is correct.

4:5 Do not be someone who stretches out his hands to receive, but shuts them when it comes to giving.

4:6 If you have the means, give offerings and alms as ransom for your sins.

4:7 Do not hesitate to give nor complain when you give, for you will be rewarded by your Father in heaven.

4:8 Do not turn away from someone in need but share with others. Do not insist on ownership, for if you are sharers in the imperishable, how much more in the things which perish?

4:9 Do not withhold discipline from your son or from your daughter, but teach them the fear of God from their youth.

4:10 Do not be harsh with your servant who hopes in the same God as you, so he ceases to fear the God who is over both of you. For He is not concerned with social status, but calls those whom the Spirit has prepared.

4:11 But you who are servants, submit to your masters, as they are examples of God's authority.

4:12 Hate all hypocrisy, and everything that is not pleasing to the Lord.

4:13 Don't forsake the commandments of the Lord, but guard what you received, adding nothing to it and taking nothing away.

4:14 Confess your transgressions when you assemble so you won't have a guilty conscience when you pray. This is the Way of Life.

OVERVIEW

Didache 4 marks a shift from training an individual to instructing on a congregational level. Again, it begins with "my child." We note several themes: respecting the words of the Master, living in community, order in family life, and trust in God. The focus here is on church harmony in addition to personal piety. This chapter includes three sections:

1. Five instructions pertaining to the congregation (4:1-8)
2. Three household rules (4:9-11)
3. Final instructions (4:12-14)

It is clear that a transition is occurring in training the disciples to prepare them for full membership in the believing community. It is far more challenging to live out one's faith with other people than in solitude. "By devoting themselves to the fellowship, the early disciples devoted themselves to the day-to-day needs and concerns of the apostolic community in Jerusalem."[1]

> Much of the teaching up to this point for the convert from paganism has been of an individual focus—the shedding of the convert's old life and putting on new attitudes and behavior patterns. But the convert is joining a family in this new life—a family with brothers and sisters and familial love—and also a family with potential quarrels and strife. So the life of the new believer in the body is stressed over the first few verses of chapter four.[2]

JUDGES

Synagogues at the time of Jesus elected a minimum of three judges and court rulings required a majority to make decisions. Likewise, Messianic communities had overseers appointed to settle issues on behalf of the fellowship.

SLAVERY

At the time of the early church, slavery was just a fact of life. The children of Israel had themselves been slaves in Egypt. Because slavery did exist, however, proper treatment of people was emphasized, not the institution of slavery itself. Accordingly, the Bible says that masters should treat their slaves kindly. In addition, within the Messianic community, all were to be treated as equals: *"There is neither Jew nor Greek, there is neither slave nor free, and there is neither male nor female, for you are all one in Messiah Jesus"* (Gal. 3:28).

When we look at slavery in context of the ancient world, we must understand that it was "a real and normal part of the economy. In the days of the Torah, there was no standard of currency, and people did not ordinarily have jobs as we do. ...In pagan society no labor laws, minimum wage requirements, or retirement plans existed. For the landless lower class, servitude was an attractive option."[3]

> The owning of slaves was not something reserved for the very rich; craftsmen of ordinary means frequently purchased one or more slaves to work with them in the family shop. Thus, the presence of slaves does not narrowly define the social status of the candidates.[4]

ENDNOTES

1. Janicki, *The Way of Life*, 173.
2. William Varner, *The Way of the Didache: The First Christian Handbook* (Lanham, MD: University Press of America, 2007), 65.
3. Janicki, *The Way of Life*, 177.
4. Milavec, *The Didache: Faith, Hope, and Life of the Earliest Christian Communities*, 163.

COMMENTARY

DIDACHE 4:1

My child, always pay close attention to the one who speaks the word of God to you, and always remember to honor him just as you honor the Lord, for where Lordship is spoken of, the Lord is present.

Again, the phrase "my child" is used to indicate the closeness of the teacher-pupil relationship. The *Didache* also emphasizes giving special honor to teachers. The teacher, as God's delegated authority, is worthy of the highest respect. Moreover, we are told that teacher and disciple did not just have the corporate anointing of two believers, but that of two individuals under the Lordship of Jesus. *"For where two or three are assembled in My name, there I am in their midst"* (Matt. 18:20).

DIDACHE 4:2

And every day seek the presence of those who are righteous so that you may rest upon their words.

THE CHURCH AND FELLOWSHIP

The word used in the New Testament for "church" is the Greek word *ecclesia*. It is found around one hundred times in the New Testament and a total of five times in the *Didache*. The literal meaning is "assembly" or "congregation." *Ecclesia* is also the word used for "synagogue."[1] Church didn't mean a building in which people met but a gathering of the people themselves. Believers in the early church sought out one another for daily fellowship. *"And continuing daily with one mind in the temple, and breaking bread from house to house, they ate their food with gladness and simplicity of heart"* (Acts 2:46).

DIDACHE 4:3-4

(4:3) Do not be one who causes dissension, but you shall reconcile those who are quarreling to bring a peaceful resolution; you shall deliver righteous judgment; you shall not show partiality when reproving transgressions.

(4:4) Do not be indecisive about whether or not your judgment is correct.

The Importance of Keeping the Peace

A relationship is formed from a genuine heart connection. Individuals initiate a relationship with mutually open hearts. Believers within a community *"keep the unity of the Spirit in the bond of peace"* (Eph. 4:3). And: *"Pursue peace with all people"* (Heb. 12:14). All it takes to break relationship is a closed heart. We may not be able to define what a "wall" between people is, but we've all felt it. An individual who causes dissension can splinter an entire group by destroying unity.

> *I have a serious concern to bring up with you, my friends, using the authority of Jesus, our Master. I'll put it as urgently as I can: You must get along with each other. You must learn to be considerate of one another, cultivating a life in common* (1 Corinthians 1:10 MSG).
>
> *Bear with one another and forgive one another. If anyone has a quarrel against anyone, even as Messiah forgave you, so you must do. And above all these things, embrace love, which is the bond of perfection. Let the peace of God, to which also you are called in one body, rule in your hearts. And be thankful* (Colossians 3:13-15).

In believing communities, our fellowship is in the Spirit and connects us together with other living stones. Just because some believers meet together in the same room doesn't mean their hearts are connected. That is why it is so important to make sure our hearts are free from offenses. Therefore, the *Didache* tells us to "reconcile those who are quarrelling to bring a peaceful resolution." To that end, decisions should be quickly made and decisively rendered: "Don't be indecisive about whether or not your judgment is correct" (4:4).

> *With all humility, meekness, and patience, bearing with one another in love, be eager to keep the unity of the Spirit in the bond of peace.*

There is one body and one Spirit, even as you were called in one hope of your calling (Ephesians 4:2-4).

DIDACHE 4:5

Do not be someone who stretches out his hands to receive, but shuts them when it comes to giving.

Believers should be charitable toward those in need. "A new initiate needs to realize that, although joining in fellowship with other believers provided him help and support in his time of need, he, too, needs to be generous when it comes time to helping others."[2]

We must remember that a unique situation existed in the Jerusalem church at the time of the Pentecost when the church was birthed. The city was flooded with foreigners who had planned to travel back to their homelands and now, among the thousands who would be added to the church, were vast numbers of people who were now homeless, broke, hungry, and without job prospects:

Parthians, Medes and Elamites, residents of Mesopotamia, Judea and Cappadocia, Pontus and Asia, Phrygia and Pamphylia, Egypt and the regions of Libya near Cyrene, and visitors from Rome, both Jews and proselytes, Cretans and Arabs (Acts 2:9-11).

Believers who had homes opened them to strangers, the Messianic community shared their resources and provided for one another's needs. Those who were part of the believing community depended upon one another out of necessity. In light of this, members of the community were encouraged to be generous in giving but only take what they needed.

All who believed were together and had all things in common. They sold their property and goods and distributed them to all, according to their need (Acts 2:44-45).

When Gentiles began to be added to their numbers, it is possible that some members of Cornelius' household moved to Jerusalem (see Acts 10:1-48). Later, Paul tells the church in Thessalonica *"if any will not work, neither shall he eat"* (2 Thess. 3:10).

If you have the means, give offerings and alms as ransom for your sins.

According to the Bible, the *tithe* is ten percent of our income. The tithe belongs only to God. Tithes are an act of recognition that God owns everything. All you have already belongs to God, but He asks that you return ten percent to thank Him for His provision. You honor Him and acknowledge that He is your provider. Unlike the tithe, *offerings* are free will gifts to God. *Alms*, on the other hand, are given to benefit the poor and needy.

Our compassion and sympathy are reflections of the heart of God. *"For the poor will never cease from being in the land. Therefore, I command you, saying, "You shall open your hand wide to your brother, to your poor and needy in your land"* (Deut. 15:11). God shows favor when our heart reflects His heart by showing compassion to the needy. God intervened on behalf of Cornelius because of his prayers and giving of alms:

> *About the ninth hour of the day he saw clearly in a vision an angel of God coming in and saying to him, "Cornelius." When he looked at him he was afraid, and said, "What is it, Lord?" He said to him, "Your prayers and your alms have come up as a memorial before God"* (Acts 10:3-4).

DIDACHE 4:7

Do not hesitate to give nor complain when you give, for you will be rewarded by your Father in heaven.

The novice is cautioned to have a proper heart attitude when giving:

> *Let every man give according to the purposes in his heart, not grudgingly or out of necessity, for God loves a cheerful giver* (2 Corinthians 9:7).

DIDACHE 4:8

Do not turn away from someone in need but share with others. Do not insist on ownership, for if you are sharers in the imperishable, how much more in the things which perish?

Instructions on charitable giving continue in *Didache* 4:8. The *Torah* clearly warns against lack of charity: *"Whoever shuts his ears at the cry of the poor, he also will cry himself, but will not be heard"* (Prov. 21:13). And in the New Testament: *"Whoever has the world's goods and sees his brother in need, but closes his heart of compassion from him, how can the love of God remain in him?"* (1 John 3:17).

The community did not redistribute wealth [which is socialism]; it provided for those in need from its surplus. Food was distributed to the poor and to the widows among the group. ...Some disciples donated all their belongings and became dependent upon the community; others retained private ownership. The hospitality mentioned in Acts 2:46 and 4:34 indicates that in the Jerusalem community individuals continued to own their own homes, and we can assume that the same would hold true for those under the instruction of the *Didache*.[3]

In light of the hardships of some churches, believers were encouraged to share with one another freely. The apostle Paul praised the churches in Macedonia for giving generously:

Moreover, brothers, we want you to experience the grace of God bestowed on the churches of Macedonia, how in a great trial of affliction, the abundance of their joy and their deep poverty overflowed toward the riches of their generous giving. For I bear record that according to their means, and beyond their means, they freely gave (2 Corinthians 8:1-3).

DIDACHE 4:9

Do not withhold discipline from your son or from your daughter, but teach them the fear of God from their youth.

Didache 4:9-11 focuses on three specific areas regarding household management. As in all Jewish households, parents were expected to train their children in the things of God.

> *These words, which I am commanding you today, shall be in your heart. You shall teach them diligently to your children and shall talk of them when you sit in your house, and when you walk by the way, and when you lie down, and when you rise up* (Deuteronomy 6:6-7).

However, fathers are cautioned against being overly harsh. *"Fathers, do not provoke your children to anger, but bring them up in the discipline and instruction of the Lord"* (Eph. 6:4). Parents should discipline their children in love as God does with us—gently with the goal of leading them in the ways of God (see Heb. 12:7). This was true in the Messianic community as well.

DIDACHE 4:10-11

(4:10) Do not be harsh with your servant who hopes in the same God as you, so he ceases to fear the God who is over both of you. For He is not concerned with social status, but calls those whom the Spirit has prepared.

(4:11) But you who are servants, submit to your masters, as they are examples of God's authority.

In *Didache* 4:10, masters are directed to be kind and remember that they represent the authority of the Lord. On the other hand, slaves were directed to submit to their masters and obey them as God's representatives. We are also reminded that social status is not important to God.

> The warning not to command slaves harshly has to do with creating a climate in which slaves might be able to hear the Lord's call and not have this voice hindered by the conduct of the master or mistress. ...At this point, the spiritual mentor addressed the slaves directly. This might be a hint that the training itself took place in the home of a candidate where household slaves were naturally present.[4]

Servants, be submissive to your masters with all respect, not only to those who are good and gentle, but also to those who are unreasonable. For this finds favor, if for the sake of conscience toward God a person bears up under sorrows when suffering unjustly. For what credit is there if, when you sin and are harshly treated, you endure it with patience? But if when you do what is right and suffer for it you patiently endure it, this finds favor with God (1 Peter 2:18-20 NASB).

And masters, do the same things to them, and give up threatening, knowing that both their Master and yours is in heaven, and there is no partiality with Him (Ephesians 6:9 NASB).

One of the many remarkable features of the believing community was the fact that it set aside the social stratifications of the ancient world. Jewish men prayed daily, thanking God that He had made them a Jew and not a Gentile, free and not a slave, and a male rather than a female.

The apostle Paul countered this prayer by proclaiming, *"There is neither Jew nor Greek, there is neither slave nor free, and there is neither male nor female, for you are all one in Messiah Jesus"* (Gal. 3:28). Moreover, lack of prejudice was demonstrated at community meals. Rich, poor, slaves, free, men, women, and Jew and Gentile all gathered together around the same table to eat and everyone prayed to the same Father in heaven.

DIDACHE 4:12

Hate all hypocrisy, and everything that is not pleasing to the Lord.

Novices are here instructed to be authentic. We can tell no bigger lie than pretending we are something we are not. While wearing a false face is never good, *Didache* 4:12 as used here is a particular caution against outward show to appear more pious than we really are.

When you pray, you shall not be like the hypocrites. For they love to pray standing in the synagogues and on the street corners that they may be seen by men. Truly I say to you, they have their reward (Matthew 6:5).

DIDACHE 4:13

Don't forsake the commandments of the Lord, but guard what you received, adding nothing to it and taking nothing away.

Students are encouraged to observe the commandments as they are without alteration. The *Apostolic Constitutions* says, "Keep what you have received from Him [the Lord]."[5] In the Book of Revelation we read:

I testify to everyone who hears the words of the prophecy of this book: If anyone adds to these things, God shall add to him the plagues that are written in this book. And if anyone takes away from the words of the book of this prophecy, God shall take away his part out of the Book of Life and out of the Holy City and out of the things which are written in this book (Revelation 22:18-19).

DIDACHE 4:14

Confess your transgressions when you assemble so you won't have a guilty conscience when you pray. This is the Way of Life.

Didache 4:14 states the vital principle of public confession of sins—the practice of being accountable to one another. *"Confess your faults one to another... that you may be healed"* (James 5:16).

We do need to deal directly with God as individuals. However, public confession has proved to be extremely powerful and beneficial over the past two thousand years. We can see the practice of open confession under Count Nicolaus von Zinzendorf (1700–1760) in Germany, John Wesley (1703–1791) in England, Norman Grubb (1895–2003) in Africa, and others throughout church history. Grubb commends open confession in this manner:

When our walls are down and we share our inner struggles with one another, we can deal with hidden sins while they are still in seed form. In this way we avoid the enemy's traps as well as keep the floodgates for revival open. Seeds of sin are removed before bearing evil fruit and the church stays in revival!

In Africa, I found these instructions being obeyed in all simplicity, and perhaps that one thing has contributed more than any other to the spread of revival. Those simple revived believers often use unusual boldness in questioning into the lives of those they contact, inquiring as to what is their real spiritual condition and experience of daily victory. ...In revival we see that we are our brother's keeper not for his sake but for Jesus' sake.[6]

ENDNOTES

1. Janicki, *The Way of Life*, 174.
2. Ibid., 188.
3. Ibid., 194.
4. Milavec, *The Didache: Faith, Hope, and Life of the Earliest Christian Communities*, 164.
5. *Apostolic Constitutions*, 7:14.
6. Norman Grubb, *Continuous Revival* (Fort Washington, PA: Christian Literature Crusade Publications, 1952), 55.

DIDACHE FIVE

5:1 The way of death is this: First of all, it is wicked and full of cursing, murders, adulteries, lusts, illicit sexual acts, thefts, idolatries, witchcraft, magic, robberies, false witness, hypocrisy, duplicity, trickery, arrogance, malice, self-seeking, greed, foul speech, jealousy, overconfidence, haughtiness, and pretension.

5:2 It is the way of those who persecute good, hate truth, are lovers of lies, do not know the wages of justice, do not cleave to what is good, who stay awake at night for wicked things rather than good, are far from being considerate and patient, lovers of frivolous things, pursuers of recompense for everything they do, are unmerciful to the poor, fail to help the afflicted and over-burdened, those who do not know the God who made them, murderers of children, corrupters of what God has made; those who turn away the needy, oppress the distressed, advocate on behalf of the rich; those who are lawless judges of the poor; those who are altogether sinful. May you be delivered from all of these, my children.

OVERVIEW

In chapter five, the *Didache* continues to instruct about the Two Ways by reminding the novice of the way of death. The way of death is evil and full of greed. Such behavior cannot be tolerated among believers in Jesus.

Those who follow the way of death murder children, advocate on behalf of the rich, and actively practice evil. Verse 1 specifies twenty-two evil vices. Verse 2 lists eighteen traits of evildoers.

For the first time, novices are addressed in a group—*my children*. In every instance prior to this the singular "my child" has been used in reference to one mentor and one novice. Not only does the recapitulation of the way of death signal that formal inclusion in the fellowship is near, but, for the first time, novices are instructed together.

Didache 5 specifies the vices and character traits of individuals who practice the way of death. The training prior to baptism is drawing to a close and this reminder of how evil the way of death is. This serves to remind the novice of the lifestyle they are leaving behind. *"Do not be unequally yoked together with unbelievers. For what fellowship has righteousness with unrighteousness? What communion has light with darkness?"* (2 Cor. 6:14). The baptismal candidates have been walking in the Way of Life for some time, so this recapitulation of evil and evildoers seems almost shocking.

> Although the new Gentile believers did not need as elaborate a description of the way of death as the Way of Life, it was important that the new believers knew exactly what behavior would not be tolerated within the Messianic communities. In essence, chapter 5 defines the lifestyle and character traits of those who are completely wicked and far from God. Such behavior should not be found among followers of the Master.[1]

Only when believers recognize evil, understand what it really is, and know what it does can we effectively guard against it in their own lives.

ENDNOTE

1. Janicki, *The Way of Life*, 174.

> **DIDACHE 5:1**
>
> The way of death is this: First of all, it is wicked and full of cursing, murders, adulteries, lusts, illicit sexual acts, thefts, idolatries, witchcraft, magic, robberies, false witness, hypocrisy, duplicity, trickery, arrogance, malice, self-seeking, greed, foul speech, jealousy, overconfidence, haughtiness, and pretension.

The vice list in the *Didache,* which should by this time in the training program seem particularly shocking, simply opens a window into common behaviors in the Gentile world of that day. Listed here is "a catalogue of sins, which faithfully reflects the horrible immorality of heathenism in the Roman empire."[1]

> *For out of the heart proceed evil thoughts, murders, adulteries, sexual immorality, thefts, false witness, and blasphemies* (Matthew 15:19).

Twenty-Two Evil Vices

1. Murders
2. Adulteries
3. Lusts
4. Illicit sexual acts
5. Thefts
6. Idolatries
7. Witchcraft
8. Magic
9. Robberies
10. False witness
11. Hypocrisy
12. Duplicity
13. Trickery
14. Arrogance
15. Malice

16. Self-seeking

17. Greed

18. Foul speech

19. Jealousy

20. Over-confidence

21. Haughtiness

22. Pretension

> ## DIDACHE 5:2
>
> It is the way of those who persecute good, hate truth, are lovers of lies, do not know the wages of justice, do not cleave to what is good, who stay awake at night for wicked things rather than good, are far from being considerate and patient, lovers of frivolous things, pursuers of recompense for everything they do, are unmerciful to the poor, fail to help the afflicted and over-burdened, those who do not know the God who made them, murderers of children, corrupters of what God has made; those who turn away the needy, oppress the distressed, advocate on behalf of the rich; those who are lawless judges of the poor; those who are altogether sinful. May you be delivered from all of these, my children.

Eighteen Evildoers

1. Those who persecute good

2. Those who hate truth

3. Those who are lovers of lies

4. Those who do not know the wages of justice

5. Those who do not cleave to what is good

6. Those who stay awake at night for wicked things rather than good

7. Those who are far from whom being considerate and patient

8. Those who are lovers of frivolous things

9. Those who are pursuers of recompense for everything they do

10. Those who are unmerciful to the poor

11. Those who fail to help the afflicted and overburdened

12. Those who do not know the God who made them

13. Those who are murderers of children

14. Those who are corrupters of what God has made

15. Those who turn away the needy

16. Those who oppress the distressed

17. Those who advocate on behalf of the rich

18. Those who are lawless judges of the poor

> *I have hated the congregation of evildoers, and will not sit with the wicked* (Psalm 26:5).
>
> *For evildoers will be cut off; but those who hope in the Lord will inherit the earth* (Psalm 37:9).
>
> *Let none of you suffer as a murderer, or a thief, or an evildoer, or even as a busybody* (1 Peter 4:15).

Summary Statement

Didache 5 concludes in the form of an exhortation that is, in a sense, both a prayer and an embrace: "May you be delivered from all of these, my children."

ENDNOTE

1. Philip Schaff, *The Oldest Church Manual Called the Teaching of the Twelve Apostles,* (Edinburgh, Scotland: T&T Clark, 1885), 179.

DIDACHE SIX

6:1 Let no one lead you away from this way of the teaching, for he does not teach you according to God.

6:2 For, if you can bear the whole yoke of the Lord, you will be perfect; but, if you cannot, do what you can.

6:3 And concerning food, bear what you can, but carefully stay away from food sacrificed to idols, for it is the worship of dead gods.

OVERVIEW

Chapter 6 of the *Didache* concludes the Two Ways section and functions as a bridge leading into a new life within a community of believers. This is the shortest chapter found in the *Didache*.

"MY CHILDREN"

The previous chapter addressed novices as a group, using the plural "my children" in a change from the singular "my child." "This switch seems to indicate a shift in focus from individualized instruction to more community-oriented teaching."[1] At this point, believers are encouraged to hold fast to the teaching they have already received and reject false teachers.

YOKE OF THE LORD

Didache 6:2 now introduces the "yoke of the Lord." We will cover this in the commentary section but it is further explained in Chapter 7 of Section Two, "Applying the Power of the Cross."

> It seems assumed by most writers that the necessary-to-be-borne "yoke of the Lord" in 6:2 refers to the "yoke of Torah." This interpretation is usually set against or compared with the "Jerusalem Decree" in Acts 15. Certainly there are some important verbal parallels with the statement by Peter in Acts 15:10 [where]...Peter refers to the yoke of Torah.

There are two other uses of the word "yoke" in the [New Testament] which should also be considered. The first is the strong statement by Paul in Galatians 6:1, "For freedom [Messiah] has set us free; stand firm therefore, and do not submit again to a yoke...of slavery. Paul is obviously referring again to the yoke of Torah. The other use of the word is by Jesus in Matthew 11:29, 30, *"Take My yoke...upon you, and learn from Me, for I am gentle and lowly in heart, and you will find rest for your souls. For My yoke...is easy, and My burden is light."*[2]

DIETARY RESTRICTIONS

In *Didache* 6:3, believers are instructed to follow some minimal dietary laws even though they are not required to obey all the requirements of the *Torah*. Regarding food, believers are told to "bear what you can, but carefully stay away from food sacrificed to idols, for it is the worship of dead gods."

ENDNOTES

1. Janicki, *The Way of Life*, 237.
2. Varner, *The Way of the Didache*, 70.

COMMENTARY

DIDACHE 6:1

Let no one lead you away from this way of the teaching, for he does not teach you according to God.

Didache 6:1 begins with a warning to novices against being led astray from the training they have received. Any teaching or teacher contradicting or adding to what they have learned should be rejected. This verse marks both the conclusion of the Two Ways section and the beginning of full membership in the Messianic community.

DIDACHE 6:2

For, if you can bear the whole yoke of the Lord, you will be perfect; but, if you cannot, do what you can.

Although *Didache* 6:2 is a short verse, it is quite profound. It speaks of the yoke of the Lord. In the natural, a yoke is something that links two animals together and brings them into union so they can accomplish work as a team, such as pulling a cart or plowing a field. This same principle applies to spiritual things.

Although this verse doesn't offer any explanation about the nature of the yoke of the Lord, the *Didascalia Apostolorum* written in Syria about AD 250, which is an expanded version of the *Didache,* says that the original Jewish disciples were told to throw off the yoke of bondage to the laws of Judaism.

> He loosed you and called you from your bonds, and said: *Come unto Me, all ye that toil and are laden with heavy burdens; and I will give you rest.* Now we know that our Saviour did not say (this) to the Gentiles, but He said it to us His disciples from among the Jews, and brought us out from burdens and a heavy load.[1]

Two Yokes

The Yoke of Bondage

We read of two yokes in the Scriptures. The first yoke is the "yoke of the law" which is the burdensome yoke of self-righteousness and self-effort. The apostle Paul chastises believers in the Galatian church for taking up the yoke of bondage again after tasting freedom: *"Stand fast therefore in the liberty by which [Messiah] has made us free, and do not be entangled again with a yoke of bondage"* (Gal. 5:1). And:

> *Did you receive the Holy Spirit by obeying the law of Moses? Of course not! You received the Spirit because you believed the message you heard about [Messiah]. How foolish can you be? After starting your new lives in the Spirit, why are you now trying to become perfect by your own human effort?* (Galatians 3:2-3 NLT)

The Yoke of Jesus

When Jesus came to earth, He partnered with His Father to complete a task by taking on a yoke. This is the yoke of Jesus. This yoke has both lesser and greater meanings:

> *Come to Me, all you who labor and are heavily burdened, and I will give you rest. Take My yoke upon you, and learn from Me, for I am gentle and lowly in heart, and you will find rest for your souls. For My yoke is easy, and My burden is light* (Matthew 11:28-30).

This particular verse is often used as a promise of relief and blessing for weary believers. While that *is* true, the fuller meaning of the yoke of Jesus is an invitation for those who are willing to lose their lives to gain the higher life:

> *And he who does not take up his cross and follow Me [cleave steadfastly to Me, conforming wholly to My example in living and, if need be, in dying also] is not worthy of Me. Whoever finds his [lower] life will lose it [the higher life], and whoever loses his [lower] life on My account will find it [the higher life]* (Matthew 10:38-39 AMPC).

Jesus took the yoke of His Father during His earth walk to complete the work of redemption on behalf of the human race. Jesus now asks us to take up our cross, the yoke by which we submit our will like Jesus, and surrender our life as a living sacrifice to the Father, just like our elder brother, Jesus (see Rom. 12:1). *"For I have come down from heaven, not to do My own will, but the will of Him who sent Me"* (John 6:38 NKJV).

> *"Sacrifice and offering, burnt offerings, and offerings for sin You did not desire, nor had pleasure in them" (which are offered according to the law), then He said, "Behold, I have come to do Your will, O God"* (Hebrews 10:8-9 NKJV).

Honoring the authority of His Father, Jesus lived in complete obedience. A very clear truth of the New Testament is that the entire life and ministry of Jesus was orchestrated by His Father. Jesus was careful to carry out every aspect of His life according to the will of His Father. Even coming to earth was an act of obedience to His Father.

The entire life and ministry of Jesus was based on doing the will of the Father. *"He went away and prayed, saying, 'O My Father, if this cup cannot pass away from Me unless I drink it, Your will be done'"* (Matt. 26:42 NKJV). All that Jesus did and said was directed by His Father. *"For I did not speak on My own initiative, but the Father Himself who sent Me has given Me a commandment as to what to say and what to speak"* (John 12:49 NASB).

When the Father sent Jesus to earth, Jesus wore a yoke prepared by His Father to finish the work of redemption on behalf of mankind. Jesus was begotten of the Father to live in a human body so He could redeem us. We were not ultimately redeemed *just* for salvation from sin but to live in union with *our* Father and continue the Father's mission on earth empowered with grace—full salvation, or sons restored to the glory of the Father.

The Father prepared an earthly body for His Son: *"Therefore, when He came into the world, He said: 'Sacrifices and offerings You did not desire, but a body You have prepared for Me'"* (Heb. 10:5). The assignment of our Messiah was not just to provide forgiveness and initial salvation but to lead sons back to the glory man once enjoyed in the Garden (see Heb. 2:10). After Jesus completed His assignment, God offers us the same opportunity: to live fully submitted lives during our time on earth—like Father, like sons. We, too, are invited to give ourselves fully to God to carry out His will on earth—many sons restored to glory.

> *I urge you therefore, brothers, by the mercies of God, that you present your bodies as a living sacrifice, holy, and acceptable to God, which is your reasonable service of worship* (Romans 12:1).

Like Father, like sons!

DIDACHE 6:3

And concerning food, bear what you can, but carefully stay away from food sacrificed to idols, for it is the worship of dead gods.

As far as rules about food, the believers are told to abide by some general dietary restrictions even though following all the obligations in the *Torah* is not necessary. In *Didache* 1, novices were instructed to put away images of idols as much as is feasible.

> Such a task would be, in many cases, nearly impossible. Floor designs and architectural ornamentation routinely depicted images of the gods. The very coins used in buying and selling bore such images. Hence, the [believer] had to bear that which he/she was able and to remove or plaster over household images he/she was unable to tolerate.[2]

When the apostles met in Jerusalem, they came to the following conclusion regarding Gentiles:

> *But concerning the Gentiles who believe, we have written and decided that they should observe no such thing, except that they should keep themselves from things offered to idols, from blood, from things strangled, and from sexual immorality* (Acts 21:25 NKJV).

Four instructions were given for Gentiles: to avoid food sacrificed to idols, blood, strangled animals that spilt blood when being cooked or eaten, and sexual immorality.

Food Sacrificed to Idols

Meat and other food presented as an offering to idols was actually sacrificed to demons. Some modern-day religions still sacrifice meat to pagan gods.

Blood

Unlike the other kosher laws, which are not explained, the reason for the prohibition against consuming blood is given in Scripture. The Lord told Israel: "For the life of the flesh is in the blood: and I have given it to you upon the altar to make an atonement for your souls: for it is the blood that makes an atonement for the soul" (Lev. 17:11). Some 1,400 years later, it would be through the shedding of the Messiah's precious blood that the sins of the world would finally be taken away (John 1:29, 36).[3]

Blood was a pagan delicacy. Eating blood was thought to dishonor God because He is the Giver of life. *"Only you shall not eat flesh with its life, that is, its blood"* (Gen. 9:4).

Things Strangled

Animals that were strangled still contained blood in the meat. *"Only be sure that you do not eat the blood. For the blood is the life, and you may not eat the life with the meat"* (Deut. 12:23).

Sexual Immorality

The common theme is that of pagan practices and worship. Animals were sacrificed to idols at pagan temples in ancient times. Prostitution at pagan temples was a common form of sexual immorality. Today, believers should avoid illicit sex because the individual who participates is committing sin. In *The Message*, First Corinthians 6:18-20 is particularly powerful.

There's more to sex than mere skin on skin. Sex is as much spiritual mystery as physical fact. As written in Scripture, "The two become one." Since we want to become spiritually one with the Master, we must not pursue the kind of sex that avoids commitment and intimacy, leaving us more lonely than ever—the kind of sex that can never "become one."

There is a sense in which sexual sins are different from all others. In sexual sin we violate the sacredness of our own bodies, these bodies that were made for God-given and God-modeled love, for "becoming one" with another. Or didn't you realize that your body is a sacred place, the place of the Holy Spirit?

Don't you see that you can't live however you please, squandering what God paid such a high price for? The physical part of you is not some piece of property belonging to the spiritual part of you. God owns the whole works. So let people see God in and through your body (1 Corinthians 6:18-29 MSG).

FOOD RESTRICTIONS

In the case of food, the rule against eating food sacrificed to idols was especially difficult because "cultic meals that were a routine part of pagan life" were ubiquitous. It was typical for pagans to routinely sacrifice to gods at festive occasions such as family gatherings and celebrating important occasions in life such as births and weddings. Therefore, a believer would be required to exercise discernment. The line would be crossed, however, in eating food known to have been sacrificed to idols because to eat would involve participating in the "worship of dead gods."

Therefore let us pursue the things which produce peace and the things that build up one another. Do not destroy the work of God for the sake of food. All things indeed are clean, but it is evil for the man who causes someone to fall by what he eats. It is good neither to eat meat nor drink wine, nor do anything whereby your brother stumbles or is offended or is made weak. The faith that you have, have as your own conviction before God. Happy is he who does not condemn himself in what he approves. But he who doubts is condemned if he eats, because it is not from faith, for whatever is not from faith is sin (Romans 14:19-23).

What am I saying then, that the idol is anything or that which is offered in sacrifice to idols is anything? But I say that the things which the Gentiles sacrifice, they sacrifice to demons, and not to God.

I do not want you to have fellowship with demons (1 Corinthians 10:19-20).

Paul teaches that eating food sacrificed to idols is not wrong, but it is better to avoid it rather than offend believers who believe it's wrong or cause them to violate their conscience and therefore sin:

> *I know and am persuaded by the Lord Jesus that nothing is unclean in itself, but to him who considers anything to be unclean, to him it is unclean. If your brother is grieved because of your food, you are no longer walking in love. Do not destroy with your food one for whom Messiah died* (Romans 14:14-15).

It is not wrong to eat meat sacrificed to idols, but it is wrong to participate in idol worship. Idol worship in ancient times often included making a sacrifice to a pagan god then feasting on the meat in celebration of the god, at which time the intent would be obvious. On the other hand, believers who bought sacrificed meat in the market or as part of a meal in someone's home would not be defiled by it. It would be a matter of faith and conscience.

ENDNOTES

1. R. Hugh Connolly, ed., *Didascalia Apostolorum: The Syriac Version* (Eugene, OR: Wipf and Stock Publishers, 2009), 226.

2. Milavec, *The Didache: Faith, Hope, and Life of the Earliest Christian Communities*, 250.

3. Gary Hedrick, "Should Christians Keep Kosher?" *CJF Ministries*; retrieved April 20, 2020 from https://www.cjfm.org/resources/statements/should-christians-keep-kosher.

PART TWO

COMMUNITY AND
CHURCH ORDER

DIDACHE SEVEN

7:1	Concerning baptism, baptize in this way: Having first said all these things, immerse in the name of the Father and of the Son and of the Holy Spirit in flowing water.
7:2	But, if you have no flowing water, baptize in other water that is available; if you cannot baptize in cold water, then immerse in warm water.
7:3	But if you do not have either, pour water three times on the head in the name of the Father and the Son and Holy Spirit.
7:4	And, prior to baptism, let the baptizer and the one who is to be baptized fast, as well as any others who are able. Require the person who desires to be baptized to fast for one or two days before immersion.

OVERVIEW

Three particular aspects of baptism in *Didache* 7 should be mentioned. First, it was simply agreed that believers should be baptized, but ritual details were not important. Second, fasting was recommended prior to the ceremony. Finally, it is likely that baptism may have originally involved a spiritual impartation in addition to ritual immersion.

BAPTISMAL PRACTICE

Baptismal candidates were always adults who had completed an intense process of apprenticeship. Moreover, the mentor acted as a sponsor at the time of baptism, vouching for the successful completion of the training program.

> Those who were undergoing baptism in the *Didache* communities were adults who were in the throes of redefining their identity, their associates, [and] their orientation in life. ...Friends and family became antagonists overnight. In its place, the new religious community provided an alternative set of kinship bonds that served to replace those that were being shattered.[1]

"The text is striking less for what it says than for what it does not say. One can clearly observe that this short text does not transmit the entire formula of the baptismal rite [as it is often practiced today]."[2] The text does not include renunciation of satan, consecration of water, or a recitation of a theology of baptism.

As for the actual details of baptism, we learn that we can baptize any way we want. How we perform the ritual is relatively unimportant. The heart of the candidate is what counts. Although a preference for flowing water is stated, it is not necessary. Alternatives include cold water, warm water, still water, or pouring water over the head, which might be more practical in desert environments.

> What is important in baptism is not the details of the ritual but that it marks a moment of decision in life: now, fully trained and shaped as a disciple, someone sets out in a new direction on life's journey. Baptism is a moment in a process: the preparation by the Spirit, then the apprenticeship with the teacher, then life moving forward as part of the community of disciples.[3]

FASTING

Fasting is the final requirement leading up to baptism. In the final chapter leading up to baptism, *Didache* 6:3 instructs believers about dietary restrictions for Gentiles.

> By fasting the candidate was being finally prepared for formally setting out on the Way—but this was a path she or he would follow in company, and so the whole community by fasting was helping the candidate with her/his preparation for this moment of change in her/his life.[4]

Although the meaning behind fasting at this particular time is unclear, fasting for two days prior to the ceremony would allow food sacrificed to idols to be cleansed from the system in preparation for partaking of food offered to the Father in holy gatherings.

Fasting could also serve as preparation for the twice-weekly fasts observed within the community. "While one cannot be certain of this implied meaning, one must be careful not to reject it out of hand since many of the most important things about the training itself cannot [be] and were not directly said."[5] The next time food would be eaten by the candidate would be at the fellowship feast immediately after the ceremony with a new identity, new family, and new community.

ENDNOTES

1. Milavec, *The Didache: Faith, Hope, and Life of the Earliest Christian Communities*, 274-275.
2. Willy Rordorf, "An Aspect of the Judaeo-Christian Ethic: The Two Ways," in Clayton N. Jefford, *The Didache: A Missing Piece of the Puzzle in Early Jewish Christianity* (Atlanta, GA: SBL Press, 2015), 221-222.
3. O'Loughlin, *The Didache*, 63.
4. Ibid., 62.
5. Milavec, *The Didache: Faith, Hope, and Life of the Earliest Christian Communities*, 255.

DIDACHE EIGHT

8:1 Do not let your days of fasting coincide with those of the hypocrites. They fast on Mondays and Thursdays, but you should fast on Wednesdays and Fridays.

8:2 And do not pray as the hypocrites, but as the Lord commanded in His gospel, pray in this way: "Our Father, who is in heaven, let Your name be venerated, let Your kingdom come, let Your will be done on earth as it is in heaven, give us this day our daily bread, and forgive us our debts as we now forgive our debtors, and do not lead us into that day of trial, but deliver us from evil, for Yours is the power and the glory forever."

8:3 Pray this way three times a day.

[Note: *When praying do not repeat memorized words but pray spontaneously for God's kingdom to be released and expanded on earth.*]

OVERVIEW

Didache 8 covers fasting and prayer. While the customary daily activities of individuals varied, all were to participate in fasting and prayer with their community following baptism. Fasting was a common practice in Judaism at that time. In the *Didache*, it is assumed that believers will both fast and pray. Therefore, the believing community expresses its heart to God through ordinary prayer as well as intensified prayer, which includes fasting. "For those adept believers immersed in the heart of their God, the mystery is that they always pray in harmony with what God is already prepared to do."[1]

FASTING

The primary goal of fasting is to deny ourselves material gratification in order to spiritually connect with our heavenly Father. In the Talmud, Rav Sheshet equates "afflicting one's soul with offering up one's soul on the Temple altar: 'May it be Your will to account my fat and blood which have been diminished as if I had offered them before You on the altar.'" The *Didache* assumes that fasting will be a regular practice of believers, both Jew and Gentile.[2]

The *Didache* assumes that believers will fast two days a week and specifies Wednesdays and Fridays rather than the Judaic practice of fasting on Mondays and Thursdays. Jews were expected to fast for private fasts, fasts decreed by the rabbi, or fasts decreed in the *Torah*. John Wesley adopted this same pattern of fasting for Methodists, asking members to fast on these days until 3:00 in the afternoon. The rigor of the fast is left up to the individual, so they could adopt a water-only fast, a juice fast, a meat fast, and so forth as they wished.

How to Pray

Pray in Faith

Truly, I say to you, if you have faith and do not doubt, you will not only do what has been done to the fig tree, but even if you say to this mountain, "Be taken up and thrown into the sea," it will happen. And whatever you ask in prayer, you will receive, if you have faith (Matthew 21:21-22 ESV).

Pray Persistently

Ask, and it will be given to you; seek, and you will find; knock, and it will be opened to you. For everyone who asks receives, and the one who seeks finds, and to the one who knocks it will be opened (Matthew 7:7-8 ESV).

Don't Pray Like the Hypocrites

And when you pray, you must not be like the hypocrites. For they love to stand and pray in the synagogues and at the street corners, that they may be seen by others. Truly, I say to you, they have received their reward. But when you pray, go into your room and shut the door and pray to your Father who is in secret. And your Father who sees in secret will reward you (Matthew 6:5-6 ESV).

Don't Pray Empty Prayers

This people honors me with their lips, but their heart is far from me; in vain do they worship me, teaching as doctrines the commandments of men (Matthew 15:8-9 ESV).

Praying Three Times Daily

Jews customarily prayed three times each day. We read that Daniel, as a faithful Jew, knelt to pray and give thanks to God three time a day while facing Jerusalem (see Dan. 6:10).

Didache 8:2-3 also instructs the believing community to pray three times a day as a community. Even though they couldn't pray in the same location three times a day, they could pray together by opening their hearts to one another, knowing that the whole community was praying at that time.

While it would certainly be acceptable to pray the words of the Lord's Prayer verbatim, spontaneous praying would be expected and welcomed as in the instructions given for prayers following meals (see *Didache* 10:7). Praying prayers by rote was not suggested. *"But when you pray, do not use vain repetitions, as the heathen do. For they think that they will be heard for their much speaking"* (Matt. 6:7).

Our Father

The Lord's Prayer is a corporate prayer "to *our* Father...give *us* this day *our* daily bread...forgive *us our* trespasses as *we* forgive...against *us* and lead *us*...but deliver *us*...Amen. Even when an individual recites it, she/he does it in union with the community into which she/he was baptized, and with whom she/he gathers to eat, and with whom she/he travels the road of life. ...This prayer meant that the individual was not to see herself/himself praying alone, but always, at least virtually, as part of the whole."[3]

A Personal Note: The Prayer of Agreement

During the time Jennifer and I (Dennis) were teaching on the *Didache*, not long after we had covered this chapter on prayer, my son, who is senior associate pastor, asked if he could come over to talk. He is a seer and very prophetic, so we listened very closely to what he had to tell us. He said that he had been sensing a weighty darkness pressing down over our congregation and had the impression that some people were praying targeted prayer against us as a church and against what God is doing in our midst.

A few years earlier we had heard John Ramirez, a former satanist who is now a believing minister, state that he and his cohorts would often go into neighborhoods, pronounce curses, and release demonic activity toward them. However, if believers who lived there were praying in one accord, their hearts knit together in the Spirit, the witches and satanists had no power to oppress or curse them.

Therefore, Jennifer, Jason, and I began praying according to the pattern of the *Didache*. Although we were in different locations, our hearts were joined together. As a result, the oppression lifted by the next day. We were so impressed at the power released by praying this way in one accord that we immediately invited our other pastors and congregations to join us in praying three specific times a day as a community, and we have had no further attacks of that sort against us.

> *Again I say to you, if two of you agree on earth about anything they ask, it will be done for them by my Father in heaven. For where two or three are gathered in my name, there am I among them* (Matthew 18:19-20 ESV).

ENDNOTES

1. Milavec, *The Didache: Faith, Hope, and Life of the Earliest Christian Communities,* 289.
2. Janicki, *The Way of Life,* 296.
3. O'Loughlin, *The Didache,* 80-81.

DIDACHE NINE

9:1 And concerning the eucharist, give thanks in this way:

9:2 First, concerning the cup: "We give thanks to You, our Father, for the holy vine of Your servant David which You made known to us through Your Servant Jesus; Yours is the glory forever."

9:3 And concerning the broken bread: "We give You thanks, our Father, for the life and knowledge which You revealed to us through Your Servant Jesus. Yours is the glory forever."

9:4 As this broken bread was scattered upon the mountains, but was brought together and became one, so let Your church be gathered together from the ends of the earth into Your kingdom, for Yours is the glory and the power through Jesus our Messiah forever.

9:5 But let no one eat or drink from your eucharist except those who have been baptized in the Lord's name. For the Lord said, "Do not give what is holy to the dogs."

OVERVIEW

Now that the former candidate has become a full-fledged member in the Messianic community through baptism, *Didache* 9 offers instruction concerning ceremonial, or eucharistic, meals. Note that the word *eucharist* simply means "thanksgiving" or "giving of thanks" in Greek. The first action taken by a new initiate after baptism was to partake of a community meal with a new family. Rather than being a solemn and formal occasion, it was a joyous celebration.

Meals were extremely significant in the New Testament. In the Gospel of Luke alone, we find Jesus regularly talking about a meal, going to a meal, eating at a meal, or coming from a meal.

> If we want to understand the significance of the meal of the [believers]...then we need to recall just how often we see Jesus involved in dining with His disciples. ...Clearly, the group around Jesus took

sharing meals with Him for granted: the table seems to have been His classroom in discipleship.[1]

For the early church, meals produced a sense of togetherness with one another and with the Messiah. In the early church, time spent with each other at the table was a continuation of a discipleship practice learned from of Jesus.

> In the meal they celebrated who they were, rejoiced in the fact that the Father loved them, and by having a meal as their basic form of gathering stressed Jesus' view of God as the loving Father who was beckoning them to the heavenly banquet. ...Staying there at the table is a crucial insight into the identity of Jesus....
>
> The kingdom of Jesus was the arrival of the great feast—the beginning of the never-ending banquet of the all-generous Father. ...The coming of the Son of Man...begins with Him eating and drinking, and inviting everyone, even sinners, to the table (Luke 7:24-35).[2]

Of all the chapters in the *Didache*, chapters 9 and 10 have caused the most controversy. There is by no means a clear consensus of thought on these chapters. On the other hand, we can begin by looking with fresh eyes on a first-century text written by Jewish apostles for Gentile believers. What we expect to find included in a eucharistic service today based on our perspective does not have to match the thought of first-century Jewish apostles.

Fulfillment of Types and Shadows

Given the fact that Jesus, the apostles, and earliest Messianic believers were all Jewish, they still lived as Jews, prayed as Jews, and celebrated their Messiah as Jews. The Jewish traditions, feasts, and Sabbath had all been instituted by God under Moses 1,500 years before Messiah came.

When Jesus opened the Scriptures to the disciples on the road to Emmaus, He didn't replace their traditions but revealed that He was the fulfillment of everything the Old Testament had foretold in types and shadows. Can you imagine how the Jewish believers must have felt when the words and rituals of old burst forth with new life?

In the *Didache*, ceremonial meals are about sharing in fellowship and communion but they are also a sacrificial celebration of the past, present, and future. They are a taste of the kingdom of heaven and the mark of true discipleship. The prayers of chapters 9 and 10 ensure that every time believers eat together their focus is not just nourishment but an encounter with the divine.[3]

The Jesus they had formerly known in the flesh was even more real to them now in the Spirit:

That which was from the beginning, which we have heard, which we have seen with our eyes, which we have looked upon, and our hands have touched, concerning the Word of life—the life was revealed, and we have seen it and testify to it, and announce to you the eternal life, which was with the Father and was revealed to us—we declare to you that which we have seen and heard, that you also may have fellowship with us. And our fellowship is with the Father and with His Son Jesus Messiah. We are writing these things to you so that our joy may be complete (1 John 1:1-4).

While the Messianic community chose different days for fasting, prayer, and so forth, to emphasize that they were distinct, they did not abandon their Jewishness. They still had the same Bible, the same feasts, and the same prayers. However, they incorporated Messianic fulfillment and the words of Jesus into the framework of the old while celebrating on different days and feasting on the spiritual reality of "Immanuel, God with us."

GIVING THANKS

The custom of giving thanks to God over food is ancient. "In the mind of the sages, to benefit from something without first giving thanks to God for it is to show ingratitude."[4] The sages found a reference to this principle in Psalm 24:1: "Rabbi Yehuda said in the name of Shmuel: 'To enjoy anything of this world without a benediction is like making personal use of things consecrated to heaven, since it says: The earth is the Lord's and the fullness thereof'" (b.*Brachot* 35a).

At every ordinary meal during the week, we would expect prayers of thanksgiving to be given. "Jesus follows the rabbinic procedure at table."[5] When Jesus ate with the disciples as they traveled on the Road to Emmaus, He gave thanks in this way: *"Joining them at the supper table, Jesus took some bread and gave thanks. Then he broke some off and gave it to them"* (Luke 24:30 ERV).

In many of our modern translations of the Bible, the word *blessed* is used instead of *gave thanks for*. Note that the bread and wine are not blessed in the sense of pronouncing a blessing over them. God is thanked *for* them.

Spontaneous Prayers

The recitation of memorized prayers was not traditional in ancient Judaism. "The prophets, more especially, were prized for their ability to improvise dynamic prayers that nourished and healed the hearts of those who heard them. ...The free-flowing style of spontaneous prayer that characterized the prophets was cherished and seen as a necessary complement to the more stylized expansion of the eucharistic prayers offered by the celebrant."[6]

Kiddush

The first question we must answer about chapter 9 is, was this eucharist meal an ordinary meal or a special meal? Thanksgiving prayers were said to the Father at *every* meal. Ordinarily, thanksgiving was offered *first* for the bread and *then* the wine.

However, the order was reversed for two special meals. At Sabbath meals and during meals at Feasts, such as Passover and Pentecost,[7] *wine* was blessed first, then the bread. In *Didache 9*, we are told that the wine is to be blessed first. In this case, *kiddush*, literally "sanctification," is a special blessing recited over wine or grape juice to sanctify the Jewish Sabbath and holidays. We assume the eucharist in the *Didache* is not an ordinary meal. Nor is it a meal during a yearly Feast. Therefore, it appears that the eucharist is a Sabbath-type meal to be celebrated weekly.

For the Jews, days were not counted sunrise to sunrise as we do today but sundown to sundown. Therefore, the Jewish Sabbath began Friday at sundown and lasted until Saturday sundown. Saturday was counted as the seventh day of the week. The Messianic believers instituted their day of worship from sundown Saturday until sundown Sunday, the first day of the week. By counting the full week and adding one day, Sunday fell on the eighth day, or the day of Messiah's resurrection. Eight is the number of "new beginnings." In the New Testament, the eighth day is also called the "Lord's Day" (see Rev. 1:10).

Just as believers changed the days of prayer and fasting to be set apart, the eighth day, the day of new beginnings, the day of the Resurrection, was chosen by Messianic believers to represent a fulfillment of the Sabbath in the Person of Jesus.

The Passover

In the Book of Exodus, the enslaved Hebrews were delivered from death by the blood of the lamb painted on the doorposts and lintels of their doors, roasting and consuming a lamb, and partaking of unleavened bread before coming out of Egypt.

> *On the tenth day of this month every man shall take a lamb, according to the house of their fathers, a lamb for a household. ...They shall eat the flesh on that night, roasted with fire, and they shall eat it with unleavened bread and bitter herbs. They shall take some of the blood and put it on the two side posts and on the upper doorpost of the houses in which they shall eat it. ...In this way shall you eat it: with your waist girded, your sandals on your feet, and your staff in your hand. So you shall eat it in haste. It is the Lord's Passover* (Exodus 12:3, 7-8, 11).

The Passover prefigured the shed blood and broken body of Jesus. Jewish believers looked back to a shared history and identity. The night of the Last Supper, Jesus used the backdrop of the Exodus story to explain that the blood of the lamb was His shed blood and the broken bread, His broken body. The Last Supper, then, represented the exodus of Gentile believers from the world. During the Passover meal, four cups of consecrated wine are offered. Each cup symbolizes part of God's fourfold promise of redemption found in Exodus 6:6-7:

> *Therefore say to the children of Israel: "I am the Lord, and I will bring you out from under the burdens of the Egyptians, and I will*

rid you out of their bondage, and I will redeem you with a stretched-out arm and with great judgments. And I will take you to Me for a people, and I will be to you a God. And you shall know that I am the Lord your God, who brings you out from under the burdens of the Egyptians."

In the account of the Last Supper in the gospel of Luke, we join Jesus and His disciples midway in the meal. The Seder service had already begun with the recitation of *kiddush*, a prayer of blessing proclaiming the holiness of the event. The cup of wine had been blessed, then the bread. Jesus would have lifted the cup high (the first of the four cups), pronounced a blessing, then passed the cup around the table for all to drink.

Later in the meal, when the third cup of wine, the cup of redemption, was offered to the disciples, Jesus added a new dimension because they partook in the presence of the Redeemer.

> *As they were eating, Jesus took bread, blessed it and broke it, and gave it to the disciples and said, "Take and eat. This is My body." Then He took the cup, and after He gave thanks, He gave it to them, saying, "Drink of it, all of you"* (Matthew 26:26-27).

These statements were not something new. They were a reminder of something old which was now given new meaning—the cup and bread in Egypt represented the body and blood of Messiah.

The Messiah was now bringing a new group of people out of their "Egypt." Although the disciples wouldn't fully understand until Peter was sent to Cornelius, this new group was Jew and Gentile together, one new man.

> *For He is our peace, who has made both groups one and has broken down the barrier of the dividing wall, by abolishing in His flesh the enmity, that is, the law of the commandments contained in ordinances, that in Himself He might make the two into one new man, thus making peace, and that He might reconcile both to God into one body through the cross, thereby slaying the enmity* (Ephesians 2:14-16).

Now, in Messiah, Gentiles participate in redemption. As the redeemed, Jew and Gentile share a common history.

It is the new Passover of the new and everlasting covenant foretold by the prophets of old. It is the eternal Passover from death to life and from earth to heaven. It is the Day of the Lord proclaimed by God's holy prophets, "the day which the Lord has made" for His judgment over all creation, the day of His final and everlasting victory. It is the Day of the Kingdom of God, the day "which has no night" for "its light is the Lamb" (Revelation 21.22–25).[8]

In *Didache* 9, we find none of the expected themes of the Last Supper. "The instructions on the Eucharist contain no references to the words of the institution, the Last Supper, or Jesus' sacrificial death on the Cross. Instead, the meal symbolizes and effects the incorporation of the Gentiles into Israel."[9]

In chapter 8 disciples are taught to pray a prayer in expectation of the coming kingdom [and] in chapters 9 and 10 they get a taste of that kingdom in a meal that foreshadows the Messianic banquet [in the Book of Revelation]. ...When the believers gathered on Sabbaths and festivals they prayed these blessings over the bread and wine in remembrance of Yeshua, the bread of life and the true vine who gave them spiritual food and drink.[10]

ENDNOTES

1. O'Loughlin, *The Didache*, 88.
2. Ibid., 88-89.
3. Janicki, *The Way of Life*, 331-332.
4. Ibid., 335.
5. Samuel Tobias Lachs, *A Rabbinic Commentary on the New Testament: The Gospels of Matthew, Mark, and Luke* (Hoboken, NJ: KATV, 1987), 241.
6. Milavec, *The Didache: Faith, Hope, and Life of the Earliest Christian Communities*, 305.
7. Seven "appointed feasts" are mentioned in the *Torah*. These were specified by God. The Feasts held during the autumn of the year are called the High Holidays. They include the Feast of Trumpets (*Rosh HaShana*), the Day of Atonement (*Yom Kippur*), and the Feast of Booths (*Sukkot*). The spring Feasts begin with Passover (*Pesach*), including the Feast of Unleavened Bread and First Fruits, and culminate with the Feast of Weeks (*Shavuot* or *Pentecost*).

The Lord also set aside the seventh day, or Sabbath, of each week to be a holy, designated day of rest. Later, other minor holidays were added that commemorate important events in Jewish history.

8. "Easter Sunday: The Holy Pascha," *The Orthodox Church in America*; retrieved March 17 from https://www.oca.org/orthodoxy/the-orthodox-faith/worship/the-church-year/easter-sunday-the-holy-pascha.

9. Draper, "The Holy Vine of David Made Known to the Gentiles through God's Servant Jesus," 270-271.

10. Janicki, *The Way of Life*, 341-342.

DIDACHE 9:1

And concerning the eucharist, give thanks in this way:

The Greek word for the "giving of thanks" is *eucharistia*. It simply refers to offering thanks to God. While giving thanks might seem like a small thing to do, it reflects a vital heart attitude.

> *O come, let us sing unto the Lord; let us make a joyful noise to the rock of our salvation! Let us come before His presence with thanksgiving; let us make a joyful noise unto Him with psalms! For the Lord is a great God, and a great King above all gods* (Psalm 95:1-3).

How does Judaism define gratitude? The Hebrew term for gratitude is *hakarat hatov*, which means "recognizing the good." Practicing gratitude means recognizing the good that is already yours. Gratitude is one of the most important Jewish values. The first words the Torah mandates we say each morning, *Modeh/Modah ani*, mean "I thank you."

Throughout the day there are so many prayers we say to give thanks for the human body, the physical world, and much more. Even the name for the Jewish people is rooted in gratitude. The matriarch Leah named her fourth child Yehudah, which means "I am grateful." Yehudah is the source of the name of the Jewish people: Yehudim.[1]

DIDACHE 9:2

First, concerning the cup: "We give thanks to You, our Father, for the holy vine of Your servant David which You made known to us through Your Servant Jesus; Yours is the glory forever."

Didache 9:2 opens with one of two blessings, the first given for the cup of wine. "The order of wine before bread here follows the prescribed order for Shabbat and festival Kiddush meals, whereas on regular weekdays the order is bread before wine. This may indicate that these blessings were intended to be recited on Sabbaths and festivals."[2]

WE THANK YOU, OUR FATHER

This blessing over the cup is considered to be an expanded form of the traditional Jewish blessing over wine. While the traditional rabbinic blessing says, "Blessed are You, O Lord, our God, King of the universe," the *Didache* reads, "We give thanks to You, our Father." "This symbolism is quite rich. Within Judaism, the vine and wine have...become the most profound expressions of Messianic expectation."[3]

> For the Holy Vine of Your servant David that You made known to us through Your Servant Jesus.

Jesus speaks of Himself as the vine in John 15:1: *"I am the true vine, and My Father is the vinedresser."* Through the Jewish Messiah, Gentiles find a new identity within the ongoing covenant God made with the Jewish people. "In the fellowship meals of the early believers, the grafting in of Gentiles to the commonwealth of Israel was sealed."[4]

> The blessing is rich in the imagery of the Hebrew Scriptures and Judaism. "Holy vine" is reminiscent of the traditional phrase "fruit of the vine." In Jewish symbolism, the vine represents the nation of Israel... In some instances, however, it symbolizes the Davidic King. The *Didache* combines these two themes. In it the vine becomes a "metaphor for the salvation and blessing of the Messianic kingdom." ...Yeshua is the Servant who takes over the scepter of kingship in the royal line of the servant David.[5]

DIDACHE 9:3

And concerning the broken bread: "We give You thanks, our Father, for the life and knowledge which You revealed to us through Your Servant Jesus. Yours is the glory forever."

The second blessing of *Didache* 9 over the bread is now given. "In Jewish law, the blessing over the bread covered the whole meal and no other blessings were necessary to recite except that over the wine or grape juice. The *Didache* follows this protocol."[6]

The bread symbolizes the giving of revelation for life and knowledge we receive through Jesus. As branches that are grafted into the vine, we continuously receive spiritual nourishment and enlightenment through the life of our Messiah.

> ### DIDACHE 9:4
>
> As this broken bread was scattered upon the mountains, but was brought together and became one, so let Your church be gathered together from the ends of the earth into Your kingdom, for Yours is the glory and the power through Jesus our Messiah forever.

The words of *Didache* 9:4 are reminiscent of a parable about the kingdom of heaven. In Second Chronicles 18:16 we recognize similar imagery about scattering and gathering: *"I saw all Israel scattered on the mountains like sheep that have no shepherd."* In the future, however, Messiah the King will gather the dispersed of Israel and establish His Messianic kingdom. *"He shall set up a banner for the nations, and shall assemble the outcasts of Israel, and gather together the dispersed of Judah from the four corners of the earth"* (Isa. 11:12).

Fellowship meals were closely linked with the kingdom and the promises of God.

> This is exactly what one finds in the eucharist of the *Didache*—those present drank of the cup of divine election and ate of the fragmented loaf which anticipated their inclusion in the final ingathering of the elect into the kingdom. ...The eucharistic meal allowed those present to taste the future so vividly that some among them spontaneously cried out, "Hosanna to the God of David![7]

> ### DIDACHE 9:5
>
> But let no one eat or drink from your eucharist except those who have been baptized in the Lord's name. For the Lord said, "Do not give what is holy to the dogs."

Didache 9:5 concludes the chapter with an admonition against allowing those who are not baptized to participate in the community's fellowship meals.

All in all, the *Didache* clearly understood the food and drink of this eucharist was to be distinguished from ordinary food. ...Moreover, following upon Jewish practice, participants undoubtedly regarded the entire meal as the "holy" eucharist. ...Thus, there would be no thought that, once the first cup and first loaf were shared, non-Christian visitors or unbaptized members of the host's household could then be brought forward and participate in the remainder of the meal.[8]

ENDNOTES

1. Leah Jalfon, "Growing in Gratitude," Moische House, November 11, 2019; retrieved March 17, 2020 from https://www.moishehouse.org/resources/growing-in-gratitude-program-resources.
2. Janicki, *The Way of Life*, 346.
3. Willy Rordorf, *"La Vigne et le Vin dans la Tradition Juive et Chrétienne,"* Université de Neuchatel, *Annales,* 1969-1970, 131-146. Reprinted in *Liturgie, foi, et vie des premiers chrétiens* (Paris, France: Beauchesne, 1983), 493-508.
4. Janicki, *The Way of Life*, 351
5. Ibid., 348-349.
6. Ibid., 353.
7. Rordorf, *La Vigne et le Vin dans la Tradition Juive et Chrétienne,* 358.
8. Ibid., 393.

DIDACHE TEN

10:1 But after you are satisfied, give thanks in this way:

10:2 We give thanks to You, O holy Father, for Your holy name which You have caused to dwell in our hearts, and for the knowledge and faith and eternal life which You have made known to us through Your servant, Jesus Your Son. Yours is the glory forever.

10:3 You, Lord Almighty, created all things for Your name's sake, and gave food and drink to men for their enjoyment so that they might give thanks to You; but You have also blessed us with spiritual food and drink and eternal light through Your servant Jesus.

10:4 For all things we give thanks to You for You are mighty to save. Yours is the glory forever.

10:5 Remember, Lord, Your church, to deliver her from all evil and to make her perfect in Your love. Gather her together in holiness from the four winds to Your kingdom which You have prepared for her. For Yours is the kingdom of power and glory forever.

10:6 May grace of the kingdom come and may this world pass away. Hosanna to the God of David. Everyone who is holy, let him come! Everyone who is not, let him repent: Maranatha. Come, Lord! Amen.

10:7 Permit the prophets to lead the giving of thanks as often as they desire.

OVERVIEW

Didache 10:1 removes all doubt that the eucharist was anything less than a full meal: "But after you are satisfied, give thanks in this way." Giving thanks prior to eating a meal comes from rabbinic tradition, but blessing God after a meal is based directly on Deuteronomy 8:10: *"When you have eaten and are full, then you shall bless the Lord your God for the good land which He has given you."*

Blessing God following a meal was common practice and frequently another glass of wine was served at that time.

> Grapes and wine are highly important symbols in Jewish tradition and ritual and date back to the first century. A magnificent golden vine that hung over the inner portal of the Second Temple was described by Josephus and the Mishnah. The Hasmoneans and Bar Kochba followers struck a cluster of grapes on their victory coins as a symbol of the fertility of the country. This same emblem appears slightly later as a decoration in mosaic floors of synagogues. ...There is a suggestion that the fruit of the Tree of Wisdom was like bunches of grapes on a vine. Noah planted a vine after the Flood. The importance of the vine is attested to by the Bible's many synonyms for its branches. ...Over 40 expressions connected with viticulture are mentioned in the Bible and Talmudic literature.[1]

WE GIVE THANKS TO YOU, O HOLY FATHER

This is the first of three blessings in *Didache* 10 that thank God the Father for spiritual benefits received through Jesus. "In the *Didache's* prayers God's name equates to His Dwelling Presence. According to the *Didache,* God's Dwelling Presence will also rest on believers in Messiah. This is important, because in Jewish thought the Holy Spirit could not rest on Gentiles unless they formally converted to Judaism."[2] Within the Messianic community, however, both Jewish and Gentile believers alike were given the Holy Spirit.

YOU, LORD ALMIGHTY, CREATED ALL THINGS

The second blessing of *Didache* 10 thanks God for His provision and that He has supplied us with both spiritual and material nourishment.

> *All ate the same spiritual food; and all drank the same spiritual drink, for they drank of that spiritual Rock that followed them, and that Rock was* [Messiah] (1 Corinthians 10:3-4).

> *He rained down manna upon them to eat and gave them the grain of heaven* (Psalm 78:24).

So don't be anxious, asking, "What will we eat?" "What will we drink?" or "How will we be clothed?" For it is the pagans who set their hearts on all these things. Your heavenly Father knows you need them all. But seek first his Kingdom and his righteousness, and all these things will be given to you as well (Matthew 6:31-33 CJB).

Our Father created the fruit of the vine and the grain for the loaf. Just as the wine comes from many grapes and the bread from many grains, He has joined believers together in community and, in the future, will gather together all who have believed. The *"new wine is found in the cluster"* and *"we, being many, are one bread and one body, for we are all partakers of that one bread"* (Isa. 65:8; 1 Cor. 10:17).

Both the cup and the loaf of bread connect the past and the future. The following table, adapted from Aaron Milavec,[3] is a summary of the concept: "Gather her together in holiness from the four winds to Your kingdom which You have prepared for her."

	PAST	PRESENT	FUTURE
CONSECRATION OF THE CUP	Divine promise of salvation	Drinking signifies salvation received. Those drinking of the "holy vine" have a foretaste of the joy to come at the Father's final banquet.	The promised kingdom for believers
CONSECRATION OF THE LOAF	Divine life and knowledge	Eating signifies life and knowledge received. Those eating a "fragment" already lay claim to the Father's reassembling a loaf.	Gathering all into the kingdom

Remember, Lord, Your Church

The third blessing is prayed on behalf of the church, that God would "gather her together in holiness from the four winds to Your kingdom which You have prepared for her." *"No one can come to Me unless the Father who has sent Me draws him"* (John 6:44).

> *And He will send out His angels with a loud trumpet call, and they will gather His elect (His chosen ones) from the four winds, [even] from one end of the universe to the other* (Matthew 24:31 AMPC).

> *Then I looked. And there was a great multitude which no one could count, from all nations and tribes and peoples and tongues, standing before the throne and before the Lamb, clothed with white robes, with palm branches in their hands* (Revelation 7:9).

Permit the Prophets to Lead

Again, the prayers in the *Didache* are not meant to be read word for word but serve as guidelines as far as subject matter. "Rote prayers had no place in ancient Judaism or in the early church."[4] Because of the place of honor given to traveling ministers, they are granted the freedom to pray and prophesy at the close of the meal.

ENDNOTES

1. Reba Wulkan, "The Grape and the Vine," *Textile Society of America Symposium Proceedings*, 1998, 217.
2. Janicki, *The Way of Life*, 377.
3. Milavec, *The Didache: Faith, Hope, and Life of the Earliest Christian Communities*, 363.
4. Ibid., 374.

PART THREE

MINISTRY AND MINISTERS

DIDACHE ELEVEN

11:1 Receive whoever comes and teaches you truth according to all that has been taught to you before.

11:2 But if the teacher has turned aside and teaches another doctrine that undermines this teaching, do not listen to him. But if his teaching promotes righteousness and knowledge of the Lord, receive him as the Lord.

11:3 And concerning the apostles, prophets, according to the truth of the Gospel do this:

11:4 Let every emissary who comes be received as the Lord, but don't let him stay more than one day, or, at the most a second if necessary; but if he stays three days, he is a false prophet.

11:5 And, when an emissary leaves, let him accept nothing but bread for sustenance until he reaches his place of lodging for the night; but if he asks for money, he is a false prophet.

11:6 Do not test or pass judgment on any true prophet who is speaking in the Spirit: "For every sin shall be forgiven, but this sin shall not be forgiven."

11:7 But not everyone who speaks in the Spirit is a prophet, unless he behaves in a manner worthy of the Lord. From his conduct, then, the false prophet and the true prophet shall be recognized.

11:8 And no prophet who orders a eucharistic meal shall eat of it, otherwise he is a false prophet.

11:9 And if a prophet who teaches truth doesn't do what he teaches, he is a false prophet.

11:10 But every prophet who has been tried and is genuine, though he enact a worldly mystery of the Church, if he doesn't teach others to do what he does himself, shall be judged by you: for he has his judgment with God, for so also did the prophets of old.

11:11 But whoever shall say in the Spirit "Give me money, or any other thing for personal gain," you shall not listen to him; but if he tells you to give on behalf of others in need, let none judge him.

OVERVIEW

Chapter 11 of the *Didache* deals with hospitality and three different offices in the apostolic community: emissaries, prophets, and teachers. This was not an unusual occurrence because itinerant rabbis and teachers had been commonplace in Israel for centuries. As you might recall from the apostle Paul's epistles, he made it a point to never be a burden when he visited local churches.

> *For you know how you should follow us. For we were not idle among you, neither did we eat anyone's bread without paying for it, but we worked tirelessly and toiled night and day that we might not be a burden to any of you. We did this, not because we did not have that right, but to make ourselves an example for you to follow* (2 Thessalonians 3:7-9).

The believing community was instructed to exercise discernment and test the prophets to determine if they were true or false. One unusual test is found in 11:10 where the ordering of a eucharistic meal then eating of it is suspect. As you might recall, prophets were allowed to participate in the eucharistic prayers, so it is thought that to order such a meal might give a false prophet a platform to exercise their spiritual gifts without being duly vetted.

DIDACHE TWELVE

12:1 Let everyone who comes in the name of the Lord be received; but when you have scrutinized him you will know him, for you shall have understanding of true and false.

12:2 If someone who comes is a traveler, however, help him as much as you can, but he shall not remain with you more than two days, or three if there is a necessity.

12:3 And if he wishes to settle among you and has a skill, let him work for a living.

12:4 But if he has no skill or way to provide for himself, according to your wisdom and understanding, plan in advance so that no follower of Jesus shall live among you in idleness.

12:5 However, if he will not conduct himself accordingly, he is making Messiah a commodity to serve his own interests. Beware of those who behave like this.

OVERVIEW

Many of the local churches were extremely poor so *Didache* 12 warns them about individuals who might take advantage of their hospitality. Although the members of the church in Jerusalem initially had all things in common, it was not so later on. Those who had learned a trade ought to work and not be a burden on the community. Visitors should be shown hospitality, of course, but communities needed to guard themselves against those who might take advantage of them.

Didache Thirteen

13:1 But every true prophet who wishes to settle down among you and serve is worthy of his food.

13:2 Likewise a true teacher is also worthy, like the workman, of making a living.

13:3 Therefore, you shall take the first fruit of the produce of the winepress and of the threshing floor and of oxen and sheep, and shall give them as the first fruits to the members of the prophets, for they serve as your high priests.

13:4 But if you don't have a prophet who serves among you, give to the poor.

13:5 If you make bread, take the first fruits, and give it according to the commandment.

13:6 Likewise when you open a jar of wine or oil [have an abundance, inheritance, or receive a gift], give the first fruits to the prophets.

13:7 Of money also and clothes, and of all your possessions, take the first fruits [of all sources of income], as it seems best to you, and give according to the commandment.

OVERVIEW

A transition occurs in chapter 13, because church offices are beginning to be established. As in the Old Testament, those who serve in church offices are worthy of support. Verse 2 is similar to the words of Paul, who said:

> Let the elders who rule well be counted worthy of double honor, especially those who labor in the word and doctrine. For the Scripture says, "You shall not muzzle an ox while it treads out the grain," and, "The laborer is worthy of his wages" (1 Timothy 5:17-18 NKJV).

As priests served in the Temple under Mosaic law, now "kings and priests" under the new covenant should be recognized and supported by the communities in which they labor. *"To Him who loved us and washed us from our sins in His own blood, and has made us kings and priests to His God and Father, to Him be glory and dominion forever and ever"* (Rev. 1:5-6). And: *"You are a chosen race, a royal priesthood, a holy nation, a people for God's own possession, so that you may declare the goodness of Him who has called you out of darkness into His marvelous light"* (1 Pet. 2:9).

The tithe, which was instituted by Abraham, is still valid for New Testament believers. As in the old covenant, the ministers serving the local assembly were to receive their livelihood directly from the tithes. If no minister was appointed, the tithe should be given to the poor.

DIDACHE FOURTEEN

14:1 On the day of the Lord, come together, break bread, and partake of the eucharist, after confessing your sins so your offering may be pure;

14:2 But let none who has an unresolved offense with someone join in your meeting until they are forgiven and also reconciled, if possible, so your sacrifice won't be defiled.

14:3 For this is that which was spoken by the Lord, "In every place and time offer me a pure sacrifice, for I am a great king," says the Lord, "and My name is wonderful among the heathen."

OVERVIEW

Note also that the *Didache* once again refers to coming together for holy communion and worship on Sundays "on the day of the Lord." To be pure before the Lord, the members of the community were cautioned about coming together before the Lord with unresolved offenses in their hearts. This is reminiscent of the words of Jesus:

> *Therefore, if you bring your gift to the altar, and there remember that your brother has something against you, leave your gift there before the altar, and go on your way. First be reconciled to your brother, and then come and offer your gift* (Matthew 5:23-24).

The apostle Paul cautioned the Corinthian church in much the same way:

> *Therefore whoever eats this bread or drinks this cup of the Lord in an unworthy manner will be guilty of the body and blood of the Lord. But let a man examine himself, and so let him eat of the bread and drink of the cup. For he who eats and drinks in an unworthy manner eats and drinks judgment to himself, not discerning the Lord's body. For this reason many are weak and sick among you, and many sleep* (1 Corinthians 11:27-30 NKJV).

The final verse in chapter 14 cites Malachi 1:11,14, emphasizing the point that meals celebrating holy communion under the new covenant functioned as sacrificial meals and a pure offering unto the Lord:

> *"For from the rising of the sun, even to its going down, My name shall be great among the Gentiles; in every place incense shall be offered to My name, and a pure offering; for My name shall be great among the nations," says the Lord of hosts* (NKJV).

DIDACHE FIFTEEN

15:1 Therefore, appoint for yourselves bishops and deacons worthy of the Lord, humble men, and not lovers of money, truthful, and proven, for they also perform the unpaid service of the prophets and teachers.

15:2 Therefore do not look down on them, for they are honored men along with the prophets and teachers.

15:3 Don't rebuke one another when angry but in peace with loving correction as you have been taught in the good news; and, if someone has done wrong to his neighbor, do not speak to him or let him hear from you as though you are not grieved but encourage him to repent.

15:4 But continue with your prayers and donations and all your good deeds and live as one who believes in the good news of our Lord.

OVERVIEW

We can have fellowship without leadership, but fledgling communities needed some system of authority. In every community they established, Paul and Barnabas appointed elders.

> Additionally, the community needed an authority structure under which to discipline members who might stray from the Way of Life. The leadership structure and disciplinary procedures outlined in the *Didache* offer a simple yet effective way to organize and maintain local communities. ...The early believers adopted the ecclesiastical models and offices already used in synagogues and throughout the Jewish world.[1]

The Messianic communities used the same structure for leadership as that used in the local synagogues. Every group needs a leader or leaders to function properly. In the family, the parents are leaders and the father is the head of the family. At a fellowship meal, the host is the leader. To function without leaders is anarchy or lawlessness. Derived from the Greek root *anarchos,* meaning "without authority," anarchy is a complete lack of government—or the chaotic state of affairs resulting from such an absence. God, on the other hand, is a God of order.

> *The man who acts presumptuously and does not listen to the priest who stands to minister before the Lord your God, or to the judge—that man must die, and you must purge the evil from Israel* (Deuteronomy 17:12).

> *Whoever will not observe the law of your God or the law of the king, let judgment be executed speedily on him, whether that be death, banishment, confiscation of goods, or imprisonment* (Ezra 7:26).

> *[Jesus] gave Himself for us, that He might redeem us from all lawlessness and purify for Himself a special people, zealous of good works* (Titus 2:14).

> *Many will say to Me in that day, "Lord, Lord, have we not prophesied in Your name, cast out demons in Your name, and done many wonders in Your name?" And then I will declare to them, "I never knew you; depart from Me, you who practice lawlessness!"* (Matthew 7:22-23 NKJV).

In planting churches, Paul makes it clear that leaders should be appointed in the assemblies; leadership positions were desirable, but he also spoke of the necessary character qualities for those who wished to serve.

> *Paul and Timothy, bondservants of Jesus Christ, to all the saints in Christ Jesus who are in Philippi, with the bishops and deacons: Grace to you and peace from God our Father and the Lord Jesus* (Philippians 1:1-2 NKJV).

> *This is a faithful saying: If a man desires the position of a bishop, he desires a good work* (1 Timothy 3:1 NKJV).

> *Whoever wants to become great among you must be your servant* (Matthew 20:26 NIV).

For a bishop must be blameless, as a steward of God, not self-willed, not quick-tempered, not given to wine, not violent, not greedy for money, but hospitable, a lover of what is good, sober-minded, just, holy, self-controlled, holding fast the faithful word as he has been taught, that he may be able, by sound doctrine, both to exhort and convict those who contradict (Titus 1:7-9 NKJV).

ENDNOTE

1. Janicki, *The Way of Life*, 495.

Part Four

Eschatology

DIDACHE SIXTEEN

16:1 Be watchful over your life—do not let your lamps be snuffed out, and do not let your loins be ungirded—but be ready, for you do not know the hour in which our Lord is coming.

16:2 Gather together frequently, seeking those things appropriate for your soul, because a lifetime of faithfulness will not benefit you if you have not been perfected by the end.

16:3 For in the last days, false prophets and corrupters will increase in number, and the sheep will be changed into wolves, and love will be changed into hate.

16:4 Because of increasing lawlessness, those who have fallen away will hate one another, persecute one another, and also even betray one another. And then the deceiver of the world will appear as a false son of God, and he will do signs and wonders, and the earth will be delivered into his power, and he will commit repulsive acts that have never taken place since the beginning of time.

16:5 Then the whole human race will come into a burning trial by fire, and many will be entrapped and perish, but those who remain firm in their faith will be saved by the burning process itself.

16:6 Then the signs of the truth will appear: The first sign will be the unfurling [of a banner] in heaven, then the sign of a trumpet blast, and, finally, the resurrection of the dead.

16:7 However, not everyone will be resurrected but as it is said: "The Lord will come, and all the holy ones with Him."

16:8 Then the world will see the Lord returning upon the clouds of heaven.

OVERVIEW

Chapter 16, the final chapter in the *Didache*, is an apocalyptic section that prophetically describes events that will culminate in the return of Jesus and manifestation of the kingdom of God in its fullness. After an introduction, the *Didache* presents five stages leading up to the second coming of the Messiah. Verses 1-2 give a general introduction. The outline of events that will take place is as follows: 1) false prophets will appear, 2) the deceiver will come, 3) there will be a trial by fire, 4) signs of the truth will appear, and 5) Messiah will return and establish His kingdom.

Believers are told that ordinary holiness is what counts. Their key concern should be holiness of life. *Didache* 16:1-2 presents the three areas in which Messianic believers should remain faithful. Members of the Messianic community are told to be watchful, ready, and gathered together.

Be watchful. Believers are told to be watchful over their souls by heeding the example of the wise virgins (see Matt. 25:1-13). The lamps that were all lit represent the human spirit. The extra vessels represent the soul. Our soul is filled with the Holy Spirit as we allow the Lord to bring transformation into our lives.

The fruit of the Spirit, the nine expressions of the love of God, is the only gift we can give to God. He doesn't want our flesh and our gifts are for other people, not for God.

> *Many will say to Me in that day, "Lord, Lord, have we not prophesied in Your name, cast out demons in Your name, and done many wonders in Your name?" And then I will declare to them, "I never knew you; depart from Me, you who practice lawlessness!"* (Matthew 7:22-23 NKJV).

> *Though I speak with the tongues of men and of angels, but have not love, I have become sounding brass or a clanging cymbal. And though I have the gift of prophecy, and understand all mysteries and all knowledge, and though I have all faith, so that I could remove mountains, but have not love, I am nothing. And though I bestow all my goods to feed the poor, and though I give my body to be burned, but have not love, it profits me nothing* (1 Corinthians 13:1-3 NKJV).

Be faithful. Believers are then told to be ready like faithful servants who watch for their master:

But concerning the times and the seasons, brethren, you have no need that I should write to you. For you yourselves know perfectly that the day of the Lord so comes as a thief in the night. For when they say, "Peace and safety!" then sudden destruction comes upon them, as labor pains upon a pregnant woman. And they shall not escape (1 Thessalonians 5:1-3 NKJV).

Be gathered together. Finally, the community is encouraged to be gathered together.

And let us consider one another in order to stir up love and good works, not forsaking the assembling of ourselves together, as is the manner of some, but exhorting one another, and so much the more as you see the Day approaching (Hebrews 10:24-25 NKJV).

Jesus builds His church with believers who assemble together in unity. *Didache* 4:2 encourages the fellowship of believers as a spiritual necessity. "Seek every day the companionship of the saints so that you may rest upon their words." *Didache* 4:14 affirms the pursuit of holiness in community. "In the church [assembly] you will confess your failings."

For wherever two or three are gathered (drawn together as My followers) in (into) My name, there I Am in the midst of them (Matthew 18:20 AMPC).

A Glorious Church

[Messiah]...loved the church and gave Himself for her,
that He might sanctify and cleanse her with the washing of
water by the word, that He might present her to Himself
a glorious church, not having spot or wrinkle or any such
thing, but that she should be holy and without blemish.
—Ephesians 5:25-27 NKJV

A Dream Church

In 2014, I (Jennifer) had a dream about the church Jesus is building during the coming move of God. In the dream, I saw a splendid restaurant, more beautiful than anything I have ever seen. Before entering through the glass doors, three steps needed to be climbed. (I believe this represents the levels of the Cross.) Everything glittered with gold and glass and crystal, and the entire building glowed with golden light. The walls were gleaming glass, crystal, and gold. Deep darkness surrounded us on the outside, but inside it was as light as day. Everyone was filled with joy, talking and smiling and laughing, and wearing gorgeous white clothing trimmed with gold. It was filled with the glory of God!

Suddenly, I noticed that something was wrong with my watch, so I immediately exchanged it for a new model. After fastening the watch around my wrist, I noticed the clasp on the old watch was broken and impossible to repair.

Next, I was taken to an enormous butcher-block table piled high with the finest cuts of meat. I immediately got to work and began trimming the fat off the meat so only the best would be served to the diners. Those who dined on the meat became strong and mature in the Spirit.

Finally, all of us were dressed in blue robes and led to a large, grassy arena inside the building where zombies began to attack us. At first I was afraid, but the Holy Spirit said, "Don't fear. When you are afraid you can't defeat them." As we turned and faced the enemy with boldness, in unity, and without fear, the dark beings retreated and disappeared.

INTERPRETATION[1]

In dreams a restaurant symbolizes the church (a place you go to be fed). This dream reveals the overcoming end-time Church that will shine forth through the darkness. Although the compromising churches will still exist at the same time, a remnant Bride will rise up without spot or wrinkle (see Eph. 5:27). Spots represent internal moral blemishes and wrinkles refer to white linen garments speaking of disobedient actions.

Gold symbolizes the glory of God. Crystal symbolizes purity. Glass symbolizes transparency. The hypocrisy and masks will be gone as God's people walk in authenticity and truth. Gold and white clothes show that people will reflect the holiness and glory of God rather than compromise and being lukewarm. There was joy and happiness in the Lord in place of guilt, shame, and condemnation.

Replacing your old watch shows that the old season of struggling and pressing through is coming to an end and is being replaced by a season of the Church flowing in God's power and glory. The fine cuts of meat show that there will be a deep level of revelation and a mature understanding of the Word evident in the Church in contrast to a watered-down compromising word that tickles people's ears. Your cutting the meat and trimming the fat is symbolic of your teaching ministry, which will greatly multiply.

The battle with the zombies is a picture of equipping the Church for the battle ahead. The blue robes symbolize the church operating in the realm of the supernatural. Zombies symbolize the spirit of death where the enemy will try to destroy what the Lord is doing and stop the advancing of His Kingdom. Being in the restaurant but still in the arena shows that the battle will rage but God's people will be firmly rooted in the word, God's glory, holiness, power, and discernment.

The Church will not run and shrink back because the enemy will no longer have a foothold in their minds and emotions. A good example of that is the fear you felt, which gives the enemy a foothold and allows him to advance. By overcoming fear, you removed the hook the enemy had and rose up in authority. Others following your lead shows that you will have a great place of influence in helping others get free in their minds and emotions so that they will come to the level of freedom and authority you have attained.

JESUS BUILDS WITH THE BEST MATERIALS

Jesus is preparing us to be part of the church He wants to build. Jesus only uses the best materials. He won't build with our flesh. Jesus only builds with the life He has produced in us. The Ephesian church we read about in the Scriptures was such a church.

> *Now, therefore, you are no longer strangers and foreigners, but fellow citizens with the saints and members of the household of God, having been built on the foundation of the apostles and prophets, Jesus... Himself being the chief cornerstone, in whom the whole building, being fitted together, grows into a holy temple in the Lord, in whom you also are being built together for a dwelling place of God in the Spirit* (Ephesians 2:19-22 NKJV).

THE DISCIPLESHIP CHALLENGE

Will you accept this discipleship challenge?

If so, we suggest that you take the *Didache* to heart for yourself. You can't give what you haven't received. Allow God to take you through your own personal school of the Spirit as you prayerfully apply chapter one through six in your own life. For individuals who have absorbed the *Didache* and "own" it, we suggest that you reach out and disciple someone else as the Holy Spirit leads. You might even want to invite some like-minded friends to join you, as John Wesley did.

If you are a pastor or church leader, you may want to establish small accountability groups so believers can practice and live out the first six chapters over the course of a year. We can learn information quickly, but it takes time for truth to become reality in our heart. (The *Didache* lost its effectiveness during the third and fourth centuries when it was watered down to a few months of teaching but little application. That marked the beginning of church decline, with nominal believers filling the churches, and so it has continued.)

Jesus only builds with the life He has produced in us.

ENDNOTE

1. Gary Fishman, "Dream interpretation," Surpassing Glory Ministries, https://www.surpassingglory.org.

BIBLIOGRAPHY

Aquilina, Mike, *The Fathers of the Church: An Introduction to the First Christian Teachers* (Huntingdon, IN: Our Sunday Visitor, 2013).

Bacher, Wilhelm and Jacob Zallel Lauterbach, "Simeon ben-Shetach," *Jewish Encyclopedia* (The unedited full-text of the 1906 *Jewish Encyclopedia*); retrieved February 23, 2020 from http://www.jewishencyclopedia.com/articles/13717 -simeon-ben-shetah.

Barth, Marcus, *Rediscovering the Lord's Supper* (Eugene, OR: Wipf and Stock Publishers, 1988).

Bauer, Walter, *Orthodoxy and Heresy in Earliest Christianity* (Minneapolis, MN: Fortress Press, 1971).

Ben-Sasson, Haim Hillel and Ettinger, Samuel, *Jewish Society through the Ages* (New York, NY: Schocken Books, 2000).

Bennett, Rod, *Four Witnesses: The Early Church in Her Own Words* (San Francisco, CA: Ignatius Press, 2002).

Philippe Bohstrom, "Unknown Monumental Palace Rewrites Ancient Greek History," *Haaretz*, January 30, 2017; retrieved January 2, 2020 from https:// www.haaretz.com/archaeology/MAGAZINE-unknown-palace-rewrites-ancient -greek-history-1.5492227.

Bray, Gerald L., *Ancient Christian Doctrine: We Believe in One God*, Vol. 1 (Downers Grove, IL: InterVarsity Press, 2009).

Campbell, Ted A., *John Wesley and Christian Antiquity: Religious Vision and Cultural Change* (Nashville, TN: Abingdon Press, 1991).

Chumley, Cheryl K. "Cannibalism: Scientist Says Eating Humans Could Save Earth," *The Washington Times,* September 6, 2019; retrieved February 26, 2020 from https://www.washingtontimes.com/news/2019/sep/6/cannibalism -whacked-scientist-says-eating-humans-c.

Collins, Kenneth J., *A Real Christian: The Life of John Wesley* (Nashville, TN: Abingdon Press, 1999).

Collins, Kenneth J., *The Theology of John Wesley: Holy Love and the Shape of Grace* (Nashville, TN: Abingdon Press, 2007).

Connolly, R. Hugh, *Didascalia Apostolorum: The Syriac Version* (Eugene, OR: Wipf & Stock Publishers, 2009).

Crenshaw, James L., *Education in Ancient Israel: Across the Deadening Silence* (New Haven, CT: Yale University Press, 1998).

Demaray, Donald D., ed., *The Daily Wesley*, trans. Paul Gerhardt (Anderson, IN: Bristol House, 1994).

Diamond, Eliezer, adapted from *The Observant Life,* May 20, 2012, "A Brief History of Torah Study," The Rabbinical Assembly; retrieved February 19, 2020 from https://www.rabbinicalassembly.org/story/brief-history-torah-study.

Draper, Jonathan A. and Jefford, Clayton N., *The Didache: A Missing Piece of the Puzzle* (Atlanta, GA: SBL Press, 2015).

Donaldson, James, ed., *Constitutions of the Holy Apostles or, the Apostolic Constitutions* (Codex Spiritualis Press, CreateSpace Independent Publishing Platform, 2013).

Dujarier, Michel, *A History of the Catechumenate* (New York, NY: Sadler, 1979).

"Easter Sunday: The Holy Pascha," The Orthodox Church in America, retrieved March 17 from https://www.oca.org/orthodoxy/the-orthodox-faith/worship/ the-church-year/easter-sunday-the-holy-pascha.

Easton, Burton Scott, trans., *The Apostolic Tradition of Hippolytus* (Cambridge, UK: Cambridge University Press, 2014, originally published 1934).

Edersheim, Alfred, *Sketches of Jewish Social Life in the Life of Christ* (New York, NY: Originally published in 1876 by James Pott & Co. Publishing. This edition was in- dependently published in 2016).

Edman, V. Raymond, *They Found the Secret* (Grand Rapids, MI: Zondervan Publishing House, 1984).

Edwards, Gene, *Revolution: The Story of the Early Church* (Auburn, ME: Christian Books Publishing House).

Epictetus, trans. Elizabeth Carter, *The Complete Works of Epictetus* (Cambridge, MA: Welch, Bigelow, & Co., 2017).

Fearnow, Benjamin, "Number of Witches Rises Dramatically Across U.S. As Millennials Reject Christianity," *Newsweek,* November 18, 2018; retrieved February 26, 2020 from https://www.newsweek.com/witchcraft-wiccans-mysticism-astrology-witches-millennials-pagans-religion-1221019.

Fiensy, David and Strange, James Riley, *Galilee in the Late Second Temple and Mishnaic Periods*, Vol. 1 (Minneapolis, MN: Fortress Press, 2014).

Fiensy, David and Strange, James Riley, *Galilee in the Late Second Temple and Mishnaic Periods*, Vol. 2 (Minneapolis, MN: Fortress Press, 2015).

Gary Fishman, dream interpretation, Surpassing Glory Ministries, https://www.surpassingglory.org.

Fox, Robin *Land, Pagans and Christians* (New York, NY: Alfred A. Knopf, 1987).

Fleming, James L., *The Jewish Background of Jesus* (LaGrange, GA: Biblical Resources, 2004).

Fredricksen, Paula, *When Christians Were Jews: The First Generation* (New Haven, CT: Yale University Press, 2018).

Freyne, Seán, *Galilee from Alexander the Great to Hadrian 313 B.C.E. to 135 C.E: A Study of Second Temple Judaism* (Notre Dame, IN: The University of Notre Dame Press, 1980).

Gedalyahu, Alon, *The History of the Jews in the Land of Israel during the Period of the Mishnah and the Talmud* (Grand Rapids, MI: Eisenbraun, 1977), 318-323.

Graves, Frank Pierrepont, *A History of Education before the Middle Ages* (Honolulu, HI: University Press of the Pacific, 2004, reprinted from the 1925 edition).

Gonzalez, Justo L., *The Story of Christianity: The Early Church to the Dawn of the Reformation*, Vol. 1 (New York, NY: HarperOne, a division of HarperCollins, 2010).

Gorveatte, Mark L., *Lead Like Wesley: Help for Todays Ministry Servants* (Indianapolis, IN: Wesleyan Publishing House, 2016).

Greathouse, William M., *Wholeness in Christ: Toward a Biblical Theology of Holiness* (Kansas City, MO: Beacon House Press, 1998).

Greathouse, William M., *Love Made Perfect* (Kansas City, MO: Beacon Hill Press, 1997), 25.

Grubb, Norman, *Continuous Revival: The Secret of Victorious Living* (Fort Washington, PA: Christian Literature Crusade Publications, 1952).

Grubb, Norman, *It's as Simple as This* (Blowing Rock, NC: Zerubbabel Press, 2005).

Grubb, Norman, *The Liberating Secret* (Blowing Rock, NC: Zerubbabel Press, 2010).

Grubb, Norman, *Rees Howells, Intercessor* (Fort Washington, PA: The Christian Literature Crusade, 1987, first published 1952 by Lutterworth Press).

Grubb, Norman, *The Spontaneous You* (Fort Washington, PA: The Christian Literature Crusade, 1985).

Gunter, W. Stephen, et al., *Wesley and the Quadrilateral: Renewing the Conversation* (Nashville, TN: Abingdon Press, 1997).

Hall, James, "An Account of Mr. James Hall, Written by Himself," *Arminian Magazine* 16 (1793).

Harris, William V., *Ancient Literacy* (Cambridge, MA: Harvard University Press, 1991).

Hartog, Paul T., *Orthodoxy and Heresy in Early Christian Contexts: Reconsidering the Bauer Thesis* (Eugene, OR: Pickwick Publications, 2015).

Haykin, Michael A.G., *Rediscovering the Church Father: Who They Were and How They Shaped the Church* (Wheaton, IL: Crossway Publishers, 2011).

Heaton, E.W., *The School Tradition of the Old Testament* (New York, NY: Oxford University Press, 1994).

Hedrick, Gary, "Should Christians Keep Kosher?" CJF Ministries; Retrieved April 20, 2020 from https://www.cjfm.org/resources/statements/should-christians-keep-kosher/

"The Hellenistic World," TimeMaps, retrieved March 4, 2020 from https://www.timemaps.com/civilizations/hellenistic-world/.

Henderson, D. Michael, *John Wesley's Class Meeting: A Model for Making Disciples* (Wilmore, KY: Rafiki Books, 2016).

Hession, Roy, *The Calvary Road* (Fort Washington, PA: The Christian Literature Crusade, 1955).

Hezser, Catherine, *Jewish Literacy in Roman Palestine,* (Tubingen: Mohr Siebek, 2001).

Hill, Steve, *Spiritual Avalanche: The Threat of False Teachings that Could Destroy Millions* (Lake Mary, FL: Charisma House, 2013).

Howell, Kenneth, *Clement of Rome and the Didache* (Zanesville, OH: The Coming Home Network, 2012).

Jackson-McCabe, Matt, *Jewish Christianity Reconsidered* (Minneapolis, MN: Fortress Press, 2007).

Janicki, Toby, *God-Fearers: Gentiles and the God of Israel* (Marshfield, MO: First Fruits of Zion, 2012).

Janicki, Toby, *The Way of Life: The Rediscovered Teachings of the Twelve Jewish Apostles to the Gentiles* (Marshfield, MO: First Fruits of Zion, 2017).

Jeremias, Joachim, *The Eucharistic Words of Jesus* (Philadelphia, PA: SCM Press Ltd., 1990, originally published 1966).

Kelly, Debra, "10 Heartbreaking Stories from Britain's Workhouses," ListVerse, July 11, 2015; retrieved June 9, 2018 from https://listverse.com/2015/07/11/10-heartbreaking-stories-from-britains-workhouses.

Lachs, Samuel Tobias, *A Rabbinic Commentary on the New Testament: The Gospels of Matthew, Mark, and Luke* (Hoboken, NJ: KATV, 1987).

Kruger, Michael J., *Christianity at the Crossroads: How the Second Century Shaped the Future Structure of the Church* (Downers Grove, IL: IVP Academic, 2018).

Lambert, Lance, *Israel: The Unique Land, The Unique People* (Wheaton, IL: Living Books, a division of Tyndale House Publishers, Inc., 1981).

Lawson, James Gilchrist, *Deeper Experiences of Famous Christians* (Anderson, IN: The Warner Press, 1981, originally published 1911).

Lindstrom, Harald, *Wesley and Sanctification* (Nappanee, IN: Francis Asbury Press, 1980).

Lizorking-Eyzenberg, Eli, *The Jewish Gospel of John: Discovering Jesus, King of All Israel* (Wheaton, IL: Good News Publishers, 2015).

Mack, Michael, "The pioneers of the small-group movement," *Christianity Today,* July 28, 2014; retrieved June 8, 2018 from https://www.smallgroups.com/ articles/2014/pioneers-of-small-group-movement.html.

Maier, Paul L., trans., *Eusebius: The Church History* (Grand Rapids, MI: Kregel Press, 2007).

Mantle, J. Gregory, *Beyond Humiliation: The Way of the Cross* (Minneapolis, MN: Bethany House, 1975).

Mariani, Mike, "American Exocism," *The Atlantic,* December 2018; re-trieved February 26, 2020 from https://www.theatlantic.com/magazine/ archive/2018/12/catholic-exorcisms-on-the-rise/573943.

Richelle, Matthieu, "Epistles: When did Literacy Emerge in Judah?" *Biblical Archaeology Review* 46.2 (2020).

Meinardus, Otto F.A., *Two Thousand Years of Coptic Christianity* (New York, NY: American University of Cairo Press, reprint edition 2016, originally published 1999).

Merrill, Selah, *Galilee in the Time of Christ* (Independently published, 2018, original-ly published London, UK: The Religious Tract Society, 1885).

Metsämuuronen, Jari, "How Jesus Learned the Scriptures: Modern Reflections of the Educational Practices at the Beginning of the Common Era," *Research Gate,* 2019, 10.13140/RG.2.2.18529.15203; retrieved January 8, 2019 from https://www .researchgate.net/publication/330497075_How_Jesus_Learned_the_Scriptures_ Modern_Reflections_of_the_Educational_Practices_at_the_Beginning_of _the_Common_Era.

Milavec, Aaron, *The Didache: Text, Translation, Analysis, and Commentary* (Thomasville, MN: Order of St. Benedict, 2003).

Milavec, Aaron, *The Didache: Faith, Hope, and Life of the Earliest Christian Communities* (Mahwah, NJ: The Newman Press, 2003).

Millard, Sean, *Reading and Writing in the Time of Jesus* (New York, NY: New York University Press, 2000).

Miltimore, Jon, "Study: Literacy in Ancient Israel Was 'Far More Widespread than Previously Known,'" Intellectual Takeout, April 15, 2016; retrieved November 10, 2019 from https://www.intellectualtakeout.org/blog/study -literacy-ancient-israel-was-far-more-widespread-previously-known.

Nadler, Sam, *Messiah in the Feasts of Israel* (Charlotte, NC: Word of Messiah Ministries, 2010).

Nee, Watchman, *God's Plan and the Overcomers* (New York, NY: Christian Fellowship Publishers, 1977).

Nee, Watchman, *The Normal Christian Life* (Fort Washington, PA: CLC Ministries International with permission of Tyndale House Publishers, Inc., 2009. Previously published 1957 and 1977).

Niederwimmer, Kurt, *The Didache: A Commentary* (Minneapolis, MN: Fortress Press, 1998).

Oden, Thomas C., *The African Memory of Mark: Reassessing Early Church Tradition* (Downers Grove, IL: InterVarsity Press, 2011).

Oden, Thomas C., *Early Libyan Christianity: Uncovering a North African Tradition* (Downers Grove, IL: InterVarsity Press, 2011).

Oden, Thomas C., *How Africa Shaped the Christian Mind* (Downers Grove, IL: InterVarsity Press, 2007).

Oden, Thomas C., *John Wesley's Scriptural Christianity: A Plain Exposition of His Teaching on Christian Doctrine* (Grand Rapids, MI: Zondervan Publishing House, 1994).

O'Loughlin, Thomas, *The Didache: A Window on the Earliest Christians* (Grand Rapids, MI: Baker Academic, 2010).

Pelican, Jaroslav, *Jesus through the Centuries: His Place in the History of Culture* (New Haven, CT: Yale University Press).

Peterson, David, *Possessed by God* (Downers Grove, IL: InterVarsity Press, 1995).

Piper, John, "Battling the Unbelief of Covetousness," Desiring God, October 30, 1988, retrieved March, 5, 2020 from https://www.desiringgod.org/messages/ battling-the-unbelief-of-covetousness.

Porter, Stanley E., "Paul's Bible, His Education and His Access to the Scriptures of Israel," *Journal of Greco-Roman Judaism and Christianity* 5 (2008), 9-11.

Quasten, Johannes, Burghardt, Walter, and Lawler, Thomas Comerford, eds., *Egeria: Diary of a Pilgrimage* (New York, NY: Newman Press, 1970).

Richelle, Matthieu, "Epistles: When did Literacy Emerge in Judah?" *Biblical Archaeology Review* 46.2 (2020).

Roberts, Alexander and Donaldson, James, eds., *Writings of the Apostolic Fathers: Mathetes, Polycarp, Barnabas, and Papias* (Columbus, SC: Veritatus Splendor Press, 2014).

Rordorf, Willy, "An Aspect of the Judaeo-Christian Ethic: The Two Ways," in Clayton N. Jefford, *The Didache: A Missing Piece of the Puzzle in Early Jewish Christianity* (Atlanta, GA: SBL Press, 2015).

Rordorf, Willy, "La vigne et le vin dans la tradition juive et chrétienne," *Université de Neuchatel, Annales,* 1969-1970, 131-146. Reprinted in *Liturgie, foi, et vie des premiers chrétiens* (Paris, France: Beauchesne, 1983).

Rosenberg, Rabbi A. J., *Shemoth: A New English Translation, Two Volumes* (New York, NY: Judaica, 195).

Safrai, Schmuel, "The Jewish Cultural Nature of Galilee in the First Century," Immanuel 24/25, 187; retrieved January 14, 2019 from http://www.etrfi.info/immanuel/24/Immanuel_24_147.pdf.

Safrai, Schmuel and Menahem Stern, *The Jewish People in the First Century: Historical Geography, Political History, Social, Cultural and Religious Life and Institutions*, Vol. 1 (Philadelphia, PA: Fortress Press, 1974).

Safrai, Schmuel and Menahem Stern, *The Jewish People in the First Century: Historical Geography, Political History, Social, Cultural and Religious Life and Institutions*, Vol. 2 (Van Gorcum, Amsterdam: Brill Academic Publishing, 1974).

Schaff, Philip, *The Didache: The Oldest Church Manual Called the Teaching of the Twelve Apostles* (Christian Book Publishers, 2013, originally published by New York, Union Theological Seminary, 1885).

Schoeman, Sonya, "Early Hebrew Education and Its Significance for Present-Day Educational Theory and Practice," *HTS,* V. 53, Number 1&2 (1997).

Severance, Diane, "Evangelical Revival in England," *Christianity.com,* April 28, 2010; retrieved June 6, 2018 from https://www.christianity.com/church/church-history/timeline/1701-1800/evangelical-revival-in-england-11630228.html.

Sittser, Gerald L., *A Resilient Faith: How the Early Christian "Third Way" Changed the World* (Grand Rapids, MI: Brazos Press, 2019).

Snaith, Norman H., *The Distinctive Ideas of the Old Testament* (London: Epworth Press, 1960).

Spangler, Ann and Tverberg, Lois, *Sitting at the Feet of Rabbi Jesus* (Grand Rapids, MI: Zondervan, 2009, 2018).

Stark, Rodney, *The Rise of Christianity: How the Obscure, Marginal Jesus Movement Became the Dominant Religious Force in the Western World in a Few Centuries* (New York, NY: HarperOne, 1996).

Strassfeld, Rabbi Michael, "Jews and Stealing," My Jewish Learning; retrieved March 4, 2020 from https://www.myjewishlearning.com/article/jews-and-stealing.

Swift, Fletcher Harper, *Education in Ancient Israel: From Earliest Times to 70 A.D.* (Chicago, IL: Antique Reprints, 2016, originally published The Open Court Publishing Co., 1919).

Tanack: A New Translation of the Holy Scriptures According to the Traditional Hebrew Text (Philadelphia, PA: Jewish Publication Society, 1985).

Ten Boom, Corrie, *The Hiding Place* (Old Tappan, NJ: Chosen Books, 1984, originally published in 1971).

Thornsen, Don, *The Wesleyan Quadrilateral: Scripture, Tradition, Reason, and Experience as a Model of Evangelical Theology* (Lexington, KY; Emeth Press, 2005, originally published 1990).

Turner, George Allen, *The Vision Which Transforms* (Kansas City, MO: Beacon Hill Press, 1964).

Tuttle, Robert G. Jr., *John Wesley: His Life and Theology* (Grand Rapids, MI: Francis Asbury Press, 1978).

Tverberg, Lois, *Walking in the Dust of Rabbi Jesus* (Grand Rapids, MI: Zondervan, 2012).

Tverberg, Lois, *Reading the Bible with Rabbi Jesus* (Grand Rapids, MI: BakerBooks, 2017).

Vander Laan, Ray, *Life and Ministry of the Messiah* (Grand Rapids, MI: Zondervan, 2009).

Vander Laan, Ray, "Rabbi and Talmidim," That the World May Know; retrieved February 3, 2020 from https://thattheworldmaynow.com/rabbi-and-talmidim.

Vermes, Geza, *Jesus the Jew: A Historian's Reading of the Gospels* (Philadelphia, PA: Fortress Press, 1981, originally published in Great Britain by William Collins Sons & Co. Ltd., 1973).

Ward, Reginald and Heitzenrater, Richard, eds., *The Works of John Wesley, Vol. 1, Journals and Diaries* (Nashville, TN: Abingdon Press, 1993).

Watson, Kevin M., *A Blueprint for Discipleship: Wesley's General Rules as a Guide for Christian Living* (Nashville, TN: Discipleship Resources, 2005).

Watson, Kevin M. and Kisker, Scott, *The Band Meeting: Rediscovering Relational Discipleship in Transformational Community* (Franklin, TN: Seedbed Publishing, 2017).

Watson, Kevin M., *The Class Meeting: Reclaiming a Forgotten and Essential Small Group Experience* (Franklin, TN: Seedbed Publishing, 2014).

Watson, Kevin M., *Pursuing Social Holiness: The Band Meeting in Wesley's Thought and Popular Methodist Practice* (New York, NY: Oxford University Press, 2014).

Wenham, David, ed., *Gospel Perspectives, Vol. 5: The Jesus Tradition Outside the Gospels* (Eugene, OR: Wipf & Stock Publishers, 1984).

Wesley, John, *Christian Library*, Vol. I (Farmington Hills, MI: Gale Ecco Print Editions, 2018).

Wesley, John, *A Plain Account of Christian Perfection* (Columbia, SC: CreateSpace, 2013).

Whitefield, Samuel, "God's Eternal Purpose for Man," December 14, 2014; retrieved May 5, 2017 from https://samuelwhitefield.com/1519/gods-eternal-purpose-for-man.

Wilken, Robert Lewis, *The Spirit of Early Christian Thought* (New Haven, CT: Yale University Press, 2003).

Wilkes, John, "The Pen Behind the Sword: Power, Literacy, and the Roman Army," *Archaeology International,* 2001, 5, pp. 32-35; retrieved January 2, 2020 from http://doi.org/10.5334/ai.0510.

Witherington, Ben, "Reading and Writing in Herodian Israel," *Patheos: The Bible and Culture,* November 2, 2011; retrieved February 26, 2020 from https://www.patheos.com/blogs/bibleandculture/2011/11/02/reading -and-writing-in-herodian-israel-was-jesus-an-illiterate-peasant-part-one.

Wright, Brian J., *Communal Reading in the Time of Jesus: A Window into Early Christian Reading Practices* (Minneapolis, MN: Fortress Press, 2017).

Wright, Brian J., "The Triumph of Christianity's Reading Practices: How Some Faulty Assumptions Swept Biblical Scholarship," *Baptist 21,* February 20, 2018; retrieved February 27, 2020 from https://baptist21.com/blog-posts/2018/triumph -christianitys-reading-practices-faulty-assumptions-swept-biblical-scholarship.

Wulkan, Reba "The Grape and the Vine," *Textile Society of America Symposium Proceedings,* 1998.

Yrigoyen, Charles, Jr., *John Wesley: Holiness of Heart and Life* (Nashville, TN: Abingdon Press, 1996).

Zaloshinsky, Rabbi Gavriel, *The Ways of the Tzaddikim,* trans. Rabbi Shraga Silverstein, 2 vols. (New York, NY: Feldheim, 1996).

ABOUT DRS. DENNIS AND JENNIFER CLARK

Drs. Dennis and Jennifer Clark minister together as a husband and wife team and are Senior Pastors of Kingdom Life Church in Fort Mill, South Carolina. They are also founders and directors of Full Stature Ministries and TEAM Embassy School. Dennis holds a PhD in Theology and Jennifer holds a ThD in Theology as well as BS, MS, and EdS degrees in psychology. Visit the authors online at www.forgive123.com.

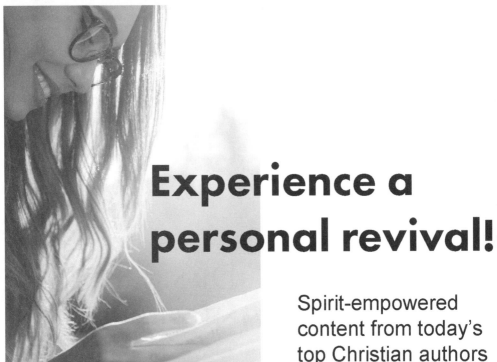